SECOND FALL:

OUR DISABLING LEGACY

&

Introducing the Theology of the Holy Spirit

By

Eugene C. Shults Sr.

ISBN: 0-7596-6137-5

This book is printed on acid free paper.

Printed in the United States of America

1stBooks - rev. 3/29/02

iv

Foreword to Second Fall

There are few writings that will challenge our accepted beliefs about man's purpose on earth as will this book. For nearly 2000 years we have foundered trying to understand Jesus' full mission and how His Kingdom can be established here on earth. Jesus told His disciples that there was only so much He could tell them because they were unable to accept or understand more. To correct the problem, we must diligently pursue His Kingdom and Righteousness and new knowledge will be revealed to us. The Gentiles, under Paul, have failed miserably to establish any kind of kingdom. Instead, our Christian churches have been feeding us "baby food" for centuries, controlling our beliefs and, in recent times, trying to make us feel good. Blindly we have accepted much dogma and doctrine as God's Word. All Christianity is connected to the early church, and whether we like it or not we share a common heritage in rejecting the leadership of the Holy Spirit. Often we think that proclaiming Jesus' message of Salvation is all we have to do, failing to see He desires our total commitment to the pursuit of His Righteousness and Truth. Accepting Christ is more than a one-time installation. It is a relentless lifetime journey. Yet, in this we have failed. Where did our church forefathers and our current church leadership go wrong? How did we reject God once again and fall from His grace into a Second Fall? In the message of this book you will find Christ's richest and most profound spiritual food and answers to these agonizing and overpowering questions. Read it with the Spirit's Blessing!

Floyd Schlosser
Sebastopol, California
April 15, 2001

iii

Preface

The contents of this book, revealed by the Holy Spirit over a period of 15 years, are profound, presenting a new and powerful perspective on Christianity. Especially mesmerizing is the set of disabling blunders made by our spiritual fathers, which we Christians unthinkingly accept as our legacy.

Largely unknown by culture and church is that our human civilization is directly dependent upon the status of the Christian churches for societal health. In the age of mass destruction weapons, this dependency has become critical, with the Spirit of God revealing that the very survival of the human species is dependent upon the renewal of the spiritual vitality of the Christian churches. Only then, can we gain the moral direction so necessary to avoid mass self-inflicted suicide.

So, how are the churches doing? Is there an awakening, a revival at hand? Brownsville, Florida stirs, but generally, no.

The theologians have struggled to understand the historical Christ, believing that then they can more clearly define true Christianity; strongly implying that our current Christology is seriously faulted. In this effort, the theologians have taken us through the New Quest, Second Quest, and the Third Quest, plunging through Source-criticism, then Form-criticism and from there to Redaction-criticism. The frustration has mounted until one reporting theologian exasperatedly said: 'our chances of recovering early forms, let alone sources, are at the mercy of so much speculation and so many unverifiable hypotheses that we are in a bad state indeed. How then can we advance?'[1] Clearly, advancement comes only from the abandonment of the intellect-only study of Scripture confined exclusively to the physical realm to move into an interactive dual realm study of the problem related to the aims of Jesus and the churches' failures therein. Only then can we progress. Indeed, by accepting the conditions of the rational and secular world's intellect only analyses, we shall always be defeated, left frustrated and disappointed. We must incorporate the Spirit of God into our analyses in order to gain vision that transcends the capacities of our physical senses. For it has become quite apparent that the current Christian churches and their rational-only theologians are unable to guide humanity to Jesus' innate expectation, the restoration of humanity to paradise.

So where are we? Undeniably, the current secular advocates of rationalism, the humanists, those that control our culture, would lead us to the global village.

---

1. Neill, Stephen & Wright, Tom *The Interpretation of the New Testament*, London: Oxford University Press, 1989, page 402.

This is another utopian dream of the intellect; a death trail, void of the presence of God, which like Marxism is an intellectual invention destined only to harvest an overwhelming abundance of human misery. Yet, to date, no effective Christian opposition has arisen to contend with this terrible turn in human events, thus permitting the continued deterioration of both church and culture.

Therefore, the purpose of this book is to expose the reasons for the current passivity of the Christian faith, to identify the main legacy blunders in our inheritance, to trace the historical events that led to our current demise, especially the current sifting of America by Satan, and to look for the correction of our faith inaptitude. It was then that the Spirit of God shocked us.

It is too late! Humanity cannot save itself. The window of opportunity for human reform has been closed. Humanity is condemned unless we receive the intervention of God. This intervention will come to us as both God's discipline and the Spirit's love touch. Yet, an obstacle to this intervention of God looms. To fully receive these two great intervention gifts of God we must reach six objectives:

1. We must comprehend the purpose, capacities and responsibilities of the Holy Spirit.
2. We must apologize for our centuries-long neglect of the Holy Spirit.
3. We must discern that humanity sits at a decisive turning point in history.
4. We must recognize that this decisive turning point is aggravated by Satan's attempt to prevent God's intervention by his own preemptive intervention.
5. We must turn to intercessory prayer, massively, in order to beat back this preemptive intervention.
6. We must grasp and then utilize the power positions in spiritual warfare that God has waiting for His beloved ones.

The Spirit of God has promised to intervene in America to return our country back to its originating covenant as the light of Christ to the world, if we can beat back the sifting of America by the enemy of God. For clearly, the sifting is Satan's attempt to turn aside God's intervention to save humanity. If we yield and accept Satan's sifting, God has nothing left for which to intervene. It is a high stakes war, with the Spirit of God stating that the entire focus of creation, the total reason for the generation of the universe and the creation of humankind are now focused here, at our time, in this moment of existence. And clearly, the essence of this conflict is fixed upon America. So, the Spirit of God added additional perspectives to the purpose of this book, all to assist humanity to reach victory in this ultimate conflict. To the original goal to define the legacy problems within the church, He added these orientations, revealing:

- Higher Level Justification via Overcoming, closing the gap in Pauline Theology
- Centuries-old human limitations in our thinking frame of references and their impact on our understanding the great teachings of Jesus, as reflected in the Bible and the Holy Spirit
- Fullness of Jesus' Rescue and the church's failure to fully embrace all of Jesus' *redemptive capacities*
- Church's comfort in its compromise with the curses of the Adamic fall, which has sharply limited its mission
- Advanced Christ-Walk with the Holy Spirit, given in the form of the Theology of the Holy Spirit
- The **Holy Junction** between the human spirit and the Holy Spirit and its role in true worship, intercession, and spiritual warfare
- Truth of the *impersonator* and the means to defeat this terrible deception
- Hierarchy of Intercession
- Advanced spiritual end-time tools to combat the enemy
- The Hidden Manna.

Hence, this book offers an introduction to new tools of Spiritual Warfare, including the primitive theology of the Holy Spirit, with the expectations that great things shall flow from this humble start, enabling humanity to survive the difficult adjustment times ahead. Praise God!

Do not be discouraged if this new vision on Christianity, with its emphasis on the theology of the Holy Spirit, tends to overwhelm you. Instead, let the Holy Spirit help you break those bonds that restrict our Christ-Walk today to reach and understand Jesus' planned path for tomorrow. Always remember the mission of our Savior is enthralling as well as dynamic, meaning that our current church's immobility and inertia results from the church's obsession that they possess all of God's truth, which is impossible, even unrealistic, and invalid!

Come, the Lord is calling us to the great overcoming adventures of tomorrow, both individually and societally. Will we answer, or will we scoff, allocating to ourselves the status of a mere observer?

Table of Contents

Introduction

The Biblical book of Genesis tells of Adam and Eve and their fall from paradise. Human exploitation quickly followed, coming to characterize the curse derived from this prodigious human mistake, the **first fall** of humanity from the embrace of God. As a direct result from this fall, wickedness, deception, and debasement characterized humankind whenever civilization was built. So, whether the story of the Adamic fall is taken literally or metaphorically, we cannot escape our past and its impacting embrace. Representing a huge break with God, the mistakes of our ancestors stalk us, defining our thinking frame of reference to unacceptable levels of hate and passion, limiting our capacities to experience agape love and deep personal compassion for each other, even in the deepest misery. Our species stumbled badly, generating cultural and personal curses of the first rank, eliciting unbounded misery and suffering upon ourselves.

Jesus came to rescue us from these problems.

All these events, the Adamic fall and Jesus' rescue, have been spoken of for two millennia, dominating European and Western Hemisphere religious thinking. Yet, Jesus' rescue has never been fully realized or embraced by humankind. Perhaps worst, those cultures that did embrace Jesus managed to sabotage His rescue by introducing a set of mission changing mistakes, nineteen in total.

Yet today, who knows about these mistakes, which collectively are equivalent to a **second fall of humankind**? Who today, realizes how seriously humanity managed to botch Jesus' rescue, and the tremendous repercussion that these stupendous miscues portent for all of us? Blissfully ignorant, humanity has operated through the centuries as if all is well with Christ's rescue, when it is not! We need to listen to this word of Isaiah quoted by Jesus:

They worship me in vain; their teachings are but rules taught by men (Matthew 15:9).

Today, and for some time in the past, the totality of Christendom has engaged in grossly weakened worship, leaving the entire Christian community in a position of wholesale spiritual futility. In fact, the Holy Spirit says the Body of Christ now approaches that position described by Matthew 15:9.

Despite exceptions, especially those found in the persecuted lands like China, the Body of Christ has been seriously and critically weakened by the second fall affliction. Indeed, the Holy Spirit indicates that most – even all - parts of the

Christian faith system worship God in vain. The Gospel by John defines true worship of God:

God is spirit, and His worshippers must worship in spirit and in truth (John 4:24).

But a simple study of history reveals that the leadership propensity of the Holy Spirit and the truth of the Gospels have been dampened by the legacy mistakes of our spiritual ancestors, generally leaving the human spirit in a weakened position under the dominance of a renegade intellect. Hence, unbelievably but accurately, widespread true worship of God as defined by John 4:24 has been missing from our worship services for more than 1600 years! Both the emerging capacities of the human spirit and the integrity of the Gospel truth disappeared in the **second fall**, compromised away by 410 AD. And incredibly, this miserable condition has become our common and unchallenged modern inheritance, our current disabling legacy!

Truly, our current Christian situation is reprehensible and unacceptable! To continue in our present mode of indifference and passivity, especially as the forces of evil gather their end-time strength, is to miss the goal for life as set by our Savior, Christ Jesus, the adaptation and establishment of the kingdom of God upon earth.

Urgently, reevaluation and reassessment must be upon us, now, if we are to modify God's anger and His discipline. Let us start by asking, where have we traveled, and what are we doing? Or restated, what exactly is our Christian legacy after two millennia of twisted and contorted history? Does anyone really know? Indeed not! But the Spirit of God understands everything, constantly searching the mind of the Father, and He has consented to lead us to the correct answers. Praise God!

In this we must listen to the words of Jesus:

I have much more to say to you, more than you can now bear. But when He, the Spirit of truth, comes, he will guide you into all truth (John 16:12)

When the Fathers of the church cut off the Holy Spirit after the Montanus incident at Pepusa in 172, much of the input that the Holy Spirit had for Jesus' beloved ones was cut off. It has been that way for 1829 years. How, the Spirit of God wants to rectify that mistake, identified as legacy blunder 2 in this book. In addition, the Holy Spirit has much to say about our modern times, and the adjustments that He deems necessary to resist the enemy of God as we enter the end-time scenario of the Church Age.

To many readers, this will be too much to accept. Those that do not walk with the indwelling Holy Spirit and are totally based on the intellectual study of the Bible will be hard pressed to accept the material of this text. Yet, seek an open mind, for the material presented here is the gift from God, given to you to assist you in the coming difficult times. Forget the author, he has no role in this affair, except to get out of the way. Realize that this input, especially about the theology of the Holy Spirit, is given to you to prepare for the greatest spiritual awakening that the world has ever experienced. This, the third Great Awakening for America, will enable the drive to the kingdom of God adapted to earth. Break out of your brainwashing denominational mind-lock and seek the Lord and His confirmation, for the material in this text is of Him and by Him. It contains the will of God for our end-time victory, for you and your loved ones, born and yet to be born. Rejoice, for the promise of God is being fulfilled:

This is the covenant I will make with them after that time, says the Lord. I will put my laws [the will of the Father] in their hearts, and I will write them on their minds (Hebrews 10:16).

Chapter 1

Defining the Legacy Blunders

As we approach the end of the Church Age, the acknowledgement and correction of the misdeeds of our spiritual ancestors increasingly become essential if humanity is to reach its individual and cultural potential: the loving embrace of God in all human endeavors.

While all of these misdeeds are grave, some are more momentous than others. Accordingly, these legacy misdeeds are divided into major and secondary blunders.

Here is that list, composed first of the Judean mistake followed by the Gentile church legacy blunders, which together generated a **second fall** for humanity by 410 AD, continuously contributing to it, even into our times.

LEGACY BLUNDERS:

1. **First legacy blunder** was the first-century Judean rejection of Yeshua. The initial birth of the kingdom of God was aborted. Of course, this was a major blunder.
2. **Second legacy blunder** was the second century decision to forfeit the church leadership by the Holy Spirit after the Montanist debacle at Pepusa. Church leadership was shifted to the intellect of men via the development of the first church canon. This was the most serious of the major blunders by the Gentile church.
3. **Third legacy blunder** was the inability of the early church to grasp the fullness of Jesus' rescue, forfeiting many of His redemptive capacities, focusing exclusively on salvation into the spiritual kingdom. Thus, because of ignorance or laziness, the Adamic curse was not defeated and the redemption of civilization was forgotten. Of course, this was a major blunder.
4. **Fourth legacy blunder** was the inability to grasp and integrate the fullness of Paul's theology, especially his Christian mysticism that *Christ dwells within, not me* with his redemption via justification by faith and the kingdom of God concepts.
5. **Fifth legacy blunder** was the inability of the early, and current, church to understand the different stages of the kingdom

1

implementation as the various growth phases of the same kingdom entity, i.e., infant, adolescent and adult. This was a major blunder.

6. **Sixth legacy blunder** was the fourth century decisions of the Christian church fathers to adopt a pragmatic route for the survival of the church. This adaptation is called the Pragmatic Curse upon the church in this text. This decision, with its curse, generated an informal Pact of Cooperation with pagan Rome, an agreement that passed beyond the death of Rome, becoming an agreement that aborted the Gentile attempt at birthing the kingdom of God. With the forfeiture of the drive to the kingdom of God, the full Gospel message of Jesus Christ was invalidated. Pagan influences infiltrated the church. Here, it is asserted that the church lost the keys to the kingdom, i.e. the God-given authority over the affairs of Jesus' house. Obviously, this was a major blunder.

7. **Seventh legacy blunder** was early use of false authorship. To attract attention, authors often attributed their work to others, sometimes men long dead. This was intellectual dishonesty then, even as it is today. But it gets worse. As with the Ignatius letters, there have been fraudulent attempts at deception in order to win some given point of view, which has led later generations into serious scholastic question about the authenticity of some of the Epistles of the New Testament. This, we do not need. Then, there are the unanswered questions. What was the influence of Gnosticism and the mystery religions? How much did the Hellenistic environment influence the early formation of our Christian beliefs? Can we even define pure undefiled Christianity? Can we find and appreciate the historic Jesus? So, the inability of the early underground church to better monitor the authorship, the origination dates of the Holy Scriptures and the environmental influences of the early church constitutes a serious legacy blunder.

8. **Eighth legacy blunder** was the degradation of the Baptism of the Holy Spirit into the largely meaningless Sacrament of Confirmation. Most likely a gradual development lost in history, the author does not know the exact date this occurred. Yet, this degradation influenced the spiritual warfare of the church. With less Spirit-filled saints, spiritual warfare, the prime condition of the early church slipped into obsolescence.

9. **Ninth legacy blunder** was the reconstruction of the vanished church canon in Le Mans France in 850, attributing undue authority to the pope while ascribing this rewrite to men of the church long dead. The canon rewrite was deemed necessary because the original canon

was lost in the deep regression of knowledge occurring as the result of God's first discipline. Unscrupulous or ignorant men used this rewrite to centralize the authority of the church upon the papacy. This focused too much power in the hands of the few, simply inviting the mischief of the enemy of God, which was forthcoming!

10. **Tenth legacy blunder** was the church's violent thirteenth century suppression of the Spiritual Franciscans and its drive to usher in the age of the Holy Spirit. It appears that this event was significantly more important in the history of the church than understood by historians or church theologians, then or since. Of course, Jesus' special appearance to Francis of Assisi in 1205 asking for the reconstruction of His church would warrant this conclusion, but yet, even this event's significance is largely lost. Indeed, the Spirit points at this legacy blunder, as the turning point of history because enclosed within this movement, before its destructive apostasy, is the vision of our future as an agape civilization. This was a major blunder.

11. **Eleventh legacy blunder** was the Reformation's refusal to return the leadership of the church to the Holy Spirit, instead retaining church leadership via the intellect of man. This leadership flaw resulted from the second legacy blunder of the early church, and it reflected a general church naiveté about the need to shift from worldly to spiritual church orientations, the latter achievable exclusively under the leadership of the Spirit of God. Both of the major Protestant leaders, Luther and Zwingli, had followers that pushed for this correction. Yet, in both incidents, these men and their reform ideas were rejected. Conrad Grebel, Zwingli's follower was imprisoned, escaped and then hunted down, dying of the black plague before he could be found and killed. His only crime was his Spirit-led desire to return to the spiritual church. Luther told his follower, Muntzer, that he could 'swallow the Holy Spirit, feathers and all.' In the rejection of these special people, men such as Carlstadt, Muntzer and Grebel, each which believed in the dynamic role of the Holy Spirit in the church, a great opportunity for reform was missed.

12. **Twelfth legacy blunder** was the Reformation's inability to grasp the indwelling role of the Holy Spirit in the personal life of the saints (as differentiated from the church leadership). Leaders like Luther, Melanchthon and other reformers saw the action of grace, which is the Spirit of God operating outside the saint, and stopped there, thinking there was no more. But the Spirit of God functions within the human entity, making it the temple of God. So in a mystery that

3

is difficult to grasp, the Spirit aids us from outside our personage as grace, pushing us into the embrace of God, as well as inside each saint as the indwelling presence of God. To just accept one orientation of the Spirit, grace, was a grave mistake, one that the Spirit of God has attempted to correct four times in the last 160 years. The last effort was the Charismatic outpouring. Why is the indwelling presence so important? Because void of the indwelling Spirit of God, the human intellect remains supreme over the human spirit, eliminating the spiritual capacity of the saint. While many important functions of the Christ-walk became degraded, seven are especially impacted: 1) spiritual warfare, 2) inner cleansing, 3) gifts of the Spirit, especially faith and healings, 4) fruits of the Spirit especially agape love, 5) spiritual deliverances, 6) closeness to God and 7) the Spirit-directed mastery of the Word. Here is a significant sign of this blunder: The intellectual study of the Bible without the assistance of the Holy Spirit is astonishingly defined by the Holy Spirit as a largely vain process, leading to division and dissension! Shocked? The author was!

13. **Thirteenth legacy blunder** was the confusion generated between justification by faith and Jesus' call to overcome, generalized to whom do we listen and follow, Jesus or Paul? Unfortunately, the Leaders of the Protestant Reformation went with Paul with his emphasis on grace, a word that Jesus never uttered in the Bible. The Reformers reasoned this way: If the saint reached justification, a status free of sin in the eyes of God, what personal struggle to overcome could possibly remain? All men sin, and none can reach perfection on their own, but then they pointed at Paul's letters to prove that justification could be achieved as a free and unmerited gift of grace (Romans 3:24). Thus, although they admitted that all men would sin, even after grace, they reasoned that their justification would still reign supreme over these actions, allowing them to ignore Matthew 12:36, 13:19, 24:13, Hebrews 10:26 and Revelation 2:11, 3:12, 3:16 and 3:21 to name but a few warning Scriptures. The Spirit says this a major teaching mistake, which still dominates a vast number of God's beloved ones, persisting even in the face of censure by some Protestant theologians, e.g., Wilhelm Heitmuller.

14. **Fourteenth legacy blunder** was the confusion of 'seeking' with 'good deeds.' The Reformers accepted the imputation of righteousness as a free gift of grace, whereas, it is a function of faith (Romans 3:22). While Christian faith can come from grace, which justifies the Reformer's assertions, it is most profusely a gift of the

4

manifesting (indwelling) Holy Spirit (1 Corinthians 12:9). Therefore, to have Christian faith abundantly, we must seek after the deeper indwelling of the Holy Spirit, meaning that seeking is the key to receiving God's righteousness. But seeking as described in Matthew 6:33 is an action verb, too often belittled, incorrectly, by some saints as the activation of good deeds. Over the centuries, this reluctance to seek has led to the escalation of the passive Christian walk, wherein, the saint is stranded as a baby Christian, a problem of every Christian faith paradigm. This legacy blunder has degenerated into cheap salvation, dead churches and the diminution of that extraordinary kingdom spiritual power that originally emanated from the Protestant Reformation.

15. **Fifteenth legacy blunder** was the sixteenth and seventeenth century mainline Protestant rejection of the Spiritual Reformation, perhaps best epitomized by the silencing of Jacob Boehme. Reform leaders, wallowing in self-righteousness and excessive arrogance, followers of Paul, not Jesus and void of the understanding of the Holy Spirit, massacred the Reformation epicenter, the Spiritual Reformation. This blunder made the Reformation a step forward in God's restoration plan, but not its resuscitation.

16. **Sixteenth legacy blunder** was the seventeenth century Calvinist and other Mainline Protestant pollution of the Pilgrim Covenant with God. God-fearing people that believed strongly in predestination, the common saints felt that their selection to heaven only could be determined by wealth in this world despite the fact that Calvinism never officially taught this concept. Hence, Calvinist saints strove mightily to prove their selection, inadvertently generating a materialistic, carnal culture that denigrated the Pilgrim covenant with God. This blunder was so great that God introduced the First Great Awakening to correct it, occurring in the middle of the eighteenth century.

17. **Seventeenth legacy blunder** was the Jeffersonian-induced rejection of the divinity of Jesus Christ into America, spread widely by the beginning of the nineteenth century. In effect, this was the reestablishment of the fourth century Arian heresy. This blunder was so great that God sent the Second Great Awakening to correct it in the first half of the nineteenth century.

18. **Eighteenth legacy blunder** is the lingering passivity within Christian leadership in America, which, when coupled with denominational jealousies, has precluded effective Christian resistance to the secular humanistic takeover of Covenanted

5

America. This process has defeated the last phase of God's restoration plan for humanity based on the primacy of human participation. Hence, this blunder is destined to generate great misery in our land as well as in the world.

19. **Nineteenth legacy blunder** resides in our violation of God's law of Bountiful Blessings. Summarizing, this law states that the first level of God's blessings fall upon all cultures that practice justice within its civilization. The second, and higher level of bountiful blessings falls upon all cultures that contain the presence of the true church of Jesus Christ. The third, and highest level of bountiful blessings falls upon all cultures dedicated to the goals of Jesus Christ to bring His redemptive light to the world. Each level is reached only when a threshold has been attained, which means that bountiful blessings remain out of generational phase. We reap what our forefathers planted, just as our children will reap what we plant. The next corollary of bountiful blessings states that no bountiful blessings will fall upon those cultures that persecute the beloved of Christ. Yet, the martyrs of those nations can generate a measure of bountiful blessings many generations later when the persecutions are terminated. Japan is such an example. However, this nation is running out of the great harvest of bountiful blessings generated by its huge numbers of Christian martyrs, one of the largest among the nations of the world. The last and very dominant corollary states that national cultures that remain forever negative in its attitude towards the Son of God will degenerate into perpetual misery. The complete depiction of this law with the supporting scriptures can be found in *Prototypical Kingdom.*[2] The problem arises when the level two bountiful blessings of a civilization (currently Europe and America) are controlled by atheistic forces of those cultures that then, in their great and arrogant ignorance, try to level the bountiful blessings of God across the spectrum of the world's civilizations. In a generation or two, this action will provoke God's wrath upon the entire world. This huge sin is now in process, our currently generating legacy blunder!

Combined, these legacy blunders, one caused by the Jews, others by the Gentile churches, with the last one generated by the humanists have led to a pending disaster for humanity. This distressing scenario has been specifically

---

2 . Shults, Eugene C., *Prototypical Kingdom, The Promise of Dialectical Agapism* 1stbooks.com

enhanced by the abandonment of the leadership of the Holy Spirit, which resulted in the nullifying of the teachings of the Bible, especially Jesus' call to the struggle to bring the kingdom of God to earth.

Thus you nullify the word of God for the sake of your tradition. You hypocrites (Matthew 15:6-7)!

Tragically combined, these blunders lost the vision of the rebellion of Jesus Christ, forcing the withdrawal of the leadership of the Holy Spirit in the church and the societal affairs of humanity. This set of mistakes, our modern Christian inheritance, has placed contemporary Christianity in an untenable spiritual position, unable to morally and spiritually balance, and moderate, the technological developments currently exploding across the entire spectrum of human endeavors. So imbalanced, humanity faces a terrible future of massive destruction and death, leaving survivors in degeneration and debauchery.

DOES HOPE EXIST?

Is there hope? Might we, even at this late date, overcome these human-generated blunders separating us from God's loving embrace and the fullness of Jesus' redemptive rescue? Then, might the imbalance of spirituality to technology be redressed in time to save humankind from itself? Can it be done?

No! Not by human effort!

Humanity, even in the form of the church, has sinned so astonishingly that recovery and rescue is now outside the sole prerogatives of human effort. Truly, we have realized these words of our Savior:

These people honor me with their lips, but their hearts are far from me (Matthew 15:8).

Only a massive spiritual renewal, led and energized by the Spirit of God, can reach the necessary spiritual awakening required for recovery. In other words, only an immense intervention by God in the affairs of humanity can save us.

We, the people of Christian faith, must be ready to assist in this spiritual intervention leading to renewal with all that we possess: Our wealth, our comfort and even our lives.

If God blesses humanity with His corrective intervention, it will be the most important event in human history since Jesus appeared to Saul on the road to Damascus or to Francis of Assisi in the old ruined church of San Damiano.

It is strongly indicated by the Holy Spirit that this special intervention shall be the last chance for humanity. Since it is given that church cooperation can help to optimize this intervention, it is essential that the reason and the potential of these events become widespread knowledge so Christian saints can be ready to support the Spirit's massive outpouring as best we can.[3]

WHAT HAVE WE DONE?

Yet today, the saints remain largely ignorant of the need for God's intervention, the reason for it, as well those anticipated events that will lead to its implementation.

'What fall?' We might proclaim. 'This charge is ridiculous; more people attend our church services than ever before. Modern media technology spreads the Gospel across the world. Look at the number of people that have converted to Christianity in the last decade alone. Surely, this allegation is false! The church prospers! The return of the Lord is imminent. This is where we must focus our attention.'

Unfortunately, this perspective is misleading. The Lord's return will occur when the Father says it shall, and when Jesus comes back we must be busy about His work. That means we must be involved in implementing His rebellion. This, of course, demands the return of Jesus' church to His modified and updated eschatology, articulated as the arrival of the kingdom of God to this planet, initially in prototype.[4] But who knows how to do this?

Understand this: The Body of Christ has lost sight of Jesus' plan for the world, even as it is expressed in the Lord's Prayer. We no longer strive to bring the kingdom to this world, satisfied instead, that Jesus will bring it back, after rapture and tribulation, as the New Jerusalem. In affect, we have given up on the task, waiting for God to do the work He assigned to us.

The bad news is that Jesus will not, and cannot, bring in the New Jerusalem until that kingdom is born first by the prayer, faith, fervor, sacrifice, and transforming cultural drive of the Body of Christ. To understand this need, we must realize that the New Jerusalem kingdom is the grown up adult of the kingdom first adapted to earth by the church. If the first stage of the kingdom is not born, allowed to grow into adolescence, then raptured, the last, adult, stage cannot come. Clearly, the Judeans did all of humanity a gigantic disfavor when it aborted the first birth of God's kingdom come to earth. Then, we, the saints, have forfeited on God's resuscitated restoration plan, leaving us trapped between personal salvation and cultural redemption, concentrating on the former, ignoring

---

3. Know the recovery of Christ's mission would have been more pleasing to God if the primary instrument in its restoration had been humankind with only the normal assistance of the Holy Spirit.
4 As given by both scripture and the Holy Spirit!

the latter. As a religion in the corner of a neo-pagan culture, we only see our Christian faith as a private affair, failing utterly to see the shed blood of Jesus Christ as culturally transforming. This myopic vision leaves us ensnared in an erroneous spiritual course full of misunderstanding and spiritual power degradation.

So what have we done? We have exchanged God's great kingdom spiritual power for physical and societal comfort. Lost, along with God's restoration plan, is the kingdom spiritual power of Jesus' church, especially as it was founded and employed in the apostolic church. Quite wretchedly, this apostolic power has been lost to the church for so long that we can no longer comprehend it or reach for its impact from within our current ten-fold weakened spiritual power vacuum. So, unaware of our loss, we remain arrogantly ignorant of God's great power gifts to us. No longer can the Christian shadow heal, nor can most of our prayers!

We exist as Christians today, exclusively, because of the promise of Christ not to abandon His church. But this is not a happy scene for the church, for God's pleasure does not dwell in our passivity, even if His love for the church still lingers. Here then, is the charge against the church:

Within the protection of Jesus' promise, we have abandoned God's restoration plans for our world, the very reason for Jesus' incarnation. Instead, we are content to live with our adjustment to the Adamic Curse, characterized by increasing indifference to the blood rescue of Jesus Christ, yielding immorality coupled with technologically driven physical comfort, all wrapped within a societally concealed exploitation of human, earth and animal resources. This decision, of course, negates the reason for the incarnation of the Son of God to this planet, effectively generating a Western rejection of Jesus' redemptive rescue!

Let everyone be warned! Our current church orientation and attitude is extremely indifferent relative to Jesus' mission vector. Indeed, we are rapidly approaching those conditions that God cannot let stand. The very existence of the structure of the church with its massive disunity is now in question.

GOD'S CORRECTION

As a correction, the Holy Spirit indicates that God is preparing to shift Christianity into its last minor dispensation: The *subset age of the Holy Spirit.*[5]

---

5. Montanus first preached this concept in the second century. Then, Joachim of Flore reported a vision of the end-time age of the Holy Spirit to Pope Innocent III in 1200. It was declared heretical. Now, however, the Holy Spirit reaffirms the coming of His age.

There we will abandon our current *order of action,* which accepts the Adamic fall and its curses - even as we remain blissfully ignorant of our outrageous history of the church's legacy blunders - to transition to a *new order of action,* which shall correct these legacy mistakes. There we will learn to overcome sin, especially the sins of material greed, self, lust, carnality, deception, envy, hardness of the heart, indifference to the suffering of others, hypocrisy, cynicism and ambition. A renewed and re-energized Christian faith paradigm based on agape love shall arise, returning to Jesus' original mission to bring the kingdom to earth. It will be a paradigm of extreme faith and fervor, characterized by overcoming via emancipation not by suppression, all accomplished in a great abundance of kingdom spiritual power. Emancipation will be found in the maximum elevation of the human temple, within the richness and power of God experienced exclusively in the fullness of the indwelling of the Holy Spirit. Both the human soul with its intellect and the human spirit with its commune capacities will be optimized by the Spirit of God. But to soar to Jesus' mission goals, we must soar in His Spirit; hence the first task of the church must be to re-introduce herself to the Spirit of God, Jesus' Spirit of Truth, begging forgiveness for the long centuries of indifference.

Now, let us take a brief trip through history, reviewing what has happened to Jesus' mission.

To help understand this trip we need a better grip on divisions of the Church Age, called minor dispensations in this text, and their impact on humanity. To assist in this grasp of the subdivisions of the Church Age Dispensation, let us use the analogy of an educational system. Each minor dispensation is like a different grade within a school system. Each grade has its own classroom with different teaching objectives. Some children are not able, or are unwilling, to attend the more advanced grades and are left behind. And increasingly, with special assistance for the child, this becomes an individual choice. So it is in life. The school system is equivalent to the Church Age Dispensation. The children represent the human race. The grades are the minor dispensations and the classrooms represent the teaching and learning goals of each of these minor dispensations. Special assistance is analogous to the centuries of missionary efforts to the heathen lands. The unwilling students are those peoples that have rejected Christ. The students advancing in the grades are the beloved ones of God.

The following schematic reviews the minor dispensations of the Church Age. Again, this input was received from the Holy Spirit:

Let the reader understand that this is a crucial component of the theology of the Holy Spirit, that which we must understand and embrace to bring the kingdom to earth.

Minor Dispensations of the Church Age:

1	**Fervor 30 to 410 AD: Fervor of the faithful changes the world, defeating Roman paganism**
2	**First Wrath 410 to 1205 AD: Reproof for joining with paganism, rejecting the Holy Spirit's leadership**
3	**Restoration 1205 to 1317 AD: Jesus appears to Francis, asking for His church reconstruction**
4	**Second Wrath 1317 to 1734 AD: Reproof for ignoring and openly defeating Jesus' request**
a	**1st Nested Dispensation 1317 to 1563 AD: Resuscitation of Knowledge**
b	**2nd Nested Dispensation 1517 to 1734 AD: Freedom, Revolt against Catholicism**
5	**Age of Repulsion Against Religion 1734 to 1848 AD: The Enlightenment, Acceptance of Rationalism only**
6	**Age of Science & Commerce 1848 to present: Technological foundation for the Kingdom**
7	**Agape Civilization: Future Subset Age of the Spirit The Conquest of the Adamic & Second Fall**

Chapter 2

Adamic Fall

The fall of humanity from the companionship of God, described in Genesis, is the key to the comprehension of human existence on this planet. The human spirit was created in God's image, and God enjoyed human companionship. Humanity, in turn, worshipped God. This arrangement was pleasing to God, and He loved His creation.

The fact that God had created the human with a spirit made as the mirror image of His Spirit permitted a perfect and **Holy Junction** between the human spirit and God. The purity of the love that flowed between the two sparkled with brilliance surpassing anything found in the physical realm of life. Truly, this scenario constituted paradise on earth for humanity. Here, in this bliss of existence the human spirit transcended the human mind, functioning as the channel for human knowledge as provided by God.

However, it is easily discernable even at this distance in time that the mind was not totally happy in this arrangement, developing a jealousy over the human spirit's sole acquisition and retention of knowledge. Thus motivated, humankind made a mistake of the first magnitude: the human mind reached for an independent acquisition of knowledge. God was stunned, taken totally by surprise. While it is clear that these actions forever validated the freewill of humankind, it is equally clear that this freewill plunged humankind into a deep abyss. As related in Genesis, perhaps metaphorically, Adam and Eve choose to eat of the forbidden tree full of wisdom, knowing that God prohibited this. See Genesis 3:6. Humanity fell from the communion with God and lost paradise. In this act, our first parents sinned. They choose the human mind with its capacities to accumulate knowledge over the human spirit with its capacities to receive knowledge that God, in His wisdom, might decide to give us.

Our early parents forfeited bliss with God for the activities of the human mind, thus inviting God's curse upon humanity. This, the Adamic curse, disabled and forced the human spirit, with its innate power to roam among the heavenly realm as a sensor in that realm, into subjugation to the soul and the soul's human mind. So dominated, the human spirit became listless and dormant. This same curse incapacitated the huge psychic capacities of the human entity that had enhanced the powerful mind of Adam, enabling mental communications, closing it except for a small psychic capacity dedicated to the commune with the enemy of God. Thus, it has remained throughout the centuries.

The following four schematics illustrate the various inner relationships of the human entity within different environmental and spiritual developments. The first chart shows the close relationship of the human spirit with God before the Adamic fall. The second chart reveals the status of the human spirit after the fall. Notice how the human spirit is minimized and placed in subordination to the human soul under the fall of Adam. The third chart illustrates modern humanists. It is significant that there is no connection with God. Yet, an unknown, clandestine connection with Satan does exist, even though most atheistic humanists are unaware of this connection. The fourth schematic depicts the advanced saint that has the inputted righteousness of God. Notice that a strong connection with God has been established, but the impact of the Adamic curse is still with the saint, forming a path for temptations. Another chart exists, not shown but very similar in structure to the first, pre-Adamic fall chart, in which the original **Holy Junction** with God is reestablished. To this position we must all seek, there to find and overcome all those church legacies personally handicapping each of us, thus enabling the overcoming of our own sin-induced problems.

SCHEMATIC OF THE HUMAN ENTITY BEFORE THE FIRST FALL:

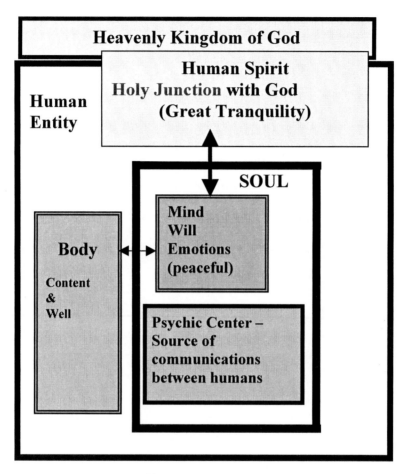

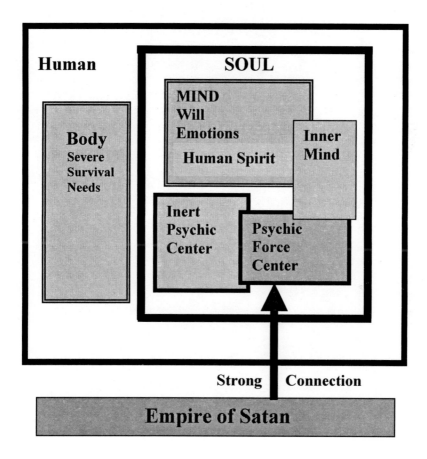

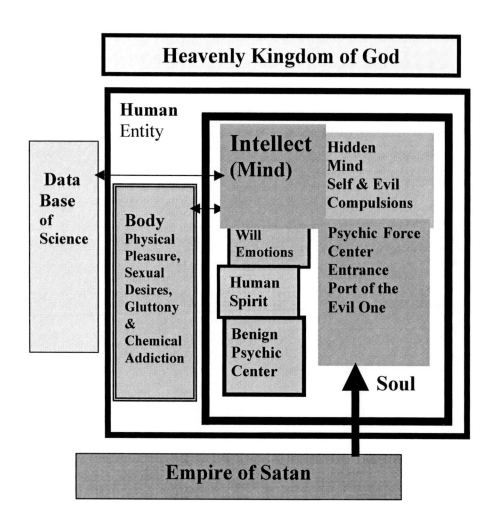

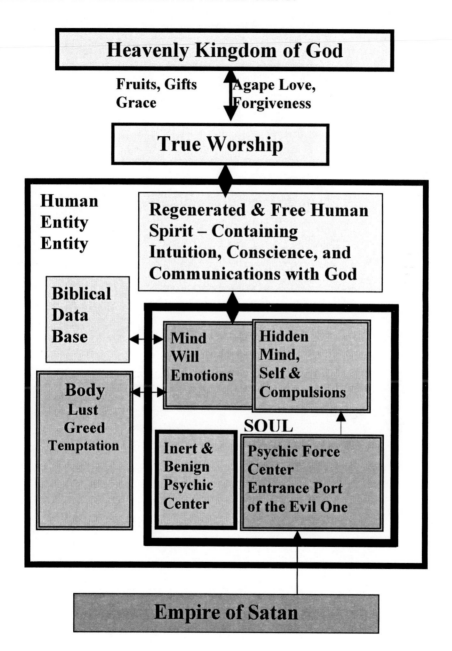

Certainly, the Genesis story of the fall of Adam and Eve is, arguably, the premier truth expressed in the Old Testament. Assuredly, it is the foundation truth for the comprehension of human existence on this planet. Here, we have in the simplest childlike expressions, the most consequential statement of the condition of human existence on earth ever recorded. Yet, most people smile and pass on. They seldom appreciate the Herculean significance of what they have read and so easily dismissed. Do not be naive or misled; the Genesis story is the basis for all that has happened on this planet since the appearance of humanity. Without this information the condition of human existence is unexplainable, and the redemptive life of Jesus Christ is inexplicable.

Scholars claim Genesis tells of human creation twice and the fall only once, attributing this to the work of a redactor.[6] This has confounded some of the saints, tending to weaken their faith in this profound scriptural revelation.[7] Regardless of the validity of the scholarly claims, the Genesis story of the fall of Adam and Eve does not lose its utter and total significance to you, the reader, to the author, or to all of humanity. Except, we must know that the fall of humanity did not concern a fruit, but rather involved the question of the power hegemony within the human. Humanity faced this decision: Would the power center of the human continue to be the human spirit that relates to God? Or would the human power center shift to the soul, to magnify the mind and pervert the human psychic, there to relate to Satan? Which one would reign within humanity? The prize offered by the enemy of God was the exercise of the mind and the independent accumulation of knowledge. The prize offered by God was the continuation of blissful physical and spiritual existence, characterized and enabled by His intimate friendship. Humanity chooses the hegemony of the soul over the hegemony of the spirit, creating a reprehensible insult to God!

---

6. Friedman, Richard Elliott *Who Wrote the Bible*, New York: Harper & Row, Publishers, 1987, page 60-61. Friedman defines a redactor as that person capable of combining documents into a single document such that it appears as a continuous narrative. Many Christian scholars have not accepted that redactors authored part of the Holy Scripture. But should the redactor allegation prove reliable, the faith of Christians should not be shattered because what reason exists that claims the Holy Spirit did not guide the redactors?

7. Estrada, David & White, William *The First New Testament*, Nashville: Thomas Nelson Inc., Publishers, 1978. Discoveries made by the Jesuit priest, Jose O'Callaghan, in the Qumran Dead Sea Scrolls cave 7 has vindicated the age of parts of the New Testament from 50 through 70 AD. From page 137-8, we read that fragments of the books of the New Testament found in cave 7, included scriptures thought by critics like Barth and Bultmann to be myths fraudulently incorporated in the Bible. The Qumran discoveries include Mark 6:48, as well as parts of scriptures found in Acts, Romans, 1 Timothy, 2 Peter and James.

After Adam and Eve decided for the accumulation of knowledge, dashing the love of God, humanity had access to a great ocean of attainable-knowledge. But while the knowledge was there to find, God's blessing on this acquisition was not there. To conquer knowledge, humanity would be forced to labor for its acquisition. This labor was so intense and the survival needs so stringent that initially humankind's attention was totally focused on knowledge that assured survival of the human species.

The question confronting humanity was which way was survival: Farming, hunting, or gathering? Indeed, perhaps the first recognition of knowledge was that humanity was desperately alone, that a serious mistake had happened!

Let us equate our ancestor's situation to the building and launching of a ship. Humankind had to build then launch its ship of human survival without shipbuilding knowledge. Imagine how difficult it would be for you, the reader, to do this survival task even with your present day knowledge. Still, if the survival ship could be built, who would direct and manage it? Where would we move it and how? Humanity lacked the position of its construction and launching site. Humankind knew no course and held no destination, possessed no navigational aids and knew no coordinates of this strange ocean of untapped knowledge. To our credit, humanity solved some of these problems by building the rudderless ship of civilization. Therein, knowledge acquisition became the keel and cross-generation knowledge retention became the hull. This ship floats, but it does not purposefully travel this ocean of knowledge. Even today, the human excursion for knowledge wanders, lost.

In effect, Satan tricked humankind into sailing upon a great and vast sea without a proper ship, course, propulsion, destination, coordinates or compass.

The rudderless ship of civilization - just a drifting ship operative only by slavery, generating unbounded human misery - defines the profound affect of the Adamic curse upon humanity. Despite the obvious progress of the ship of human civilization under the bountiful blessings of God since the Protestant Reformation, this drifting ship retains the basic conditions of human misery, especially for those lower decks [non-Christian third world nations] void of Christ and His vector back to the warm embrace of the Father.

The Adamic curse changed the physical realm of earth. But what changed after the Adamic fall? Survival existed by consuming other life forms. For the human this meant hard work to find, herd, raise and harvest these life forms. From this toil each human gained assets that provisioned that human. These assets included seeds, land, animals, water, shelter, spouse, children, and self esteem. The survival search generated the twin concepts of family units and supportive property. God permitted the survival of the family units. However, without the companionship of God, the rise of evil and misery was inevitable. Some humans discovered that in consuming the labor and the property of other humans they could attain life more luxuriant. It is conjectured that these events occurred in this order:

Sequence of Exploitation:

1. The greedy stole the property of others.
2. With their evil greed still not satisfied, they then stole the labor of others, then the freedom of others to function as humans. In this terrible escalation of sin, they despoiled the inviolability of property by forcing other humans to be their property. Slavery was born and greed flourished. They enjoyed the exploitation of others even as their victims screamed out in pain and misery. Cruelty walked the earth as sadism.
3. To solidify their gains, and to monitor the interactions of the advantaged few, these evil humans formed structured-groups called clans or tribes.
4. In subsequent trade interactions between clans, the clan leaders inadvertently founded societal economics. Once formed these economic groupings provided stability and social structure for all its members, setting rules for the advantageous few to live in safety. Primitive civilization was born.

Significantly, the culture of exploitation, initially developed as slavery, became the central orientation of all civilized, human existence. Human existence was stabilized but in the misery of the many. Thus civilizations, founded upon human exploitations, became the basis for the untold, unmeasured but continuous human misery experienced by our ancestors throughout the ages. Subsequently, it is held to be quite defensible to state these ten theorems of human civilizational maturation:

Civilizational Development Theorems:

Development Theorem One: The first fall of humankind resulted in human aggression against other humans.

Development Theorem Two: The ability of the few to systematize and monopolize this aggression became the basis for civilization.

20

Development Theorem Three: God sent his son to humanity to shift civilization from cruelty to agape love, for Jesus' message of love was too severe for humanity who diluted and polluted the word, limiting its impact on civilization.

Development Theorem Four: Eventually a higher form of civilization was developed based on some of the freedom premises of Protestant Christianity. This cultural experiment enabled the more aggressive of the disadvantaged to seek the status of an exploiter, developing this experimental culture as a Pseudo-Democratic Republic, functioning under the rule of law (America).

Development Theorem Five: God was pleased that part of His Son's work had been culturally utilized; hence He poured out His bountiful blessings upon the experiment. America, especially after WW II, shared this blessing with major portions of the world [Europe], causing modified versions of the experimental culture of limited upward mobility to be copied by large portions of the world.

Development Theorem Six: The flow of Christ-indifferent and Christ-haters to America caused the control of the experiment to shift from Christian to secular and humanistic orientations (America today). The first article of the American Constitution was interpreted as the protection of the sensitivities of the minority, generating the Tyranny of the Minority. This serious, and deliberate misinterpretation was employed as a weapon of oppression against Christianity and its dominance within the nation.

Development Theorem Seven: The progressive defeat by the Christ-haters of those portions of Jesus' mission still operating to bring God's prosperity on America will eventually reach a crisis of exploitation, threatening human, animal and environmental prosperity, instigating a severe challenge to the pseudo-democracy experiments. This crisis will generate recognition of the need for the complete defeat of the Adamic curse and its exploitations in order to reach the highest form of social groupings: agape civilization.

Development Theorem Eight: Under the intervention of God, humanity will be led to a great and wondrous spiritual awakening, followed by a revival of such dimensions that a church convolution will erupt. An Overchurch will be established that unites the brethren. Led by the Spirit of

God, the Overchurch will return the church to its first fervor and reacquaint the saints to the mission vector of Jesus Christ.

Development Theorem Nine: Following the vectored path of Jesus' mission will lead to the development of an agape civilization, and hence, the defeat of the Adamic curses of exploitation. This vectored course is mandated to pass through the challenging format of Dialectical Agapism. Here the New Covenant faith system will confront the advanced freedom civilizations. Herein, these factors exist:

Thesis: Pseudo-Democratic Republic (America)
Antithesis: Rebuilt New Covenant church freed from the impact of the Second Fall and operative as the Overchurch in all the redemptive capacities given humanity by Jesus' blood sacrifice
Synthesis: Agape Civilization, an exploitation free culture, representing the effective defeat of the Adamic fall, and which shall possess the potential to develop into the Bride of Christ, initially as the Prototypical Kingdom of God.

New Development Theorem Ten: When the Validated Societal Commune with God is added to this victory, the culture has the potential to slip into the millennium reign of Jesus Christ, either with or without Jesus' physical return. The restoration of humanity to the warm embrace of God now looms.

Summarizing our Current Civilizational Status

In this representation of human current and future existence, all civilizations formed upon the premises of human exploitation are judged as primordial or primitive in their basic nature. Astoundingly, this includes all civilizations ever devised to date, including all modern civilizations. Alarmingly then, today, human and earth exploitations remain the continuing modus operandi of all human social structures, each fully derived from and dependent upon the Adamic curse.[8]

---

8. Christians must not be led into positions of ignorance and indifference on human exploitation simply because personages of Antichrist orientations such as Jean-Jacques Rousseau (1712 -1778) and Karl Marx (1818 -1883) identified and loudly proclaimed these human problems. Three considerations exist here. First, no intellectual who walks without God can understand the fullness of the problem of human exploitation. Second, failure to fully comprehend the problem means failure to solve the problem. This truth we

Clearly, humankind has made great civilizational progress over the millennia, but over that same period humanity has made only incremental progress in moral valuation and execution. We face the squeeze of advancing technology upon every aspect of our civilization without a counterbalancing moral capacity. Exclusively, only the rescue by Jesus Christ can save us from this plight. Yet unfortunately, that rescue is now largely forgotten, marginalized or scorned.

---

have seen in the twentieth century debacle of Marxism. Third, why have the Christian communities been so slow in discovering and facing the basic human problem of life since we carry true enlightenment and freedom to be found only in the Bible? Has the enemy of God, by first stating the obvious truth, victimized us into second-class intellectualism even as the truth stares out at us from Holy Scripture? Absolutely! Now, the time approaches to project the truth of God and the salvation of Jesus into our culture, emphatically. We must lead, not follow!

Chapter 3

Lost Millennia

Initially after the Adamic fall, data acquisition was confined to the human mind with the human spirit in complete subjugation. **The human sensor into heaven was shut down.** What were left of the human entity were the physical sensors of the human body, which dictated that knowledge would be of the physical realm.

To appreciate this human struggle, to grasp human survival difficulties, the optimal analysis must focus on knowledge: its acquisition, utilization and retention.[9]

Knowledge then, especially physical knowledge became the vehicle for survival. Initially, no recording capacities existed; no methodology remained to convey survival mistakes, thus forcing each generation to repeat the mistakes of the preceding generation. Humanity was adrift upon the equivalent of an ocean of untapped data, the vast physical and spiritual creation of God, stranded without adequate tools, fearfully and desperately trying to cope. Immediately, rebellious humanity needed to capture and convert basic survival data into useful information, turning it into retained knowledge from which humanity could endure and prosper.

Truly, the task must have been formidable, for depressingly, humankind would have to probe this ocean of achievable knowledge without the blessings of God.

To purposefully travel this vast ocean, any intelligence must have coordinates and a known, fixed position within those coordinates. In effect, a set of knowledge coordinates of the knowledge-ocean is indispensable for accurate navigation over this vast sea. That is, the *knowledge of knowledge* is indispensable to knowledge travel. Humanity did not, and still does not possess these knowledge coordinates.

---

9 As used in this text, knowledge is defined as the human cognitive ability over the function or operation of some system or subsystem occurring in God's creation. It is also the unique human capacity to adjust or modify existing systems or their components into new human adapted systems.

WHAT IS EVIL?

Additional problems existed. The ocean of potential knowledge contains all the good as well as all the evil of existence. It is an ocean of deception and entrapments, an ocean of deep selfishness and brutality as well as an ocean of beauty, soaring morality, human integrity and love. What methodology existed to sort this knowledge? Without God how do we judge good from evil? Is it good to sacrifice the first born, or is it evil? Void of judgment standards for the acquisition and classification of human knowledge, who then determines the inevitable by-product, human conduct?

God, of course, determines good and evil because God alone possesses the coordinates of knowledge. He, alone, holds absolute truth. However, with the inputs from God closed, our ancestors floundered. Lacking access to absolute truth, humanity was left without a filter, void of a standard of truth, left without a method to sort information. So stranded, human attempts to gain *knowledge of knowledge* became diluted then thwarted.

RELATIVISM

The apex of human achievement without God's assistance would be the concept of relative-values, still the best plan the Christ-rejecting world can invent. Here, humanity would simply say that if any given social group agreed to a standard, that standard would be honorable. To wit, if a culture decided to execute the father after the birth of the first born son, then the concept of relativism would state that this would be a fine cultural decision even if it were societally fatal. Who knows how many cultures perished in antiquity because of strange customs, all of which would be deemed acceptable under the premise of social relativity?

Beyond the question of good and evil, other urgent questions pressed upon humanity demanding immediate answers. How do we relate to one another? Do we band together and live in social groups? If so, then who leads the group, the brightest or the strongest? What standard of conduct do we demand for the group? What value does each member of the group possess to the group? Do we have a rigid or flexible social scale? Who and how do we enforce these decisions? And what is the best course over the wide expanse of potential knowledge? What responsibilities, if any, do we have in passing our acquired knowledge to our children? These and many more questions demanded answers.

Obviously, survival knowledge became the first and most important knowledge acquisition. And yes, humanity decided to travel over this ocean in social groups and to perpetuate the group by passing survival knowledge to the children. With these decisions, humanity formed its first civilization. In hindsight these are remarkable decisions, focusing the difficulties that humanity must have suffered before it could reach that stage where it could subjugate self for the perpetuation of the group. What a metamorphosis this must have been! How many millennia did it take?

While these emerging civilizations were not comparable to the forfeited culture of paradise, now remembered only in legends, these new, primitive civilizations provided a survival format for the human species. The human species would survive! We can only ponder what God felt as He watched. Was He amused, proud, or deeply grieved?

But what course should humanity follow after survival? Do we grow to reach our lost potential, or are we content to just survive? And if we grow, do we attempt to find our lost paradise? The age-old answers are yes! We grow, and yes we seek paradise. Therein, our ancestors have bestowed upon us a strong basic urge to return to the close relationship and the pure worship of the Creator. This urge, almost an instinct, has never left our species. But left unanswered, the questions of propulsion and direction remained. Many false answers arose.

Clearly, the knowledge coordinates of paradise were not in sight, and no human knew what to do. The human situation was desperate. Humanity could wander about this great, unknown ocean of achievable-knowledge, but without God's help humanity would forever be wandering aimlessly. Yet, the knowledge-path to God remained obscure and hidden, forbidden to humankind. Driven by the compelling urge to reunite with God, but unable to find the path back, superstitions and idol worship arose. Spiritually lost without God's companionship, the viciousness of one human to another became rampant; the human attempt to discriminate good from evil was completely forfeited. A series of civilizations appeared, one after another. The faith and belief systems of each attempt collapsed under the increasing weight of human exploitation, especially as slavery escalated,[10] becoming the modus operandi of all these primitive

---

10. Somehow the injustice of the word, slavery, has lost its impact upon our generation. Seemingly, this illustration drives the concept home: You are a slave, you have a terrible need for sleep, and you have a tooth that is abscessed, generating great pain. Suddenly, your master has an unexpected guest. He beckons, demanding you get on your hands and knees to be a chair for his guest while they dine and talk the night out. That is slavery, human exploitation near its maximum repulsiveness!

cultures. This human affliction was to continue even when civilizations turned sophisticated.

The evil-one walked with the human race where God once walked, flooding human minds with evil knowledge. The situation with humankind became so hopeless that God destroyed humanity by the flood and started over again with a small family. In this destruction, we have failed to recognize that God did not just destroy the people; He also destroyed the civilizations that had emerged.

Civilization again evolved as the human populations grew. Still humanity struggled; the human race remained desperately lost. In this state, humankind continued to acquire knowledge but to what avail? No direction existed.

Then God came to the rescue. He selected a people and prepared them with selected knowledge for the coming of the Savior, His Son. These people were to prepare the way for the coming of Logos containing the vector over the knowledge-ocean to God. Theirs was to be a special civilization in the maze of lost cultures; yet these people stumbled and frequently lost sight of their mission. The human situation remained desperate.

Four classes of damage resulted from the Adamic fall. The first is the loss of soul/spirits to the presence of God for all of eternity. The second resides in the divestiture of the coordinates of paradise. The third is the misery forthcoming from God's absence, suffered individually. The fourth disaster is the dispossession of human societal potential.

The total of these losses represent the havoc of the Adamic fall with perhaps the fourth, the loss of human societal potential, that is most neglected by the theologians and religious scholars. Decidedly, even in modern times, this neglect has impacted the human search for an improved civilization.

UNDERSTANDING THE LOSS

The measurement of the Adamic havoc is definitive and precise because of God's spiritual Law of Equity and Balance between the physical and spiritual realms. Distressingly, at this moment in human history, this measurement belongs exclusively in the spiritual realm of God. However, even if humanity cannot measure this havoc, we can understand the finality of this existence-determining spiritual law. It functions as authoritatively as any law of physics. This spiritual law can be stated as follows:

LAW OF COMPENSATION AND BALANCE

God's creation is balanced, and in harmonious equilibrium. Inequities occurring within God's physical creation shall be compensated in God's spiritual creation through the judgment and punishment of individuals or by the blood of Jesus Christ.

Scriptural support (Associative):
Blessed are the poor in spirit,
...for theirs is the kingdom of heaven.
Blessed are those who mourn,
for they will be comforted.
Blessed are the meek,
for they will inherit the earth.
Blessed are those who hunger and thirst for righteousness,
for they will be filled.
Blessed are the merciful,
for they will be shown mercy.
Blessed are the pure in heart,
for they will see God (Matthew 5:3-8).

The Scriptural support for this law is also found in these Scriptures:

So the last will be first, and the first will be last (Matthew 20:16).

and whoever wants to be first must be your slave (Matthew 20:27).

Stated differently, within the two realms, the spiritual and the physical, there must be equilibrium in the harmony of God, including equity in human justice. This law recognizes the dualism of life in both the spiritual and physical realms yet functions across these realms as one realm, generating a continuum of spiritual and harmonious balance. This cross realm balance is better appreciated when the complexities of the spiritual realm are mastered.[11]

Kingdom decorum standards set the correct guide for human conduct, especially and initially as established by the Ten Commandments. These are given to humanity to assist us in maintaining this spiritual and harmonious double realm balance. Sin is therefore anything that disrupts this balance, tilting it away from God's harmony.

---

11. See Shults, Eugene C. *Prototypical Kingdom: the Promise of Dialectical Agapism* chapter 18 for details of the spiritual realm.

UNDERSTANDING THE CONSEQUENCES OF SIN

Significantly, the law of balance indicates that once sin has occurred, forgiveness of sin, although essential to the harmonious walk with Christ, may not be enough to address the inequities caused by that sin. Even while God's anger and disappointment over the sin abates, His law of balance still requires compensation for the inequities of His harmony caused by the sin of the human, for each sin generates a tilt in the harmony of existence. Some buy-back must occur. The law must be satisfied since laws of existence are ruthless and void of compassion, even spiritual laws. If you fall off the top of a six-story building, the law of gravity functions even if you are a child of God, fully justified. And as it is in the physical, so it is in the spiritual realm. Laws that have been established by God exist and function. We dare not assume that God will invalidate the law of gravity half way down the fall from the six-story building. So, in the same fashion we cannot assume that the law of Compensation and Balance (Equity) will not function just because we are saved and justified by faith. Because while John 3:3, 3:16, 3:36 and Romans 3:22-24 set our justification, freeing us from our sins, Matthew 12:36 and Hebrews 10:26 tie us to our sin's rippling consequences in two ways. One way is the sin itself if unrequited, and the second way is the affects of the sin on the harmony of God's dual realm equilibrium.

Let us examine a real life scenario to illustrate this equity problem. A couple driving near Evanston, Indiana has an argument. In a rage, the mother, who is driving, pulls the car out of the heavy traffic to pass on a hill. She hits another car coming over the hill, killing herself and the mother of five in the other car. The father, a recovering alcoholic, could not restore his life after the loss of his wife, and the lives of the five children turned tragic despite the efforts of the extended family to raise them. This tragedy has all the potential to ripple into subsequent generations, demeaning the lives of many. The harmony of God in this little family was severely disrupted, most probably with the loss of untold, unmeasured spiritual and societal potential. This was an injustice. Who pays? Does anyone pay? Yes, in the duality of existence as established by God, payment is due!

Thus unfortunately, the inequities of the double realm caused by human sin must be paid in full, usually in suffering and misery in one realm or the other, sometimes both. It is true that this payback in suffering can be Jesus' suffering at the stake and on the Cross, but is this what you want? If the saint, because of his or her love for Christ, elects to undertake his or her own obligation of suffering to ease the dynamic suffering burden of the Savior, then this act of love does not neutralize justification, it only supports and enhances it. Indeed, in a special revelation, the Spirit says that this was the way of Paul.

This entire process would then mandate that an Equity Adjustment Queue exists in the spiritual realm for those headed for heaven. The Roman Catholics were correct; there is something like their purgatory out there. The Catholics use 1 Corinthians 3:15 and Revelation 21:37 as scriptural support, maintaining that the living can pray for the dead, assisting the saved in their equity suffering. But perhaps the most important scriptural support for praying for the dead is from 2 Maccabees 12:39-45.

For if he [Judas Maccabee] were not expecting that those who had fallen would rise again, it would have been superfluous and foolish to pray for the dead. ... Therefore he made atonement for the dead, that they might be delivered from their sin (2 Maccabees 12:44-45).

Now, we must ask this question. Since the Roman Catholic Church had seriously abused this concept in a corruption of paid indulgences, did Luther and his supporters become too angry by this sinful procedure, overreacting? Did they go too far in their backlash, even to the point of modifying Holy Scripture? Is this why the Apocrypha was thrown out? Might this then be another legacy blunder, one that has precluded the aid of the living saints for the dead for five hundred years! But wait! The Holy Spirit states we are dealing with partial truths. And this is the truth that the Spirit is pushing: Only the freewill acceptance of Jesus as Savior, regardless if it is the product of grace or human evangelism, can warrant eternal salvation for a soul/spirit. And this cannot be done anywhere except among the living. Hence, those denominations that baptize their dead loved ones are wasting their time and efforts. But that is not the end of the message of the Spirit on this affair. A complicated set of retention queues exist in the Spiritual realm, and the living are empowered to assist those soul/spirits in some of those retention queues. Specifically we can help those in the Equity Adjustment Queue, those souls/spirits on the road to heaven, delayed while they work out their sin-generated inequities. We can pray to the Son, asking for relief. Love is the operative factor here. But God is not happy with the techniques of those churches that recognize this opportunity. The organized church's teachings and practices on special indulgences are groundless. Since the keys to the kingdom were lost in the second to the fourth centuries, proclaiming indulgences and similar church pronouncements are ineffective and can be insulting and abusive to the faithful, as well as the Lord. Normally, one cannot ease the burden of the dead by walking through a door or visiting a church on a given day or time. Seek the righteousness of God then pray for the dead.[12] This is the path. There is a measure of anger, no, frustration, on the part of God on this issue. Let us be careful. The Catholics need to pray out their procedure, correcting it; the Protestants need to wake up to their theological fallacy generated by 484 years of

_____

12. The methods are laid out in Shults, *Prototypical Kingdom*.

overreaction. With their living descendents indulging in self-righteousness, the Protestant dead has suffered for hundreds of years, needlessly deprived of love intercessions, included in the greatest of ironies, many of the original Reformation leaders.[13] The Spirit is grieved.[14]

That humanity is called to help their loved ones, or any other soul/spirit, through their spiritual time of punishment is a great mystery of God's creation. Yet, it is so! Perhaps, therein, reside the basic teaching tenets of agape love. And if we cannot master this tenet, we cannot grasp the fullness of God's love! And thusly, we fail the basic lessons of life!

Indeed, this is the indication of the Holy Spirit; confirm it yourself. Remember all confirmations must be one to one with the Spirit of God, not from an authority figure that might be brainwashed into a prohibitive bias of denominational doctrine. Only the truth sets us free, and that has not been our unaltered companion since 172 AD, the instigating date for the first church canon and the date that marks the beginning of the death of massive and widespread true worship of God the Father.

Hence, the distressing conclusion is that our loved ones, now dead, await our prayer assistance. Many poor soul/spirits have been waiting for hundreds even thousands of years for assistance. The numbers are staggering! Theology based on biases, hatred and arrogance has failed us.[15]

IMPACT OF THE ADAMIC FALL, OUR FIRST FALL

Now, consider the magnitude of the Adamic mistake. The enormity of that sin transcended the combined capacities of potential human compensatory suffering. The Adamic sin was so excessive that it deprived humankind of all its basic, intrinsic value. Disaster struck our species. Both power centers in the human entity, the human spirit and the human psychic, were shut down. To grasp

---

13. The Spirit of God has mandated that the names involved in the push from the Equity Adjustment Queue into heaven be held as private with one exception.

14. Two prayer partners, Floyd Schlosser and James Ashmore, and the author were shocked when the Spirit asked us to help push out the leaders of the Protestant Reformation stuck in the equity queue for the last 450 years. They are needed as implementation generation leaders following the incarnation pattern of John the Baptist. We were stunned when we pushed 82,260 such soul/spirits out of the equity queue into God's loving embrace in a mere three weeks, using the Holy Junction. God dispatched them to their momentous assignments. This information is given under the Spirit's urgings so that those who have ears to hear will hear and act. The scorn and cynicism of others will be settled after their passing.

15. See Shults, Eugene C. *Prototypical Kingdom: The Promise of Dialectical Agapism* for details about interceding for the dead.

what happened we must realize that collectively, the human race could not correct the inequities generated by the Adamic sin, not even by the combined misery and suffering of all men and women then, now and forever. Humankind could not discharge God's Law of Compensation and Balance.

Humanity was trapped; the human race could not correct its own mistake. Into this debacle, human misery exploded across the survivors. Humanity was in a desperate situation, lost in a miserable abyss of suffering and dejection, seemingly destined to live forever one notch above the animal kingdom. It was into this abyss of human misery and hopelessness, that God manifested His loving compassion for the human race.

Chapter 4

Plan of Redemption: Arrival of Yeshua Ha-Mashiach

To solve the harmony imbalance generated by the Adamic Fall, that is, to redeem humankind, our God of Love developed a plan of redemption. He selected a man, Abraham, to form a people to prepare the way for a Great Redeemer, His own Son. He then sent these chosen people multiple prophets to prepare the way for the Anointed One. The greatest among these prophets was Moses. Through Moses, God dispatched the basis of the kingdom of God's decorum in the form of the Ten Commandments. Collectively, these prophets pointed at the coming Savior of the world and established conditions for the recognition of His arrival.

However, the preparation people God had selected turned into a rebellious, strong willed people, difficult to harness to His work. To help, God had His Spirit inspire the recorded testimony of the Adamic fall of humanity. Recorded also is the work of many of His special messengers, His prophets, capturing in writing their activities and prophecies concerning the coming of the Redeemer. This is called the Old Testament in Christian scholarship.

At the selected time, God dispatched His only Son to take the body of a man upon Himself in the incarnation birth and life of Yeshua Ha Mashiach known as Jesus the Christ to western humanity.[16] The Son of God, incarnated as Yeshua, possessed a transcending, intrinsic value surpassing the value of humanity combined. This concentrated value, if forfeited in sacrifice, would enable the adjustment in the balance of God's creation, bringing it back to harmony. It would pay off the debt of human sinfulness in the life sacrifice of that one special person. Humanity could be returned to paradise via this rescue. This was God's redemption plan. It would take nine steps to complete this rescue:

---

16. Interestingly, it is presumed that God's redemptive redress had to wait for historians to arrive among humanity. Is it arguable that the Son's redress arrived a bit too soon? But what then of the souls lost by a further delay verses the souls lost because documentation was not up to modern standards? In this, we must have faith that God selected the optimum timing for Jesus' incarnation.

- **Step One:** the Sacrifice of the Son of God in atonement
- **Step Two:** The development of Jesus' church by the Holy Spirit to ensure and assist in the initial implementation of the kingdom via the Judean nation
- **Step Three:** The initial implementation of the kingdom via the Judean nation, a tribal implementation, stage one of the kingdom, its birth stage
- **Step Four:** The Judean church leads the way to a larger, mixed racial and cultural implementation with the Gentiles. This form of the kingdom would last for one thousand years as God works out the necessary human adjustments, internal cleansing and spiritual growth problems, transforming existing cultures of the participating world into the bride of Christ. This would be stage two implementation of the kingdom, the adolescent stage
- **Step Five:** The great harvest of the good seed
- **Step Six:** The removal of the bride of Christ in the rapture
- **Step Seven:** Elimination of all remaining bad seed in the Great Tribulation
- **Step Eight:** The return of the bride of Christ as the New Jerusalem Kingdom, a transcending accomplishment, stage three implementation of the kingdom
- **Step Nine:** The gift of the kingdom to the Father.

To appreciate this plan, it must be recognized that there is only one kingdom, with three stages of growth: birth and infancy (Judean), adolescence (Gentile), and adult (New Jerusalem).

Here are several scriptures that support these steps:

Scriptures supporting the infant implementation:

… Jesus replied. The kingdom of God does not come visibly, nor will people say, 'Here it is,' or 'There it is,' because the kingdom of God is within you (Luke 17:20-21).

Our Father in heaven, hallowed be your name, your kingdom come, your will be done on earth as it is in heaven (Matthew 6:9).

I declare to you that the Lord will build a house for you: When your days are over and you go to be with your fathers, I will raise up your offspring to succeed you, one of your own sons, I will establish His Kingdom. (1 Chronicles 17:11).

Scriptures that support the adolescent stage of the kingdom of God adapted to earth:

The kingdom of the world has become the kingdom of our Lord and His Christ, and He will reign forever and ever (Revelation 11:15).

This Scripture, the seventh trumpet, indicates that the kingdom arrives as a transformed not a transcendent culture. Notice the past tense of the words 'has become', which strongly points at the arrival of the kingdom as a cultural transformation. Second, it says this transformed culture is never to perish, which if the first assumption is correct, strongly supports the contention that all of the stages of the kingdom implementations are the same kingdom in different growth development. The key to this interpretation is that the seventh trumpet does not herald the arrival of the New Jerusalem form of the kingdom.

Hallelujah! For our Lord God Almighty reigns [on earth] (Revelation 19:6).

Even so, when you see all these things [the springtime of human existence], you will know that it [His Millennium Reign] is near, right at the door (Matthew 24:33).

Blessed and holy are those who have part in the first resurrection [the resurrection into the Millennium Reign of Jesus Christ]. The second death has no power over them, but they will be priests of God and of Christ and will reign with him for a thousand years (Revelation 20:6).

Scriptures that support the third stage, the adult, implementation of the kingdom:

I saw the Holy City, the New Jerusalem, coming down out of heaven from God, prepared as a bride beautifully dressed for her husband (Revelation 21:2).

Scripture supporting the harvesting of the good seed:

Then another angel came out of the temple and called in a loud voice to him who was sitting on the cloud, 'Take your sickle and reap, because the time to reap has come, for the harvest of the earth is ripe.' (Revelation 14:15).

Scripture supporting the day of the Lord, the Great Tribulation:

See, I will send you the prophet Elijah before that great and dreadful day of the Lord comes. He will turn the hearts of the fathers to their children, and the hearts of the children to their fathers; or else I will come and strike the land with a curse (Malachi 4:5-6).

There are more supporting scriptures for each step, but these verses provide necessary biblical support for the inputs of the Spirit about God's initial plan of rescue.

It is important to recognize two factors at this junction of our analysis:

One, God had created the perfect plan to reverse the Adamic fall restoring humanity to paradise.

Two, because of the severity of the human betrayal inherent in the Adamic fall – perhaps, truly outside of our comprehension and assessment abilities in the twenty-first century - God insisted that humanity must accept the plan within the fullness of human freewill. Only then, could God trust the restoration of humanity to His paradise.

Here is a schematic of God's original restoration plan:.

Step 1: Son of God would incarnate as a humble carpenter and die on the Cross to redeem the sins of humanity, freeing the human species from its Adamic chains.

Step 2: To ensure the remaining development of the Father's plan Jesus would ask the Holy Spirit to form His church.

Step 3: The Tribe of Judea would implement the first demonstration of the kingdom of God on earth becoming the light of the earth for all of humankind. This would be stage 1 initialization of the kingdom adapted to earth, the infant stage.

Step 4 : Copying the demonstration of the Kingdom shown by the Judeans, a major demonstration of the kingdom would be implemented among the Gentiles becoming (along with the Judeans) the Bride of Christ, lasting for one thousand years. This would be stage 2 of the implementation process, the adolescent stage of the kingdom.

Step 5: Harvesting and cleansing of the good seed would follow.

Step 6: Christ would come back for His bride removing her from the earth plane.

Step 7: The Great Tribulation would eliminate the remaining bad seed from the earth.

Step 8: The removed Bride of Christ would be returned as the New Jerusalem Kingdom as the transcending culture of the entire world. This would be stage 3, the last stage implementation of the kingdom of God on earth. This is the kingdom in its adult form.

Step 9: Jesus would give His Kingdom to the Father.

Jesus grew up as a normal human being fully subject to the environmental factors of human life. Thus as an adult, with the richness of human life fully valued by Jesus, the Father asked Jesus to offer up His life as payment for the sins of humanity. As stated above, God's plan was to achieve equity in the balance of existence through Jesus' suffering in the Garden, His pain at the flogging stake and His death on the Cross. But before Jesus accepted this path, He hesitated. Here, we have, perhaps inadvertently a signal sent down through the centuries that His humanity was complete and full. Yet, Jesus accepted His Father's request and redeemed humanity by His great mystery of suffering. He died on the Cross buying back all of humanity. Jesus' redemptive act was confirmed by His amazing and glorious resurrection to which the Shroud of Turin witnesses as a marvelous modern day sign, validating this incredible event in history.[17]

These events consummated the first step in the plan of human redemption set by the Father. It reset the balance of God's harmony and freed humanity to travel the path to the companionship of God. Yet this journey to the companionship of God was not forced upon humanity. Perhaps because of God's crushing disappointment in the Adamic demise, God set the requirement that human companionship must be generated from love not obligation. He went further; He decreed that each human must seek Him in difficulties. Hence the path to paradise, personally and culturally, is arduous. It is the overcoming path, that which has been so overlooked by the theology of grace. To reach overcoming, the saint must find his or her individual communion with God as a cherished prize.

What is true of the individual struggle to overcome is true of the culture of humankind. **Human civilization can only become the kingdom of God in human struggle**. Even the forthcoming intervention of God cannot succeed in bringing the kingdom of God to earth without the churches' struggle to implement it. Look upon God's intervention as a parent placing the child back on the tricycle after falling. The fallen child, the church, must once again operate the tricycle in order to move forward.

Thus, Jesus' victory on the Cross was strategic, not tactical. Christ won the war, but each of us must overcome in our personal struggles, and the church must return to its original status as a spiritual organization, fighting in harm's way for Christ Jesus. Only this process can win the tactical battle.

_____

17. Several scientists have alleged that the initial carbon 14 dating of the shroud was scientifically inaccurate. The world waits for the next official test.

Over the centuries it has remained for each saint to utilize Jesus' blood victory on the Cross to gain individual tactical success by accepting Jesus' open door of salvation, given without merit to each of us. From this position, we must obtain a personal rapport with God, reaching our personal Justification with God, a process of faith. Yet, it can be argued that Justification is not a free gift because faith is a gift of the Holy Spirit. Justification can arrive via grace but more likely, and more powerfully, it will arrive through the indwelling presence of the Holy Spirit. If you have no relationship with the Holy Spirit except through grace, then just claiming you have adequate faith without the deep indwelling presence of the Holy Spirit may not be enough. In fact, it may be a sham, a form of cheap salvation – a deception out of hell designed to capture you for the forces of evil! The Christian life is a fortuitous opportunity, a chance to join Jesus in heaven. Do not pilfer this opportunity by accepting cheap salvation, defined as that theology which satisfies your need to be both saved and an operative heathen in the secular world, busy in the maximization of personal esteem, wealth, comfort and lust!

Frequently, humans desirous of attainment, deceive themselves. And unfortunately, when it happens in our walk with Christ, the results are always devastating. Far too many saints have *display faith*, the appearance of faith put up for the societal need to appear as others. Expect God to test your faith and if it is *display faith*, it will fail. To strengthen faith, each individual must seek the indwelling presence of the Holy Spirit, becoming deeply involved agape love partners. Each saint must review Acts 8:14-17. If you have not been prayed over for the baptism of the Holy Spirit, be concerned. Your walk with God cannot be optimized, in fact, it could be that you walk the path of cheap salvation, a dangerous road leading to places you do not want to visit! But wait! This is not the worst of this personal message. The enemy of God is a beast of the first magnitude, totally interested in our undoing. He has managed over the centuries to fabricate many falsehoods to deceive us. Perhaps the worst deception resides here in the baptism of the Holy Spirit. He has introduced a set of impersonators of the Holy Spirit; evil spirits all. Sadly, your baptism of the Holy Spirit could be a fabrication. In fact, the Spirit said on 7/9/01 that 62 percent of the 'Spirit-filled saints' do not have a valid indwelling of the Holy Spirit. This is a calamity of the first magnitude! So how can we tell if we have deception? The Spirit of God is a Spirit of love and truth. He loves, and loves to be loved. If your relationship with your indwelling presence is not based on strong spiritual love, then seek the Spirit-Check, a process of spiritual cleansing.[18]

---

18. The spirit-check prayer can be found in Chapter 20 of this text. It also can be found in Shults, *Christ-Walk* pages 83-84 and in Shults, *Prototypical Kingdom* page 70. Page 232 of the *Prototypical Kingdom* best explains the spirit-check application.

Learn the secret of life embodied in this prayer: binding and self-deliverance practiced with the Spirit of God. Then use it to overcome.

Societally, it remains for the churches of Christ to utilize Jesus' victory for the ultimate tactical victory: The redemption of the culture of humanity into the kingdom of God adapted to earth. This requires cultural confrontation leading to cultural transformation. In fact, this is the central message of the Gospel, diluted by Paul who did not have enough faith in the faith of the churches, telling them to do what he said, not what he did. Hence, it would appear that this lesson has not been mastered, and in fact, we are content today to sit in a small part of the secular humanistic culture, happy with our secular bone, church tax exemptions.

Chapter 5

Judean Rejection of Yeshua: The First Legacy Blunder

Yeshua Ha-Mashiach fulfilled the prophecies for the Messiah's arrival given by the Old Testament prophets except the expectations of the Jewish people for political and military liberation. Of all the sixty major prophecies of Jewish Scripture that points at Yeshua and His life, none seems more convincing than Isaiah 53:[19]

But He was pierced for our transgressions, He was crushed for our iniquities; the punishment that brought us peace was upon him, and by his wounds we are healed (Isaiah 53:5).

And verse eight:

... for the transgression of my people he was stricken (Isaiah 53:8).

And Psalm 22:

... a band of evil men has encircled me, they have pierced my hands and my feet. I can count all my bones; people stare and gloat over me. They divide my garments among them and cast lots for my clothing (Psalm 22:16-18).

Remember, when these Holy Scriptures were written, crucifixion, as a death punishment, was unknown. Clearly, the mission of the Hebrew prophets was to focus the exact arrival of Yeshua in the history of humanity so that no informed and fair-minded person could miss the Messiah's arrival. Yet, Yeshua's own people missed Him. Why? Basically, since the ministry of Yeshua did not advocate violence, the Judeans, still immersed in a civilization of violence, despite their chosen status and special Scriptures, rejected Yeshua, killing Him by crucifixion in 33 AD – scholars believe that this date is closer to 30 AD.[20] His

---

19. For an exhaustive review of these prophecies read Lockyer, Herbert *All the Messianic Prophecies of the Bible.* Grand Rapids: Zondervan Publishing House, 1973.
20. Some scholars maintain it was several years earlier. Crucifixion was a Roman punishment, stoning was a Judean punishment. But a few scholars assert that the Judean

church immediately appeared in the Judean culture as the Nazarenes[21] and contended for the faith loyalty of the Judeans.

RISE OF THE NAZARENE CHURCH

The Nazarene church, inspired by the Spirit of God, faithfully passed out Yeshua's message of the coming of the kingdom of God to earth in agape love and brotherhood. They initially clung to His promise to return to rule over this kingdom. It was their expectation that Judea would embrace the Good News of Yeshua and that the Kingdom would arrive immediately.[22] When this did not happen, the Nazarenes, undoubtedly with a measure of regret, began to record the Good News of Yeshua for subsequent generations, establishing the materials for the Gospel and Epistles of the New Testament.[23]

Yeshua's message was revolutionary; it proclaimed a New Covenant, one that called forth accountability for our thoughts, not just our actions. It was rebellious, promoting an integration of our entire existence with the teaching and presence of God. Based on faith not religiosity, Yeshua's teachings opened the door for an entirely new civilization, the first truly new civilization since the Adamic fall.[24] To affect this, the new pact of God abolished the old pact, abrogating the old forms of worship, especially animal sacrifices and the genetic priesthood. Indeed, the aim of Yeshua's message was the very restructuring of the nature of civilization: Humanity was to live in agape love within the brotherhood of compassion, with each human as the Temple of the new faith, obtained and sanctioned by the indwelling Spirit of God. So, since each follower

---

authorities had a one-year moratorium on the death sentence placed on them by the Roman authorities. Hence the Judeans were forced to ask the Romans to kill Yeshua by crucifixion. The author cannot validate this claim but if true it would make the prophecies of Isaiah 53 and Psalm 22 even more miraculously fulfilled.

21. Gibbon, Edward, *The Decline and Fall of the Roman Empire*. New York: Random House, Inc. Volume1, page 389. Gibbon confirms that the early Jewish converts were called the Nazarenes.

22. It is noteworthy that Jesus foresaw the destruction of the temple. Might this mean that Jesus expected the kingdom to arrive after the temple destruction? If so, the Nazarene church had already forfeited their responsibilities by fleeing before the Jerusalem siege! Should the burden for this failure, the first and very decisive blunder in the **second fall**, belong to the Judean nation or to the Nazarenes, Yeshua's original church? Who carries this large burden?

23. The New Testament was initially assembled in its present form (minus Revelation) in 363 AD at the council of Laodicea.

24. This would be agape civilization, a culture free of human exploitation, achievable only via the adaptation of the kingdom of God to earth, Yeshua's great message.

of Yeshua was to be a temple onto God, the Temple at Jerusalem (Herod's Temple) was no longer the focus point of worship. Abandoned by God, God tolerated its destruction by the pagans in 70 AD.

Yeshua's sacrifice of His earthly life was the ultimate enabling triumph of this new pact, becoming the exclusive vehicle for this faith construction. All the sacrifices of every living creature within the world could not duplicate it, indeed, rendering further animal sacrifice meaningless.

The dynamics of the Gospel of Yeshua, shifting from Jewish religiosity to charismatic faith, from structure to free flowing agape love, from rigid laws to the freedom of the Holy Spirit, was colossal, requiring enormous personal belief shifts. Perhaps for the Judeans it was too demanding to grasp and accept, certainly, a huge step forward for all of humanity at this junction of human development. The dynamics of this shift is summarized in these brief words of Yeshua:

Love the Lord your God with all your heart and with all your soul and with all your mind. This is the first and greatest commandment. And the second is like it: Love your neighbor as yourself (Matthew 22:37-39).

These brief words constituted a revolution in human existence, in three sentences eliminating the rigidity of the Jewish law, replacing it with agape freedom. A wondrous, pivotal moment in human affairs, yet a destiny-shift few have fully comprehended! Assuredly, the future will carry complete human cognition either in relentless sorrow or unbounded joy!

Initially, the Nazarene church attempted to define and project Yeshua's outreach to Judea, winning a sizable number of Judean converts. But this initial success was for naught; **Judea had chosen to ignore Yeshua**. The pattern was set. In what appears to be a desperate action by Yeshua, - confirmed by the Holy Spirit - the Good News of Yeshua was shifted to the Gentiles by Yeshua's appearance to Saul on the road to Damascus. These Gentiles came to know Yeshua Ha-Mashiach as Jesus Christ. However, in the Judean rejection of Yeshua, the birth stage implementation of the kingdom adapted to earth was negated, forfeited! Who can measure this catastrophe?

Realize what happened here. God's birth of His kingdom was aborted! A tragedy of untold dimensions had occurred, generating irredeemable harm to God's plan to restore humanity to paradise by reversing the Adamic fall. Reflect on the pain that God must have felt! Betrayed again!

At first, the Judeans looked upon Yeshua's movement as another Jewish sect much like the Essenes. The Judean religious authorities were moderately, if reluctantly, tolerant of the Nazarenes. Fearful of riots and disruptions, which would bring Roman disapproval upon their remaining autonomy, they tolerated the large conversion rate. The future of the Nazarene church looked promising.

But somewhere in the fifth and sixth decade of the first-century, Judean tolerance of the Nazarenes faded. Jewish persecution of the early followers of Yeshua commenced. Nazarenes became frightened with many of their Hellenistic Nazarenes fleeing Judea. The remaining Nazarenes, seeking mainline Jewish acceptance, practiced the Torah more vigorously than the Pharisees.[25] But the mode was set and Judean confrontation replaced reluctant acceptance. Placed under strong Jewish social pressure with some persecutions, many of the remaining Nazarenes deserted Yeshua and returned to conventional Jewish beliefs. This abandonment under pressure, even torture, decided the fate of the Nazarene witness to the Judean nation. Weakened by war, the message of their own Messiah was lost to them, grieving God. Angered, God's wrath would pour out upon the Judeans and their descendants for thousands of years. Sadly, this wrath can still be still seen in our current lifetimes. The recent Christian politically correct efforts to divert the accountability of the Jews will only induce accountability upon the churches. Accountability based on reality is not bigotry! Avoiding accountability based on the political correctness myths of a social and political system simply invites the return of God's wrath.

FIRST JUDEAN WAR FOR INDEPENDENCE

In 66 AD, a short generation after the crucifixion of Yeshua, the Judean Zealots managed to start a war of independence from Rome. Seven years later, with no more towns or strongholds left to resist, the Judeans finally capitulated.

But in fact, the war was decided in September of AD 70 with the fall of Jerusalem. One month before, "Roman legionnaires erected their banners in the sacred precincts and sacrificed before them."[26] Then the Romans razed the entire city, including Herod's temple. Many Jews died in the siege of Jerusalem; a large

---

25. The Spirit indicates that this cowardice was a factor in the failure of the Nazarene church, that indeed, by embracing the Jewish law so tightly, it lost sight of the New Covenant, guaranteeing the Nazarene failure. Only the shift to the gentiles saved Yeshua's salvation message and His redemptive capacities.

26. Keller, Werner *The Bible as History*, New York: William Morrow and Company, 1981, p 371.

number went into slavery; some were able to flee, and a substantial remnant survived in Judea.

JUDEAN REVENGE

The belligerency of the first-century Jewish refugees remained intact, rising up in revolt against the Romans in 115-117 AD.[27] Before the Romans could put down these displaced Judeans, the Jews killed (massacred) four hundred thousand Greeks in Cyrenaica, Egypt and Cyprus. Clearly, their rage at the destruction of their temple and their exile still burned hot forty-five years later.

Notably, the brutal Greek holocaust by the Jews in 115-117 AD would mirror their own on-going punishment over the forsaking of God, and, at the same time, graphically outline the brutal consequences of the Judean rejection of Yeshua and His message of agape love. Even today their massacre of hundreds of thousands of innocent Greek peoples - men and women, their children and their infants - is a crime neither recognized nor repented in Jewish culture and history. They dwell in history as victims, but that perspective is not totally accurate. Why is this brought up? To facilitate the understanding that while chosen of God, the Jews are still humans with weaknesses for violence that need cleansing, just as it does for the rest of humanity. Clearly, the Jews did suffer horrific consequences from their rejection of Yeshua. Cease your false pretensions of victim-hood, recognize the implications of your ancestral actions, repenting, and join the human race in its search for agape existence, found only in Yeshua, your rejected Messiah.

DECLINE OF THE NAZARENES

Before the Romans destroyed Jerusalem in 70 AD, the Nazarenes fled to Pella where they gradually diminished as the Gentile church grew. Eventually, the Roman authorities allowed the Nazarenes to return to Jerusalem. A condition of their return was the appointment of a Gentile as their leader. Meanwhile the growing Gentile church, calling themselves orthodox Christians, became unhappy over the Nazarene church's continued worship within the Mosaic Law. It is alleged that they probably detested the Nazarene view that Yeshua was the Messiah, a doctrine that did not explicitly state that Yeshua was the Son of God. Eventually, the Gentile church declared the Nazarene beliefs heretical.[28] The differences between the Gentile and the Jewish Nazarene churches continued until the Gentiles, feeling the Nazarenes were unworthy of their name, renamed

---

27. Garraty, John A. & Gay, Peter *The Columbia History of the World*, New York: Harper & Row, Publishers, 1972, page 220.
28. Gibbon, page 390.

them the Ebionites.[29] In this fashion, the original church split apart even in the first century. Totally, in the course of these events, the Nazarenes and their outreach to the Judeans disappeared into history. Yeshua's witness to the Jews was dead.

From this point onward, the Jewish survivors saw the Gentile Christian church as a foreign faith, one increasingly employed by their conquerors. Under these conditions, it remained impossible for this faith to witness to the Judeans or their descendants even about their own Jewish Messiah. And so it has remained for almost two thousand years.

JUDEA ACCEPTS A MESSIAH: SECOND WAR FOR INDEPENDENCE

Meanwhile the Judean remnants from the first War of Independence remained restless, warlike and waiting. Then in AD 132 a new claim to the Jewish messiahship appeared. This new claimant, Simon Bar Kokhba, proclaimed the anointing of God upon himself, and the great Jewish teacher, Rabbi Akiba, supported this claim. Bar Kokhba foretold of a Judean victory over the Romans, allegedly promised by God. The Judeans accepted him as their long awaited messiah officially labeling him 'Son of a Star' on their coins.[30] He led them into an absolute disaster with the Romans, destroying the Judean nation in 135 AD in another holocaust. The Jewish Diaspora was consummated from necessity.

SUSPENSION OF YESHUA'S ESCHATOLOGICAL EXPECTATIONS

Finally, and most importantly, it is alleged that these Jewish decisions for war rejected Yeshua's peace path, grievously upsetting the eschatological plans of Yeshua, crushing God's restoration plan for humanity by elimination of the second and third steps of God's plan:

- Establishment of the Jewish church
- First implementation of the kingdom of God on earth.

It is alleged that these Judean decisions threw the timetable of God's plans for humanity into turmoil and forced the fulfillment of the eschatological expectations of Yeshua onto the unprepared Gentiles. In affect, the Chosen People failed God. The following scripture indicates that this allegation is correct:

---

29. Gibbon, page 391.
30. Keller, page 379.

The days are coming,' declares the Lord, 'when I will raise up to David a righteous branch, a King who will reign wisely and do what is just and right in the land. In his days Judah will be saved and Israel will live in safety. This is the name by which he will be called: The Lord Our Righteousness' (Jeremiah 23:5-6).

That King did come, but the Judeans did not recognize Him, killing Him instead. Perhaps reaching a bit, it is alleged that these events were the correct path for Judea:

- Acceptance of Yeshua as the Messiah
- Peaceful extraction of the state of Israel from the grasp of Rome as a self-ruled province of Rome
- Conversion to a tribal culture of agape love
- Initial birth of the kingdom of God upon earth.

Indeed, it would seem that Yeshua's kingdom was meant for the Judeans, destined to arrive and be successful through agape love. But in their myopic vision, the Judeans wanted the kingdom delivered to them through the slaughter of their enemies. They were, and remained, a culture of violence.

Somehow the basic message of Yeshua, that the Judeans were enabled to success, to victory, if they would only embrace the struggle in agape love for adaptation of the kingdom of God, never arrived in their contemplation.

The Gentiles did little more. After the promises were shifted to the Gentiles, the concept of the struggle faded in five generations and was forfeited in eight. The Holy Spirit sadly confirms these conclusions.

`kind finds itself in an increasingly difficult position. In affect, we are losing our tender grip on civilization. One only has to look at the massacres of the twentieth century to validate this conclusion. Combine this affinity to murder one another with weapons of mass destruction and extrapolate the conclusions: If humankind cannot rediscover the message of the Messiah, all will go badly for us. Now, in the drive for the resuscitation of the mission vector of Yeshua, the badly decimated Christians need these seven achievements:

1. Escape from the mistakes of the past
2. Empowerment of the Holy Spirit as a spiritual church forfeiting forever the carnal church
3. Regeneration of the mission vector of Yeshua in an **Overchurch** dedicated to the fulfillment of Yeshua's modified eschatology

47

4. Unity in agape love to affect the adaptation of the kingdom of God to earth
5. Blending of the Jewish people in unity and agape love in this **Overchurch** drive for the kingdom of God, requiring the inevitable: Jewish acceptance of their Messiah, Yeshua.
6. Defeat of the Adamic Curse
7. Successful drive to the kingdom of God.

Hence, the arguments in this chapter and indeed, in this entire book, are to be considered as a dissertation for these results.

WARNING FROM HOLY SCRIPTURE

Indeed, it is eminently arguable that the first-century Judean decisions were the first serious post redemption mistakes of humanity. Their blunder decisively affected the course of human history. To understand the magnitude of this mistake, we turn to Holy Scripture:

When Solomon finished praying, fire came down from heaven and consumed the burnt offering and the sacrifices, and the glory of the Lord filled the temple (2 Chronicles 7:1).

Thus the temple of Solomon was dedicated with the Shekinah (the Holy Spirit) presence of God, a sanctioning of unique importance. This anointed dedication, however, also carried a warning.

But if you turn away and forsake the decrees and commands I have given you and go off to serve other gods and worship them, then I will uproot Israel from my land, which I have given them and will reject this temple I have consecrated for my Name... And all who pass will...say, 'Why has the Lord done such a thing to this land and to this temple?' People will answer, 'Because they have forsaken the Lord, the God of their fathers' (2 Chronicles 7:19-22).

These events, of course, happened to the Jewish people when they were exiled to Babylon in the first Diaspora, and the Solomon temple was destroyed. But God in His mercy allowed the return of the exiled people and the reconstruction of the temple under Ezra. In the subsequent history of Judea, the temple was desecrated and plundered several times, but was always rededicated and restored. Under Herod the Great the temple beauty was renewed. Since the temple maintained its existence for centuries after its initial destruction, the warning of 2 Chronicles 7:19-22 must be considered as in effect beyond the Babylon exile and upon the restored temple. Truly, the holy warning from God contained in 2 Chronicles 7 remained applicable to the Jewish Temple as long as God maintained His presence in the Temple, even if this presence was not His Shekinah glory of the Solomon Temple. The original covenant reigned. This is the foundation premise of the following argument:

As given in Holy Scripture, the Judean nation can only be devastated and their temple destroyed through the forsaking of God by the Judean peoples.

THE ALLEGATION: JUDEA DID FORSAKE YAHWEH

In 66 AD, Judea revolted from the authority of the Roman Empire. Judea was crushed in the subsequent seven-year war. Hence, forty years after the Crucifixion of Yeshua on the Cross and almost one thousand years from the first dedication of the Jewish Temple, all the events indicated in the warning in 2 Chronicles came to pass for the Jewish people in the catastrophe of 70 AD, followed sixty-five years later by the extinction of Judea in 135 AD.

Unequivocally, the occurrences of those years – as attested to by Holy Scripture in Chronicles 7:19-22 - historically witness to the fact that God was forsaken by the Judeans through the rejection of their Messiah, Yeshua. Moreover, the first century Jewish forsaking of God has never been requited. Repentance is required followed by atonement, but the proud and stubborn Jewish people refuse to repent of their forsaking of God even in the face of their history of repetitive holocausts. It is the most remarkable display of obstinacy in the history of the world.

Certainly, after the 135 AD dispersion, it can be argued that the facts behind the forsaking that led to the first and second century Diaspora were not well held by the scattered Jewish communities. For indeed, it would be centuries before their scholars gained access to the writing of Josephus.

Nevertheless, the driving and yet unresolved enigmas associated with the rejection of the Jewish Messiah, Yeshua Ha-Mashiach, resides as an outstanding wound deep within the Jewish material and spiritual existence, unhealed, still bleeding nearly two millennia later. This wound drives the misery of the Jewish peoples. It is incomprehensible that the first Chosen of the world could reject their Messiah and never look back. But that is what happened, and the proof of this allegation is found in history.

HISTORY COMPARED TO SCRIPTURE

Scripture indicates that the wrath of God accumulates to a threshold then bursts out over the object of that wrath like a thunderclap. This has happened to many peoples in history, but it happened to the Judeans twice in sixty-five years, and has since occurred periodically to the descendants of that Judean nation.

Note that serious holocausts followed each Judean decision relative to the messiahship. A holocaust followed the decision to reject Yeshua, and another holocaust followed the acceptance of Bar Kokhba as the messiah of Judea. Each holocaust resulted in the death of millions of Judean citizens. The war of 66-73 destroyed the temple and killed millions of Judeans. The war of 132-135 eradicated the Judean nation, scattering the remnant Jews around the Roman Empire.

Who has asked: What action did the nation of Judea undertake that so angered God that He allowed His Temple to be torn down and the Judean nation destroyed in such a short period of time? Understand that we are talking about God's Chosen People. These are the people God selected to bring the Messiah to this earth. Throughout their history God had protected them despite all their stubbornness and sinful ways, seriously breaking them up only once and that for a limited time only. What happened on these first and second century occasions that were so different and so severe, and why?

Repeating, Scripture clearly states that the Chosen People could only suffer this form of destruction by forsaking God. So Judea must have forsaken God. But Judea did not explicitly forsake God. Their worship pattern did not change until after the 70 defeat. There was no general turning away from God within the population. There was no wholesale desertion to another God. If anything, the maintenance of their centuries old worship devotion was strengthened by their collective hates for the occupation of the Roman army. So, what happened?

DETAILS OF THE 70 AD HOLOCAUST

In 70 AD, the Judeans gathered by the millions at Jerusalem to lift up God on the feast of unleavened bread. It has been estimated that the city could hold up to 2,700,000 people, and several large granaries of food existed. But, as they celebrated this feast day, the gates of Jerusalem were slammed tight by the Zealots, trapping large portions of these devout Jews inside the walls of Jerusalem.[31] Then, the Zealots slaughtered the Jews until the Zealots grew arm-tired from the killings. In this slaughter, the Zealots exterminated the Sadducees

---

31. Whiston, William *Josephus, Complete Works*. Grand Rapids: Kregel Publications, 1976, page 587.

and severely massacred the Pharisees.[32] (Two years later, the Romans eliminated the Essenes.) In the ravishing of the trapped faithful, the Jewish Zealots repeatedly violated the Holy Place.[33]

Tired of killing, the Zealots called in the Idumeans, using deception to bring them into the slaughter. Again, the trapped citizens as well as the regular city occupants were raped, plundered and killed in a fresh surge of violence, this time by the Idumeans. The Idumeans and their friends for the moment, the Zealots, butchered the Jewish people as if they were animals.[34] Eventually, the Zealots and Idumeans fell to fighting among themselves. In this internal fight they destroyed the food granaries of the city. All this happened before the Roman legions appeared at the gates of Jerusalem, for the Romans had been busy systematically exterminating the rebellious Judean and Galilean cities, working their way toward Jerusalem.

When the Romans finally arrived at Jerusalem they immediately demanded the surrender of the city, and of course, the Zealots refused, triggering off the six month Roman siege. In a decision, which seems pragmatic but impossible to visualize at this distance in time, the contending Jewish factions divided up the wall defense to resist their common enemy.

And resist they did! In the ensuing conflict, the Romans were shocked and angered by the fierceness of the Jewish resistance, pouring out the blood of the Roman legions upon Judean soil. The struggle had the appearance of a stalemate, but the Romans held a tremendous advantage: food. With the prior destruction of Jerusalem's food granaries, the two million people in Jerusalem were under the worst conditions: Enduring a siege without adequate food reserves. They slowly starved!

But even in food deprivation, the Judeans continued to fight aggressively, greatly angering the Roman general, Vespasian and his son, Titus. Infuriated, the Romans, in a terrible act of intimidation, began crucifying captured Judean soldiers. They averaged over five hundred public crucifixions of captured Jewish soldiers per day each day of the siege from April until September when no more trees could be found. Food deprivation so weakened the Judeans that frequently they fell dead into the graves of those they tried to bury. Over one million, one hundred thousand Judeans were killed in the Roman siege of Jerusalem.[35] This count does not include the hundreds of thousands killed in the sieges of the other

---

32. Garraty & Gay, page 220.
33. Maier, Paul L. *Josephus*. Grand Rapids: Kregel Publications, 1988, page 316. Josephus identified those who first desecrated the temple as the Jewish Zealots. This desecration included rape and murder in the Holy of Holies.
34. Ibid. Page 319.
35. Whiston, page 587.

cities. It does not include the death of the fleeing Judean citizens trying to escape the siege. Allowing the fleeing citizens to think they had successfully bribed their way to freedom, the soldiers would recapture them, probably in a wadi, where they disemboweled women and children in their ruthless search for treasure, up to a maximum of 2000 a day.

In these city sieges the Judeans suffered terribly, even to the point that a mother ate the flesh of her baby to survive.[36] In Jerusalem, the Judeans became as animals, inflicting the most horrible crimes upon themselves even starting long before the first Roman legions appeared before the city walls in April of 70 AD. Paraphrasing from Josephus *Wars of the Jews* about the comportment of Jews to Jews in the 70 AD Jerusalem siege:[37]

Whenever the Zealots saw any indication a household had food, they broke in, and stole the food. They beat the elderly and sexually tortured the women. They would bash in the heads of the children, then leave.

One cannot read of these abominations without trembling in rage. For the sake of the reader these abominations are not quoted to their fullness. Yet this barbarism, this level of human debasement is what the Jewish people were reduced to only forty years after they demanded the crucifixion of Yeshua!

This is a difficult fact to face, especially painful for the average, unknowing Jewish person. Time may have buried their pain but that pain was unbearable and demands recognition, equaling or exceeding even the twentieth century holocaust in intensive suffering, perhaps because this pain was partially inflicted by Jew upon Jew. So intense were these Jerusalem killings that they occurred in less than a year. If the siege had lasted any longer there would have been no survivors.

This slaughter has been considered, by some, as an inferno largely without paralleled in history.[38]

The words of Yeshua ring in our ears:

When you see Jerusalem surrounded by armies, you will know that its desolation is near. Then let those who are in Judea flee to the mountains, let those in the city get out, and let those in the country not enter the city. For this is the time of punishment in fulfillment of all that has been written. How

---

36. Whiston, page 579. The woman killed her son, who was breast-feeding, then roasted him. She ate one half of him, and hid the other half. This action distressed the city and from this moment on many wanted to die.
37. Whiston, page 564.
38. Keller, page 364.

dreadful it will be in those days for pregnant women and nursing mothers! (Luke 21:20-23).

Obviously, God's judgment was upon these special people and equally obvious it remains upon them. Again, we ask why? Why would God so punish His Chosen People? The only feasible answer to the Jewish enigma is that they must have forsaken God. No other explanation can satisfy the demands of 2 Chronicles 7:19-22 and explain the terrible sufferings of the Jewish people after the rejection of the Nazarene church. It was certainly the attitude of the first century church that the wrath of God had fallen on the Judeans because they had crucified Yeshua.[39] This, then, is the postulation:

The rejection of Yeshua and His church, followed by the 70 AD holocaust, followed by the selection of Bar Kokhba specifically as their messiah, followed by its holocaust, uniquely defines the Judean problem: The Jews missed their Messiah, Yeshua Ha-Mashiach.

Summarizing, these events fix the Jewish problem.

They turned against their Messiah, Yeshua Ha-Mashiach, killing Him in 30 AD, resulting in the following grievous losses:

1. They lost their Temple and their pattern of worship in 70 AD.
2. They lost their moral integrity with the brutal slaughter of the Greeks in 115 to 117 AD.
3. They lost their nation with the incorrect selection of a messiah in 135 AD.
4. They lost the lineage of the House of David. Hence, they are prohibited from selecting a messiah in the present or future. This is God's method of requiring that the Jews look back into history to find their Messiah.
5. They lost their special status as the Chosen People, although they remained as a special people in the eyes of God.

THE LOGIC OF THE ALLEGATION

Around 100 BC the expectations for the arrival of the Messiah heightened in Judea. Many impostors appeared proclaiming themselves the messiah at this period in Jewish history with perhaps Judas of Galilee being the most accepted

---

39. Gibbon, page 389. Many early Christians claimed that the Jewish holocaust of 70 AD was the result of God's wrath on the Jews for the death of God's Son.

candidate before 30 AD. But he was defeated and killed by the Romans along with his followers who were crucified by the thousands on the plains of Galilee. Problematically, the killing of Judas set a precedent among the Judeans: The messiah cannot be anyone executed by the Romans. From that point onward to the final dispersion of the Jews from Judea in 135 AD several self-proclaiming prophets arose such as Honi the Circledrawer, Theudas and 'the Egyptian'. Honi was stoned to death by the followers of Hyrcanus II. Roman soldiers beheaded Theudas and killed the Egyptian. But none of these men were considered as more than potential prophets. Clearly, only two candidates arose that was seriously considered as plausible messianic aspirants by the people of that era. These were Yeshua in 30 AD, the man of peace, and Bar Kokhba in 132 AD, the man of war. Judea, desperate to be free of the Romans, rejected Yeshua, especially after He was crucified by the authorities, and accepted Bar Kokhba a century later. Bar Kokhba proclaimed that God had promised Judean freedom from the Romans through his messianic mission. The ensuing events, predicted in 2 Chronicles, completely and definitively indicate that Judea chose the wrong messiah. Yet, the current Jewish position, among those who consider such things, is that the selection of Bar Kokhba was simply wrong and that the messiah is yet to come.

Jewish foundations for a future messiah are weak. If there had been one punishment, one revolt, one expulsion, then it could be postulated that the door was open for a future messiah. However, the double nature of the holocaust punishments strongly validates that the Jews missed their Messiah, and that any further selections will be severely punished by God. Hence, the signal from the Lord is that continued waiting is futile. Strengthening this argument is the loss of the lineage of the Jewish families. The lineage of the house of David, the requirement for identifying the messiah, cannot be documented from among today's Jewish descendents. That is, it is impossible to identify a Jewish messiah today. It is almost as if God wanted no misunderstandings about what had happened. So clearly, since no future candidate can validate the correct lineage, the door is shut! Indeed, the Jews have no choice but to look back into history to find the Messiah they missed, and the only candidate with this house of David lineage is Yeshua, known to the West as Jesus Christ.

Another and utterly unassailable element in this contention is the fact that the destruction of the temple is associated with the punishment over the rejection of Yeshua, not the failure of Bar Kokhba. To any rational, objective observer this set of events clearly points at the truth, a truth denied for two millennia: The Judeans made a terrible mistake, one that their descendants have not yet rectified but one that they must rectify if they are to elude even more, future judgmental punishments.

Logic for Yeshua's Selection

Let us be even-handed. Is it possible that the theocratic leaders of Judea were correct, that Yeshua was an impostor? Putting aside faith for the moment, let us look deeper at the evidence of the double holocaust punishment in an attempt to find the rational truth of this exceedingly important question:

1. The punishment experienced by the nation of Judea and its population between 66 AD and 135 AD entirely fulfills the warning of 2 Chronicles 7.
2. It is an undeniable premise that guided by Jewish Scripture, the magnitude of God's punishment upon Judea - the aggregate of a double holocaust - could be warranted only by the most grave mistake: A giant forsaking of God on the part of the Jewish people.
3. A simple sinfulness of the people, or its accumulation over the centuries, would not have been adequate to implement the measure of wrath experienced by Judea. This premise is based upon the previous history of Judea in which only the severe turning away from God under Zedekiah caused holocaust type punishment.
4. Yet, premised on the warning of 2 Chronicles 7, coupled with the unprecedented magnitude of the misery of the people in 66-73 AD and 132-135 AD, it must be concluded that in the fulfillment of Holy Scripture the people of Judea turned away from their God and His plan for them in the first century, thus forsaking YHWH.
5. To grasp this first century situation, it is important to understand the reasons behind the first temple destruction, the loss of the Solomon Temple to Nebuchadnezzar. This destruction occurred because: ... **the people became more and more unfaithful, following all the detestable practices of the nations and defiling the temple of the Lord, which He had consecrated in Jerusalem (2 Chronicles 36:14).**
6. But in the first century, Judea did not explicitly turn away from God. They did not follow the detestable practices of the pagan nations. Therefore their sin must have had a different operational pattern, a new mode, from the Nebuchadnezzar holocaust.
7. Accordingly, it is concluded that since the people of Judea did not shift their worship patterns, God must have shifted His course. What Scripture had foreordained occurred: The Messiah arrived and the old worship patterns were no longer adequate. The Messiah revealed old worship stereotypes based on animal sacrifices as imperfect, not the best expression of the will of God. Even more, a shift in the covenant had

occurred; God would dwell in each spiritually regenerated human instead of the Judean Temple. The New Covenant of Yeshua had arrived.

8. Now God would not shift His Covenant without informing His Chosen People of such a shift.

9. Yeshua carried the message of the shift. He announced the good news of the New Covenant that God was Love. He also carried the good news of freedom from the Adamic curse found in His sacrifice. He revealed that true worship could only be found in each human spirit reborn to God's love. He proclaimed the coming of the kingdom of God by the Spirit of God. He stated that this kingdom of God came to earth, first, in the rebirth of the human spirit, implying that from this rebirth it would move into the culture of humanity, transforming it. He called all men to Him starting with the Judeans. Clearly, Yeshua was calling Judea to the implementation of the kingdom of God under a new and clearer covenant.

10. When confronted with the Man of Peace and His message of the New Covenant, most of the people of Judea acquiesced in the rejection of Yeshua as their Messiah.

11. In this rejection of Yeshua, the Judean people missed the will of God.

12. In the interim between 30 AD and 132 AD, the Judean people seeing that they were being severely punished, instead of looking back and reassessing their previous decision, selected another as their messiah, and in that election they rejected looking back.

13. By selecting Bar Kokhba as their messiah and in their refusal to reappraise their earlier decisions against Yeshua even in the presence of terrible punishments, the people of Judea as well as the state of Judea performed an intolerable act of rebellion against God.

14. Assuredly, then, when the Jewish leaders rejected Yeshua, they were guilty of forsaking God.

15. The decision to forsake God was accepted by the people. This decision by the Judean people, not just their leaders, subsequently brought the wrath of God upon themselves and their descendants. The most recent illustration being the Holocaust of the twentieth century.

16. Except for the fortuitous escape of Rabbi Yohanan ben Zakkai, who subsequently gained Roman recognition and reorganized Judaism, the faith of Jewish peoples might have been seriously damaged forever.[40]

17. The reorganization of Judaism is the partial product of the mind of man. As such, God's anointing is limited even as it is limited on Christian worship that is the product of the human mind.

---

40. Garraty & Gay, page 220.

18. The worship patterns of the Jewish people dramatically changed after the events of the first century. Animal sacrifice ceased. The temple was gone. Only the feast days remained. These historical facts invalidate the argument that the Jews could not accept Jesus because He changed the Mosaic worship patterns, for indeed, He did not. Yet the reality is that the Jewish worship patterns were changed as a result of the first and second century holocausts.
19. The continuing, periodic outpouring of pogroms and holocausts upon the Jewish people signal that God is neither happy with their initial decision nor their continuing stubbornness in rescinding that decision. It must be concluded that God's judgment upon the Jewish people is dynamic and ongoing. This is a horrendous and monumental conclusion!
20. The only rational decision is that Yeshua was not a hoax and that the Jews made a frightful error, waiting to be corrected.

The facts of history and the word of Scripture speak loudly in support of this analysis; indeed, they thunder forth. It is an inescapable conclusion for any rational observer:

The rejection of Yeshua was the cause-effect that resulted in the terrible punishment of Judea. No other cause-effect of significant magnitude existed in this time frame or in any other period of Jewish history that merited this level of punishment.

This conclusion only can be challenged on the basis that either Holy Scripture is not inviolate or that the warning of 2 Chronicles 7:19 did not transfer between temples. None of these arguments is substantial to men and women of God. Indeed the history of the Maccabees corroborates the contention that the warning of 2 Chronicles 7:19 did transfer between the two temples.

The inescapable conclusion based on Jewish religious text and decided without the requirement of faith and a minimum of bias is that Yeshua was not a fraud. Consider for a moment the accomplishments and impact of this one life on the world. It is without challenge the greatest of the great, surely of the magnitude only achievable by the true Son of God.

This means that the present Jewish people are living in spiritual bankruptcy within a forfeiture of their historical and messianic eschatological goals, which is their very reason for existence as a people of choice, the original chosen people of God. Surely, the most casual Jewish observer should be able to see that their religious practices were altered, with portions of their belief system modified or eliminated (animal sacrifice, priesthood, mandatory pilgrimages, etc.) in the same time frame as the appearance of Yeshua. Can no Jewish eyes see this connection?

What veil lingers over the eyes of the Jewish nation, that it, composed of the brightest and most achieving humans, cannot see this simple fact: Their original and subsequent rejection of their Messiah is an exercise of the most extreme idiocy. It is actually a process of intellectual dishonesty that has been brought down over the centuries as a cultural and religious legend, a lie that is brainwashed into each generation of Jews. Indeed today, the true facts of the first and second centuries, so critical to our present and future decisions, are not presented to the Jewish people or even to the Christian peoples. If they were, then prayer and compassion would replace hate and distrust!

This is an extremely unhappy situation, and the entire Christian community should be in shame for its indifference to the Jewish plight. Instead of a lack of sympathy, the Christians should be pouring out prayers in great abundance to God for our Jewish brothers and sisters. Never, should any follower of Yeshua look upon the Jewish people without compassion and love. This motivation must be from love; yet another reason for compassionate prayer exists. The coming struggle to lift humanity to a higher level of human existence, to the kingdom of God adapted to earth, cannot succeed without enthusiastic Jewish participation.

Chapter 6

Gentiles Assume the Mission Vector of Jesus Christ

With the rejection of Jesus' mission vector by the Judeans, Jesus switched His mission to the Gentiles using Paul as His missionary apostle. Although unprepared for this responsibility, Jesus found millions of Gentile soul/spirits willing to place everything on line for this opportunity. In fact, their fervor and willingness to work the mission vector of Jesus Christ generated the Grand Redemptive Engine of God. This was the Gentile church of Jesus Christ at its fighting best, functioning to redeem humanity by effecting the transformation of any encapsulating pagan or neo-pagan culture in which the Spirit of God moved. At its best, Gentile Christianity became Jesus' church forcefully driving on His mission vector eager to bring the kingdom of God to earth. What a pleasant surprise this must have been to God.

The appearance of the redemptive engine has only occurred with the initial Gentile church. Although the engine has attempted to break into history several times since, its advent with the first century Gentile church remains its exclusive manifestation. It is most interesting that the church's appearance in this fighting form was with the Gentile church not with the original Judean church.

To understand what was happening in this first century church the reader must grasp that the Gentile church was more than just a spiritual fighting army. More than just a religion, that church epitomized a completely different orientation in human thinking. Look, a new frame of reference to human life arrived on earth, that although rejected by one group of people, it generated a great awareness that a grand happening was occurring on earth with another group. And interestingly, it was the common folks of that group that made it happen. In this common knowledge they knew something that Christians have long since forgotten: It is an honor and a privilege to participate in God's great plan of restoration, even if their only participation vehicle remained the forfeiture of physical life.

Characterized by close and intimate relationship with a loving God, that early church was the logical extension of the incarnation of the Son of God as Yeshua, the humble carpenter. Yeshua introduced humanity to His Father, the God of Love. And in this process, He provided humanity with an exclusive vector over the knowledge-ocean to God and His paradise, the kingdom of God. The key to the vector was agape love coupled with faith in the indwelling companionship and guidance of the Holy Spirit – all assembled and recorded within the revealed truth of Christ's New Testament Gospels.

Some eighteenth, nineteenth and twentieth century scholars charge that Hellenized influences, including the impact of the mystery religions, brought about an impure, imperfect form of the Christian faith in the first Gentile church. If this influence existed, it was unable to veer Jesus' first Gentile church from its task of changing the world for Christ. Loss to these scholars is the fact that the Spirit drove this early church from the common saint up. However, when that capacity was removed in the **second legacy blunder**, then it must be acknowledged that infiltration of paganism did impact the purity of the church, polluting the vector of Jesus Christ to the kingdom of God adapted to earth, forfeiting it.

JESUS' MISSION VECTOR

So, what is a vector? A vector is a quantity defined by magnitude applied in a given direction within a given set of coordinates. Jesus' vector is a force applied toward the kingdom of God all directed and pushed by the Spirit of God. Today, it is obvious that the required coordinates are the thinking frame of references that include modern technology and cultural freedom plus the Holy Spirit. Combined in one great set of thinking coordinates, they shall enable this great human venture.

VECTOR:

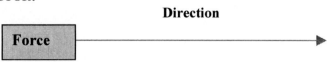

Direction

Force

The vector of Jesus Christ is His rescue of humanity, empowered by the blood of the Cross, directed and guided by the Holy Spirit all pursuant to the human individual and cultural transit over the unknown ocean of potential knowledge integrated with God's agape love to reach and enter paradise. Please note that without agape love integration we reach destruction, not paradise, our current direction.

JESUS' MISSION VECTOR:

Kingdom Spiritual Power **Holy Spirit Guidance & Direction** **Kingdom of God**

Jesus' vector has two aspects to it. One is the individual pursuit and the other is the collective or cultural pursuit. To pursue this vector as an individual is to find overcoming and the heavenly kingdom of God, but to find this vector, as a culture, is to bring the kingdom of God to our earth. This difference defines the duality of Jesus' mission to our planet; a duality that the early Gentile saints understood and lived. In affect, they subordinated their individual physical existence to the cultural cause of Christ, willing, even eager in many instances, to fall on the pagan swords to do this. The world had seen fervor before and since, but the world had not seen fervor so correctly focused as it was in this particular moment in history. Indeed, these early Christians changed the world, holding total victory in their hands, despite the many heresies and other mind-generated distractions of their time. Then, their church leaders betrayed them. But before this betrayal, these early saints fostered the greatest moment in church history: The rise of the Grand Redemptive Engine of God, that mechanism of God capable of transforming and adapting any given culture of the world into the kingdom of God. To understand the magnitude of this development, it is absolutely necessary to appreciate that this *engine of redemption works from within any encapsulating civilization.* In simpler words, the early church was transforming the culture of the time into something better, moving it from within, not from outside, along Christ's mission vector. Had it been allowed to continue, we would be in a different place today! But what is our place today? The following graph represents the orientation of our problem.

MODERN VECTOR:
Random Goals

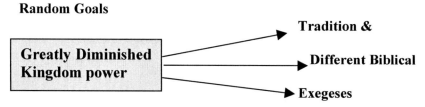

The overwhelming problem is that we have lost the leadership and guidance of the Holy Spirit, thus invalidating our direction and polluting our spiritual power. Today, we do not follow Jesus' vector, but the randomizing direction of foolish humans, each supremely confident of their direction.

This is God's original restoration plan, drawn schematically as vectors:

Judean Vector to Stage One Implementation:

BIRTH IN THE JUDEAN TRIBE:

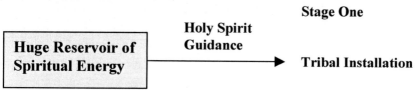

JEWISH-LED GENTILE VECTOR TO STAGE TWO COMPLETION:
GROWING UP:

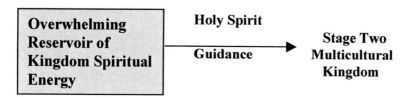

Lamb-led worldwide Stage Three Implementation:
Adult: Returned after Rapture

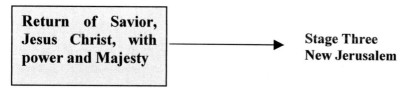

The magnitude of the damage done to the Father's plans for humanity by the Judean rejection of Yeshua is obvious from examining the above set of vectors. The inability to implement the first stage, the tribal birth of the kingdom, clearly dictated our present day disarray. With the demise of the first vector, the second vector was shifted into a birth stage, even as it still retained its adolescent kingdom characteristics. It is alleged that the early church did not possess the knowledge of this eschatological shift, making their task prohibitively difficult. Yet the spiritually unprepared, but faithful Gentiles tried. Indeed, it was not the people but the intellectuals who failed by their rejection of the leadership of the Holy Spirit. They could not keep their hands or their minds off the leadership of the church.

Chapter 7

Theorem of Maximum Assistance: Understanding the Shift to the Carnal Church

The early church functioned within the leadership of the Holy Spirit. It is imperative that the saints understand what that meant so we can appraise what was lost. To fully grasp this condition, we introduce the theorem of Maximum Assistance, that in which the early church operated. Here is that theorem:

THEOREM OF MAXIMUM ASSISTANCE

God's kingdom assistance (as grace or as an indwelling presence) to each human or social group pours forth upon the beloved of God, bounded only by the eagerness of each receiving human or group to indulge in or submit to negative physical life-force attractions.

Scriptural support (inverted):
... but when perfection comes, the imperfect disappears (1 Corinthians 13:10).

Such negative and Spirit constricting physical life forces might be intellectual pride, envy, lust, greed, ambition, self-righteousness and self-importance. Perhaps the most destructive of all life-force factors is, however, the human propensity to organize and lead. Humanity cannot stand anything that looks like anarchy. We want to organize everything, to make it execute efficiently. Of course, this is the legacy of war, especially proven in war, commerce, science and governance. But this is not necessarily the way of God.

While order is of God, it is His order and perspective, not ours. So when the human organizing forces takeover either an individual or a group, the Holy Spirit withdraws. And this is exactly what happened to the church after 172 AD.

But God understands our needs for order and hence has given humanity a corollary to the Theorem of Maximum Assistance.

FIRST COROLLARY TO MAXIMUM ASSISTANCE

Humanity and the Spirit can harmonize together in human organization when human leadership is anointed by God.

Scriptural support:

And we, who with unveiled faces all reflect the Lord's glory, are being transformed into His likeness with ever-increasing glory, which comes from the Lord, who is the Spirit (2 Corinthians 3:18).

What harmony is there between Christ and Belial (2 Corinthians 6:15)?

SECOND COROLLARY TO MAXIMUM ASSISTANCE

Harmonized organizations are many-fold more efficient than non-harmonized human organizations.

Scriptural support (implied):
For we are God's workmanship, created in Christ Jesus to do good works, which God prepared in advance for us to do (Ephesians 2:10).

THIRD COROLLARY TO MAXIMUM ASSISTANCE

Harmonized organizations receive the bountiful blessings of God upon that organization and its goals.

Scriptural support:
And I [Paul] pray that you, being rooted and established in love, may have power, together with all the saints, to grasp how wide and long and high and deep is the love of Christ, and to know this love that surpasses knowledge – that you may be filled to the measure of all the fullness of God (Ephesians 3:17-19).

FOURTH COROLLARY TO MAXIMUM ASSISTANCE

The kingdom of God brought to earth shall be a harmonized cultural organization.

FIFTH COROLLARY TO MAXIMUM ASSISTANCE

In all harmonized organizations the Spirit of God leads through the commune with the anointed human leaders of these organizations.

Scriptural support:

I will put my laws in their hearts, and I will write them on their minds (Hebrews 8:10 &10:16).

SIXTH COROLLARY TO MAXIMUM ASSISTANCE

A harmonious church is a spiritual church. The non-harmonious church is the carnal or worldly church.

Scriptural support:
Brothers, I could not address you as spiritual but as worldly – mere infants in Christ (1 Corinthians 3:1)

The rejection of the leadership of the Holy Spirit followed by the compromise of the Gospel's one hundred and forty-one years later, neutralized the effort to transform the secular and pagan cultures into the kingdom of God. The church went from a harmonized organization to a non-harmonized human structure, from spiritual to carnal in less than 150 years. Perhaps this explains why the church never mastered the eschatological information about the kingdom step implementations. This critical information could only flow from God to man within a harmonized church organization! A special, reliable commune was necessary.

This blunder has placed Christianity in a terrible state of affairs in which large portions of the Body of Christ only believe in the third vector, the New Jerusalem Kingdom, without comprehending that this vector cannot occur unless the second vector is first modified for birth, then born. If the kingdom cannot be birthed it cannot become an adult. Thus, the church's failure to recognize the dynamics of the Lord's eschatology, especially its step implementation process, has contributed substantially to the **second fall** of humanity. This is the **fifth legacy blunder** of humanity.

CONSEQUENCES FROM THE LOSS OF THE HARMONIOUS CHURCH

The **second fall** destroyed the church as a harmonized organization unwittingly forcing a Gospel accommodation upon church leaders. This inadvertent accommodation centered about the drive to the kingdom of God especially as espoused in the Sermon on the Mount. Hence, the forfeiture of the harmonized church for the leadership of human intellect generated three great obstacles.

The *first obstacle* was the huge kingdom spiritual power drain from the church with its resultant problems, too many to articulate in this space. The *second obstacle* was that the church, functioning as a non-harmonized organization, had no hope of Christianizing the world.

While it is asserted that the Catholic leaders and other prominent men of history, such as Francis of Assisi, Luther and Zwingli as well as the Anabaptists pragmatically beheld the consequences of the forfeiture of the harmonized church, they failed to understand the theorem of Maximum Assistance. Interestingly, their reaction to this forfeiture was different. The Catholics separated and isolated those who were willing to practice the Sermon on the Mount from the lay people, calling the separated ones, monks or Saints. Others, such as Luther, said that the saints should be involved in the secular governance in order to 'restrain outrageous villainy'[41]. His solution would be that individuals holding to the Sermon on the Mount should infiltrate the government to moderate it. Generally, he held a pessimistic view of the world, holding no hope for the coming of the kingdom of God. The Anabaptists called for the complete withdrawal from the secular society. They advocated a separation of church and state, including separation from the evil works of the state, e.g. technological advances.

The *third obstacle* is that without harmonizing the culture of the world, there is no hope of bringing the kingdom to earth.

Then, in the Catholic world of the thirteenth century, hope arose. It was the movement of the Spiritual Franciscans. This movement came close to awakening the Grand Redemptive Engine of God. But before that could really happen, the movement became de-harmonized in apostasy. The Protestant Reformation followed this crushed hope two hundred years later. Harmonious church structures reappeared. Hope abounded. But this movement of hope also disappeared into de-harmony under the impact of human propensity to organize the Spirit of God out of their midst. Carnal congregations and churches again replaced the spiritual churches. Their members largely forgot their charismatic, Spirit-energized Reformation founders. Although some spiritual groups remain intact, most of the mainline Protestant organizations lost their initial harmony.

So what has happened since the sixteenth century? Largely, America has accepted Luther's solution, making our religious beliefs private and non-intrusive. This, the Luther solution, combined with the general passivity of the Protestant mainline churches have resulted in a great victory for the enemy of God. From there, the secularists have practiced outrageous villainy almost unopposed. It matters not that the secularists have allowed the Anabaptists to ride their buggies in isolation with a minimum of secular interference. They are not intrusive in our culture, and they are also of no influence. Will they still be riding their buggies when the enemy of God overwhelms our culture, destroying the last

---

41. Bainton, Roland H. *The Reformation of the Sixteen Century* pages 99-100.

vestige of Christianity? Just look beyond our protected and myopic American view to see the facts. We live on a planet of unrestrained villainy! The Adamic Curse rules. Exploitation abounds, even as we sleep in our comfort. God is calling!

Chapter 8

Jesus' Lost Redemptive Capacities: Legacy Blunder Three

Aggravating the situation is our general ignorance of the fullness of Jesus' mission vector, including many of Jesus' important redemptive capacities or rescue attributes, most of which have been forgotten or forfeited. **First**, He revealed the important knowledge that God was our Father who viewed us with love not with sternness. **Second**, Jesus revealed a special indwelling help for His beloved followers willing to struggle back to God: the Holy Spirit of God. This meant that each individual saint as well as our churches and cultures could have the assistance of God in our struggles. **Third**, He opened a new avenue of human force, the human spirit. Dormant from the Adamic curse, it is enabled to regeneration in Jesus' salvation. Especially important is the fact that the human spirit contains the means to find and commune with God through the Spirit of God, therein gaining the knowledge intimacies of God. **Fourth**, He provided the knowledge vector to the intimate communion with the Father found largely in His Sermon on the Mount. However, Jesus went further. **Fifth**, He revealed that He was the exclusive gateway to that vector, and that it was His sacrifice that permitted the human search back to God, including the human acquisition of knowledge with and under the blessings of God.

Totally, Yeshua revealed nineteen redemptive capacities through the author's commune. One other redemptive capacity exists, the knowledge to which we are not enabled. Summarizing then, here is this important list.

REDEMPTIVE CAPACITIES:

1- **Spirit of God with His Gifts and Fruits**
2- Agape love enabling compassion[42]
3- **Personal Salvation**
4- Redemption of human civilization
5- View of the kingdom of God brought to earth as a societal structure[43]
6- God's assistance found through prayer
7- **Activation of the human spirit (born-again experience)**
8- Personal commune with God[44]
9- True Worship of God
10- Divine Guidance
11- Human Acquisition of Knowledge with God's Blessings
12- Dominance of the Human Spirit over the Mind
13- Emancipation of the Mind from Carnality and Self
14- **Forgiveness of sin**
15- Reduction of suffering (healing)
16- **Grace (unmerited assistance)**
17- Inner Cleansing of humanity
18- Sealing off of the enemy's human port of entry, returning humanity to the status of the pre-Adamic fall
19- Vector to paradise with Spiritual Power
20- Unknown, except it exists – perhaps as the hidden manna.

These capacities function as attributes of the vector of Jesus Christ. In the early days of Christianity, Christ's vector and its attributes were known as the 'Good News of Jesus Christ.' Totally, these attributes or capacities are the keys

---

42. Interestingly, agape love is given as a redemptive capacity even though it could be considered as included in the fruits of the Spirit.
43. The kingdom structure, especially the validated societal commune, as presented to the author can be seen in the soon to be published manuscript *Odyssey to Agape Civilization.*
44. This is much more widespread among the senior spiritual saints than the world realizes.

to knowledge, the *knowledge of knowledge*, and are important contributors to the keys to the kingdom of God.

Yet, in arrogance or ignorance, humanity let the fullness of these redemptive gifts slip by us even as we rejected the Holy Spirit as the controlling force in our church and subsequently in our personal lives. By these actions we lost the fullness of Jesus' redemption with its 20 redemptive capacities, incapacitating an important part of the mission of Christ. With this breakdown, the church lost the ability to reverse the Adamic Fall with its serious curse of human exploitations and manipulations. Without defeating the Adamic fall, the implementation of the kingdom of God cannot proceed and Jesus' restored and updated eschatology is seriously setback, in fact, destroyed. Add to this situation the misinterpreted complexities of the three stages of the kingdom development and one can sense the confusion of those first days.

Redemptive capacities generate outreach, of which the fruit of the Holy Spirit revealed in Galatians are the most famous:

But the fruit of the Spirit is love, joy, peace, patience, kindness, goodness, faithfulness, gentleness and self-control (Galatians 5:22).

Even more outreach traits are generated from the exercise of the redemptive capacities than just the fruit of the Spirit, as great as they are. Here is a list of the redemptive outreaches, including the Spirit's fruits, as received from the Holy Spirit through the author's commune. Confirm them for yourself:

REDEMPTIVE OUTREACH:

- Forgiveness
- Tenderness
- Compassion
- Generosity
- Ethics
- Human Decorum
- Civility
- Cleanness
- Charity
- Biblical Acumen
- Wisdom
- Support
- Service
- Joy

- Peace
- Patience
- Kindness
- Goodness
- Faithfulness
- Gentleness
- Self Control
- Trust
- Child-like mind
- Loyalty
- Earnestness
- Sacrifice for others
- Gifts of the Spirit
- Humbleness
- Caring
- Esteeming
- Helping
- Commiserating
- Sympathizing
- Happiness
- Joyous Laughing
- Listening
- Thoughtfulness
- Contemplation
- Integrity
- Manners
- Honesty
- Companionship
- Prayer
- Shared awe of God's hand
- Intercessional Prayers
- Unselfishness
- Spiritual Warfare
- **Holy Junction.**

WHO STOOD IN THE GAP?

By allowing the eschatology of Christ to be defined as the defeat of the Adamic Curse, followed by the race down the vector of Christ to the first implementation of the kingdom of God, the Prototypical Kingdom, followed by the millennium reign, rapture, the Great Tribulation, and Jesus' return – disregarding the various arguments of the order of these events – then the complexity of Jesus' eschatology becomes apparent. So, did the Holy Spirit teach this complexity to the early church? More decidedly so, even as witnessed by this special scripture:

I will put my laws in their minds and write them on their hearts (Hebrews 8:10).

The early church challenged the pagans and defeated them, changing the world. This was largely accomplished without the benefit of the Gospels or the letters of Paul. They did not have the Bible! They did not rely on preaching. They did not have large resplendent churches; in fact, they had no churches but met in private homes. Many were illiterate, depending on others to read the Jewish Scrolls and what letters or Gospel they could procure. They were not socially accepted. In fact, they were persecuted and frequently put to death. Yet, they prevailed. They moved down the complex highway toward the reversal of the Adamic Curse. Why? Because the Spirit of God wrote the truth of Jesus' mission on their hearts! They lived for the future, for the coming of the kingdom, content to allow their children or grandchildren to see the kingdom come to earth. To this end, they put out all images of false gods and conducted spiritual warfare to cleanse their homes and person of demonic oppression. They broke curses and prayed for spiritually clean governance. In all this, they saw the need to reverse the work of the Adamic curse. These early saints did all this in order to walk close to Jesus Christ, companioned and directed constantly by the indwelling presence of the Holy Spirit. They stood in the gap for Christ Jesus. Largely void of education, Bible, preachers, television evangelists, church buildings, and organization, they turned the tide on paganism. Their sole weapon was the Spirit of God. Assisted by Him in two modes, as grace and indwelled by Him as God's temples on earth, they overcame.

Unfortunately however, the men of intellect in those times were not tuned to the Spirit. For a while the voices of the Spirit speaking through the people prevailed. Then the Pepusa incident occurred and the voices of the common people, especially those so strongly tuned to the Spirit, were no longer heard. The church canon arrived and spiritual freedom died.

So under these dynamic and shifting conditions, those saints that had stood in the gap aged and died out without adequate replacements. A calamitous truth was found. The Spirit of God could not be inherited; He must be found in each generation. So from the beginning of the third century on, what man or woman was ready to step into the gap? Who was willing to interpret the teachings of the

Holy Spirit about the Jesus' true mission vector to the church? Who knew about the step implementations of the Kingdom or the mystery of the vector? We must conjecture that there was someone. Was it Origen, Tertullian or Irenaeus? Might it have been the three Cappadocians, Basil, and the two Gregorys? Perhaps it was a woman, unknown, whose voice never reached us, for decidedly today, we do not hear this voice. If it was articulated, it has been lost. Might the enemy of God or the bias of men or the ambition of a rival have succeeded in suffocating it? Unquestionably, it would seem that we are never to know the answer in this realm.

Look at the church void of this voice. On one hand the church is confronted with the simplicity of the salvation of the 'good thief' and on the other hand the complexities of the Adamic reversal. Which way is it? Both! Yet, it is alleged that our church fathers got lost between the simple and the complex, unable to follow both salvation and the reversal of the Adamic Curse. They selected the easy and perhaps the logical choice for the church: Salvation. **Legacy blunder three** was enacted; the cultural rescue tools, Jesus' redemptive capacities, were abandoned for the simple personalized salvation rescue. Eschatology, defined here as the reversal of the Adamic Fall, became forgotten, remaining largely so until Albert Schweitzer reacquainted the theologians to this mistake. This centuries-long neglect represents **legacy blunders four and five**.

The abandonment of the complex teachings about the reversal of the Adamic Curse became an essential component of the **second fall**, our inheritance today. This means we have long since forgotten the true mission of our Lord to reverse the Adamic Curse and pursue the vector of Jesus to the kingdom of God, except, of course, for an occasionally articulation by the theologians. Here is the charge:

Church positions of prominence, authority, respect or esteem aside, this pitiful lack of knowledge about Jesus' true mission to reverse the Adamic Fall and His redemptive capacities given to accomplish this task include the vast majority of the leaders of today's churches and the overwhelming majority of the saints.

This is why the Spirit stirs Jesus' people. We have much to do without the slightest idea of the task, its goals, its difficulties or our need to prevail. In terms of existentialism, we are at the extreme of the inauthentic existence as a church and individually as a people of the Lord.

Today, we see a mighty effort to spread the salvation message around the world using the television media. Yet, none of these efforts can save the world for Jesus (or even save the world from itself) without the equivalent effort to defeat the Adamic Curse, a process of properly employing Jesus' redemptive capacities, which is, today, largely without advocates.

74

Our problems with the Adamic Curse stem from the actions of the early church. By the fifth century and onward, only a partial set of knowledge-coordinates continued to exist in the Christian database. Basically, these are the concept of personal salvation (redemptive capacity 3), grace (redemptive capacity 16) and the forgiveness of sin (redemptive capacity 14). Three other capacities are underutilized. These are the Holy Spirit with His gifts and fruits (redemptive capacity 1), activation of the human spirit through the born-again experience (redemptive capacity 7) and access to God via prayer (redemptive capacity 6). The other redemptive capacities were lost or deemed impractical.

By default, the secular world has adopted three abandoned redemptive capacities. These are the acquisition of knowledge with God's blessing (redemptive capacity 11 which the secular world developed as Science), the cleansing of the inner human (redemptive capacity 17 which the secular world developed as Psychology/Psychiatry), and the lessening of human suffering (redemptive capacity 15 which the secular world developed as Medical Science). Unfortunately, this interference in the innate, but forfeited affairs of the church has generated the equivalence of three delta functions[45] in our culture, spearheaded by a one sided, secular optimization of science. This has occurred while many of the other redemptive capacities remained dormant, a process so culturally malnourishing that it cannot remain healthy, eventually dooming us all. Although it is difficult to schematically represent this problem, it is hoped by examining the following schematics that the reader can obtain a better appreciation of this extremely consequential problem.

Here is an attempt to schematically illustrate this problem:

---

45. A delta function is a sudden spike in an otherwise normal distribution of events.

The **second fall** has effectively neutralized Jesus' redemptive capacities. The secular world operates three redemptive capacities (green) to enhance modern culture. These pierce the Adamic and second fall. Unrealized by the secular world, the captured redemptive capacities has neutralized any potential re-energizing of the fight against the Adamic curse, thus ultimately threatening human existence.

Schematic of the Redemptive Capacities Deployment

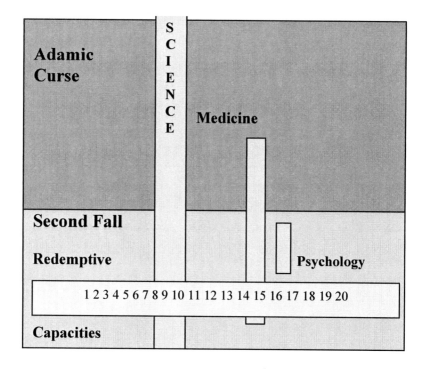

THE PERFECT DEPLOYMENT:

Civilization (in purple):

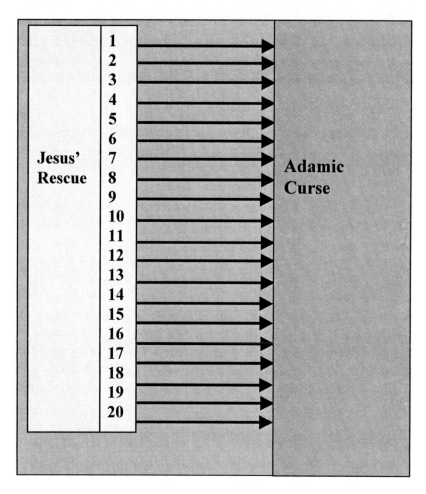

In this perfect deployment, the redemptive capacities banish the Adamic curse.

IMPERFECT DEPLOYMENT: Modern Situation using only six redemptive capacities of Jesus' rescue:

Civilization in purple & Second Fall in brown:

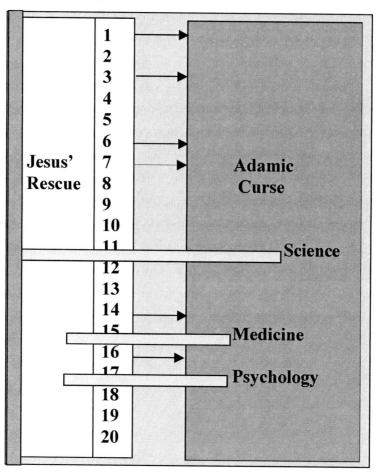

Green bars are secular assumption of church tasks. Allied with secularism, science has punctured Jesus' rescue, dividing and repudiating it, feeding the Adamic Curse.

In the perfect application of Jesus' rescue all of the redemptive capacities would be activated to their fullness. But with the church ignoring so many of these capacities, it became inevitable that some would be picked up by the secular world. This happened after the first and large portions of the second millennia had passed. Secular applications developed based on the inquisitiveness of humans and their interest in monetary rewards. Investigators, like Isaac Newton probably instigated the work since the organized Christian church was opposed to almost all efforts of knowledge acquisition. Why? Because the church had lost its way and had become corrupt in religiosity! In their myopic vision, the church generated the four-headed world that we have today:

UTILIZATION OF JESUS' REDEMPTIVE CAPACITIES

1. **Three Redemptive capacities implemented by the church**
2. **Three Redemptive capacities grossly underutilized by the church**
3. **Three Redemptive capacities implemented by the secular world**
4. **Eleven Redemptive capacities not implemented, or even known.**

The mission vector of Jesus Christ has been seriously corrupted. Now the entire mission of Christ faced extinction. The God will not tolerate this.

Chapter 9

Covering the Mission Damage: Generating the New Testament

As the fervor of the apostolic church waned and the original generation of followers died without experiencing the promised return of Jesus, restlessness and confusion settled into the new generations of followers. Every thinker wanted to know what was wrong? The realization that the promise of Jesus' return would not be immediately fulfilled prompted the church to assemble the writing of the first-generation apostles and their followers so that the wondrous acts and statements of Jesus, His Good News, could be preserved. Eventually, this collection was pulled together in 363 at Laodicea in the present form of the New Testament, minus only Revelations.[46]

MISUNDERSTANDING AND MISPLACING

Now Christendom had a document that was accepted as the word of God, Logos, by all. However, subsequent generations have made a serious mistake in their embrace of this document, the New Testament Gospels, by confusing the differences between the vector to paradise, especially as given in the Sermon on the Mount, with the position of paradise. They assumed that the recorded words and actions of Jesus reflected the knowledge-coordinates of absolute truth when, indeed, it represented the course for finding this position. In addition, the Judeans did a double disservice to the cause of Christ by writing large portions of the New Testament within the thinking coordinates of the first stage eschatology. In this, they introduced first century customs as if they were from God. Especially embarrassing are those first century ideas of the worthlessness of women and children.

The other large problem dealt with the original eschatology in which Christ forecast some events happening before witnesses in His hearing would die. Obviously, this did not happen, and the cause-effect for this failure of His eschatology must be placed on the Judeans. They rejected it. But once rejected,

---

46. This was accomplished in the Council of Laodicea in 363. (Note, some documents use 360 as the date). Gibbon, Edward, *The Decline and Fall of the Roman Empire*. New York: Random House, Inc. Volume 1

the eschatology desperately needed an update, one that could only come from divine sources.

Specifically, information about the different stages of the kingdom and the subsequently different areas of responsibilities, were urgently required.

The Gentile Christians consumed their fervor trying to implement the original Judean-generated eschatology; whereas, it is asserted [with the input help of the Holy Spirit] that God had a Gentile-modified eschatology that they could have successfully followed. Someone, perhaps Paul, had the responsibility to straighten out the eschatological confusion generated by the Judeans. However, that person did not adequately accomplish the task, contributing much to the subsequent disarray of Christianity down to our times. Indications are that when Paul disobeyed the request of God not to go to Jerusalem, Paul lost an edge in his spiritual contact with Jesus. This special edge was essential in order to correct this eschatological confusion. Hence, the possibility exists that a gap persists in our New Testament Scriptures. Could it be true? Are we missing this critically corrective letter? And pessimistically, even if this scripture had been written, would we be able to interpret it correctly in unity? For different biblical interpretations of the same scripture by men and women of sincere persuasion continue to represent the root disunity problem within our Christian faith, a reflection of the second, third, fourth and fifth legacy blunders.

REDEMPTIVE DRIVE

The early saints were spiritual warriors, each ready to give their lives for Jesus. This engine of redemption confronted the cruelty of the Roman Empire, slowly forcing that civilization into cultural crisis. But the enemy of God, initially shocked at the force of the spiritual onslaught of the saints, collected his forces and counterattacked. The church was heavily attacked on its flanks by heresies and divisiveness. It suffered from too much intellectualism, abetted in part and compromised in part, by the apologists. The church suffered from increased ambition, frequently being misled by the ambitions of the presbyters. Yet, it stayed the course and still persevered in its cultural confrontation. It remained as a culturally rebellious, spiritual, moral and redemptive underground engine of God throughout the first century of its life, and continued weakened after Pepusa for the next two centuries

Facing frequent and intermittent persecution by the pagans, these early saints gained strength through the love of Jesus and the presence of the Spirit of God. Willing to give all for the coming of the kingdom, they lived for the future.[47]

---

47. Clearly, in the belief, fervor and faith of the primitive church, Christianity was at it finest. Living for the future of humankind, disdaining the Roman culture with its human

Slowly, then more rapidly, the giant pagan empire yielded to the sacrificial love of the Christians.[48] Cultural victory over the pagan Romans, complete and uncompromising, loomed before the saints. Victory was at hand. In the battle formation of the Grand Redemptive Engine of God, the church reached for paradise.

---

misery and exploitations, Roman paganism and its human slavery, Roman pleasures and its rewards, each saint disregarded even their own earthly existence for the love of Jesus. They looked forward to the coming of His kingdom followed by the return of Jesus. These saints offered everything to Christ, often accepted. It is to this kingdom orientation that the Christian churches must return but with a more accurate eschatology. This high point in Christianity is the Grand Redemptive Engine of God.

48. Gibbon, page 474, Gibbon relates that the early Christians pushed the Roman authorities looking for accusers of the faith. They often, rudely interrupted the public services of paganism, demanding the death sentence be placed upon them. Clearly, the early Christians were extremely aggressive for the cause of Christ, pushing the pagan world into a desperate corner.

Chapter 10

Final Forfeit of the Vector of Jesus Christ: Legacy Blunder Six

The primary goal of the vector of Jesus Christ is the redemptive transformation of human civilization into the kingdom of God. This task, the early church eagerly undertook. Those precious saints, functioning with great faith in the vector of Jesus Christ, willingly sacrificed themselves in the struggle against paganism. Successful, their cultural and spiritual war against paganism constitutes the single most compelling shift in the history of the world to date. Clearly the vision of the kingdom of God danced in their minds and spirits.

However, as the struggle against the Roman pagan culture continued into the second and third centuries, six generations removed from the fanatical generations of the first century, some saints hesitated in their dedication to the eschatological missions of Jesus Christ. The Body of Christ, initially divided between the common saints who knew the Spirit of God and the intellectuals and church leaders that did not, became even more separated. Prosperity blossomed between persecutions, seriously eroding the fervor of the saints for sacrificial martyrdom. The knowledge-coordinates unique to the vector track of Jesus Christ, so dependent upon faith and trust to pursue Jesus' vector into the unknown, bent and weakened. While the common saints were willing to trust the Spirit of God, church intellectuals could only see foolishness in this trust, which would lead to anarchy. Blinded by their intellect, they could not - and still cannot - see or experience the Spirit of God.

So weakened, the kingdom of God did not come in the near term. This caused even more of the saints to vacillate in their faith,[49] triggering a spiritually destructive cycle in which the redemptive engine of God slowly but steadily lost power. Under these spiritually degrading conditions, the influence of the apologists and the church intellectuals increased among the saints. Ambition and its companion, corruption, spread through the presbyters, causing a perceptible shift of clerical integrity within the church. This generated a counter movement

---

49. Neill, Stephen & Wright, Tom *The Interpretation of the New Testament*, London: Oxford University Press, 1989, page 284, the authors state that the early church saints were concerned about the delay in the coming again of Jesus. Some of the saints held that the interval between Jesus' Ascension and His Parousia should be short. When it was not, they had to reconsider their entire theology. It was a great disillusionment. (This attitude unquestionably enabled the **second fall**.)

for the purity of the priests and presbyters known as the Donatists, which greatly disrupted the peace of the church in the fourth and fifth centuries. Confidence waned. The church was in trouble.

LOSING THE VISION

The social status and local power of the presbyters and bishops continued to increase. Since the early church did not suffer constant persecutions, the church would experience long periods of peace, perhaps as long as a generation. During these peace interims, the presbyters and bishops made the daily administrative decisions for those early Christian communities, and the communities prospered. Then in times of persecution, they made the decisions that assisted the survival of their flock. Gradually, the saints came to look upon the presbyters for spiritual guidance. Soon they looked upon them for spiritual inspiration, then protection. Through this process, the presbyters and bishops ceased to be leaders among equals and became exulted among the saints. Gradually, the bishops took advantage of the situation coming to live like kings in plush surroundings, enjoying the exaltation of the people. The simple life and near poverty of the Savior was not emulated.

Now a more fundamental shift began. Frustrated over the Pepusa incident, the church started to write a canon dictating worship patterns and acceptable beliefs. The saints, whose ancestors had looked primarily upon the Holy Spirit for leadership, now followed the leadership of men. This shift in reliance from the Holy Spirit to human church leadership reflected the eroding church confidence in the eschatological expectations of Jesus, which in turn reflected the decline in knowledge of Jesus' vector coordinates.

Within this scenario, the kingdom spiritual power of the early church began to slip away. As the prestige of the presbyters increased, opportunities opened wider for the corrupt and ambitious presbyters. More unscrupulous presbyters arose, each taking personal advantage of their positions of authority.[50] A measure of cynicism arrived within the body of saints tilting heavily against the purity of the Christian movement. A great schism arose among the people.

The Donatist of North Africa gathered support. They insisted that corrupt priests or presbyters were totally incapable of administering the sacraments. But the traditionalists replied:

---

50. Gibbon, Edward *The Decline and Fall of the Roman Empire,* Gibbon reports fraud, envy and malice existed in all congregations. Many of the presbyters' and bishops' morality collapsed.

That bequeaths some who thought they were married, unmarried; some who thought they were baptized, not baptized; some who thought they received communion, without.

The war between the two factions soared, seriously splintering Christianity in North Africa. In an equal fashion other arguments and heresies began, such as Pelagianism[51] and Manicheanism,[52] further dividing the Body of Christ. The saints were listening to men, not to the Spirit. **Legacy blunder two** was transcendent in the Body of Christ.

Increasing portions of the early church slowly shifted from the sacrificial mode of Jesus Christ to the manipulative mode of the human intellect. It shifted from the vector to the kingdom knowledge coordinates based on faith to the pragmatic knowledge coordinates of the Roman culture, based on politics. **Legacy blunder six** became transcendent.

New problems started to abound within the church. The intellectuals and theologians trampled upon the Ebionites, struggled with the Greek mystery religions and grappled with the Gnostics. They fought Marcionism (the concept of two gods, one that developed the Old Testament and the one that developed the New Testament). They rejected Montanism, which believed in the continuing revelation of the Holy Spirit.[53]

The impact and the significance of each of these struggles cannot be underestimated. Consider the Montanist: They believed that the New Jerusalem was coming immediately. Motivated by the prophecies of Montanus, the faithful gathered by the thousands at Pepusa in the eighth decade of the second century where they waited in vain. Disappointment settled into the church. Driven by this disappointment and the general disappointment of the saints over the failure of the kingdom to appear either through the effort of God or church, and blessed with prosperity between persecutions, the desire to live the good life replaced the fervor to live for the coming of the kingdom.[54]

Now a divergent situation existed in the underground church. The church was divided between the fervent of the heart and the worldlier need to prosper. And in this confused situation, most of the leaders of the church, busy with the mundane things of the world in organizing and protecting their episcopate

---

51. It held that grace was not necessary for salvation.
52. It held that two deities existed, one created the evil and the other the light of the world with our fate determined by the stars.
53. Hughes, Philip *A History of the Church*, New York: Sheed & Ward, 1949, Volume 1, p 94.
54. Gibbon, page 482, the author states that prosperity was more dangerous to Christian faith than the severest trials of persecution.

realms, lost what little contact with the Holy Spirit they had retained. Interestingly, this occurred even while a large portion of their congregations remained in rich companionship with the Spirit. The redemptive engine functioned, when it functioned, overlooked by most of the church leaders.

Then, as the generations passed, many of the bishops and presbyters forgot about Jesus' eschatological expectations over the coming of the kingdom. Even the return of Jesus faded from their minds, thus heavily influencing the faithful in their shifting attitudes. Some cynical historians have even suggested that the intellectual element of the church used the eschatological promises of Christ to jump-start the church then threw these promises away when they were no longer required to sustain the church.[55]

Yet, martyrdom still occurred, even as the church's combat with the pagan culture continued. Too often, however, the impetus for this combat came from the pagans in their renewed efforts to eradicate the Christians.

Still, in the persistence of this combat, the New Covenanted church of Jesus Christ survived and lived. Even with the drainage of kingdom spiritual power, the church remained strong enough to spiritually defeat its enemies. Perhaps it is safe to claim that God's grace and God's anointing remained on the church despite its many problems.

Large portions of the church remained in spiritual and cultural warfare with victories continuing to accrue for the Christians.[56] The early underground church converged upon the goals of Jesus' vector by initiating the transformation of the culture.

DECISION FOR ACCOMMODATION

The Roman culture bent under the cumulative weight of the early church's spiritual power and the cultural push of the church's Redemptive Engine. Divided, the western portion of the pagan culture offered truce terms in the early fourth-century. The official reason given was a prognosticating dream of the power-aspiring Roman general, Constantine. The pragmatic reason was that Constantine felt he needed the moral assistance of the Christians. In 312, the

---

55. Gibbon, on page 404 supports this idea. He states that when the institutional church was completed, the eschatology of Jesus Christ was abandoned because the church no longer required these ideas to hold the people in the church. He states that the idea of Christ's reign upon earth was degraded by degrees until it was held to be a doubtful and useless theological position. Eventually, it was rejected as the 'absurd invention of heresy and fanaticism.'

56. Williams, Don *Signs Wonders and the Kingdom of God*, Ann Arbor, Michigan: Servant Publications, 1989, page 133.

leadership of the Western Roman State was split into various warring factions, and Constantine's opponents to Caesar's seat had claimed all the major gods of his pagan religion. Constantine strongly felt he needed a god to support his military ventures.[57] So after his alleged dream, he ordered the symbol of Christ on his soldier's shields.

Immediately afterwards, Constantine's outnumbered[58] but battle-seasoned army defeated the less experienced armies of Maxentius, opening Rome to him and placing Christianity in a different perspective within the Roman culture.

Quickly, the bishops, the apologists and the political leaders of the underground church agreed; they would seize the moment. Here, at last, was their great opportunity to rupture the era of Christian persecutions. Those who did not agree had to accept the fact that an accommodation had occurred and that there could be no turning back. Together, the church fathers rushed forward into Constantine's embrace. And he received them. But now a shockingly different scenario developed. Instead of representing Christianity to Constantine as a united movement bent on converting all of the Roman Empire, the church leaders pursued Constantine for political leverage against other Christian factions.

The underground church had been splintering for decades. The Donatist, who believed in the necessity for purity in the clergy, had been active in North Africa. Now, suddenly, a new division arose. They were the Arians. These peoples claimed the Son was not of the same substance as the Father - that the Father created the Son. These factions, along with the traditional underground Christians, all pushed the Emperor for special patronage. This push for support quickly elevated Constantine, still not a baptized Christian,[59] to the de facto leadership of the new, officially approved, Christian religion. The underground church was firmly above ground but not on firm ground. They had implemented **legacy blunders two, three, four, five and six** in a mere two centuries.

NEAR DEATH EXPERIENCE

In the next five years the conflict between the different Christian factions became severe. Riots broke out in 317 AD. Christians killed Christians. This was the start of a cruel fate that would see bloodletting become common in

---

57. Fox, Robin Lane *Pagans and Christians*, New York: Alfred A. Knopf, Inc., 1989, page 613.
58. He was outnumbered four to one.
59. Hughes, page 199. Eusebius of Nicomedia, an Arian, initiated Constantine to the sacraments on his deathbed.

Christendom.[60] Constantine called the first church-wide council in Nicaea in 325 AD to settle the issue between the traditional and Arian factions of the church. Orthodoxy is the fundamental beliefs of a faith system. Would Christian orthodoxy hold on to the traditional concept of the Son made of the same substance as the Father, i.e., that Jesus was divine, or would it hold that the Father created the Son? The traditional bloc won in Nicaea in 325, forming the Nicene Creed as the direct answer to the Arians.

Now the traditional faction, calling themselves orthodox Catholics intensified their organization as an institutional church. But this initial hierarchical church continued to depend heavily upon the headship of Constantine, and Constantine was to prove unreliable. With the Nicene council as recent history, the great champion of the Arianists, Eusebius of Nicomedia, captured the emperor's ear, effectively reversing the decisions of the Nicene Council. Catholic Nicene orthodoxy staggered and almost slipped into oblivion as the Arians had the people singing: "There was a time when the Son was not."[61] The Nicene situation in 336 AD was extremely untenable. Constantine had displaced all the Catholic bishops but one, and he planned on installing Arius into that position, effectively resetting Christian orthodoxy to Arianism.

Set the scene: the entire force of the Empire was arrayed against the Nicene traditionalists. The Arians were ready to send Christianity down that path which rejected the divinity of Jesus Christ. The Christian Catholics prayed intensively for God's intervention. Yet, nothing happened; Arius was set to replace Athanasius, Bishop of Alexandria, and the last Catholic Bishop in Christendom. As the date for this replacement drew nearer, the Roman authorities finished their plan to install Arianism as the official orthodox belief of the Christian religion by elevating Arius back into the church with high ceremony. Riots broke out in Alexandria and Constantinople. The Catholics stormed heaven for relief. These prayers appeared to be in vain for the time of Arius' elevation arrived. But in 336, on the eve of Arius' official elevation back into the church, he died. Constantine died a few months later on May 22, 337 AD. The Eusebians [the Arians] lost on the eve of their triumph over the Nicenes.[62] It would seem probably that God intervened in this affair to preserve the Catholics and with it the Sonship of Jesus Christ as expressed in the Nicene Creed. The Spirit confirms this!

---

60. Riots and killings characterized the heresy disputes of the fourth-century. In one form or another, vast numbers of saints have been tortured and killed by others professing to follow Jesus Christ. It is indeed a sad situation; one that has occurred in the twentieth century, e.g., Northern Ireland.
61. Placher page 70.
62. Hughes, page 197.

Still the struggle for survival was not over for the orthodox Nicene Catholics. The Arians survived these deaths to challenge once again, regaining political favor. The new bishop of Rome, Silvester, seemingly disappeared as a political factor in Roman politics. Perhaps his heart was still with the rebellious, underground church of his youth. Regardless of Silvester's intentions, his political impact was slight, and the Nicene Catholics continued to lose heavily against the Arians. Three types of contenders strove for the throne: pagans, Arians and Nicene Catholics. The struggle intensified. Political intrigue and murders were common; riots and persecutions occurred. The struggle lasted from 337 to 360 AD with the Nicene Catholics increasingly battered and persecuted by their opponents. Their champion against the Arians remained Athanasius who precariously hung on through multiple trials and two exiles. In 361 AD, Julian became emperor and pushed a new form of paganism against all Christians. The survival light dimmed for the Nicene Catholics. Martyrdomship returned. The Roman authorities encouraged the pagans to attack Christians. Huge Anti-Christian riots occurred, which authorities encouraged. Massacres of Christians again appeared with Roman pagan authorities laughing at Christian appeals for help, mockingly taunting that Christianity called for suffering. The pagan authorities went further; they tried to annul the issue of Martyrs by using new legal excuses for killing the Christians, which never mentioned the real religious reasons for the deaths.[63]

The orthodox Nicene Catholics would survive this bleak moment in history only in Julian's early death. Julian's last words were: "Galilean, thou hast triumphed." It would be fourteen more years before Gratian, an orthodox Nicene Catholic emperor, gained the Western throne and rejected paganism in 375 AD. Meanwhile in the East, the emperor Valens insisted that all citizens be Arians.

The political intrigue of the Romans continued and the threat of the Arians remained, but the Nicene Catholics had learned their political lessons well. They would successfully play the hard game of politics from this point onward from which they would assert, and never relinquish, control over the institutional Christian church.

However, a great scare had been thrown into the orthodox Nicene Catholics. The church fathers had elected to join the political world, and the political world almost consumed them. The Nicenes narrowly survived. Now, tired of the heavy hand of the secular world, the orthodox Catholic fathers seized upon Julian's death to build their new religion around the bishop of Rome, arguing that this episcopate possessed a continuous succession to Peter. The struggle with Arianism would continue for three hundred years or more, but the mode of victory was established for the orthodox Catholic Church: Political manipulation

---

63. Hughes, page 181.

backed by an efficient organization. They would cooperate, participate, even recognize the hegemony of the state, but they would not be directly ruled by the state and they would not allow the state to judge heresy. Further, they would ruthlessly subdue any heresy that arose, and this control would start with rigid control over the faithful.

Legalism rose from fright but at a terrible price: With rigidity and codification the freedom that abetted and embraced the deep and loving presence of the Spirit of God was shut down. With these decisions the church fathers built an unyielding power hierarchy, embraced excessive authoritativeness, created syntactic worship and codified salvation. This overreaction to its near death in the fourth-century spun the institutional church into a spurious tangential vector, traveling a path away from the will of God. It is a direction from which it has yet to recover. The essence of this mistake is that salvation is found in the institutional church. This weakness is still found in most denominations of Christianity. And however diluted, it is wrong! Salvation is found in Jesus Christ, not a church. And saints, the two are not the same!

Sadly, the inherited conditions for the existence of the organized, orthodox Catholic Church had been set by the middle of the fourth century. The church embraced a Pact of Cooperation with the pagans and their pagan based culture. The underground and rebellious church of Jesus Christ was dead. The church had slipped and fallen from its eschatological mandate, which it did not even understand.

SATAN'S ROLE

As stated earlier, the essential condition of the fourth-century underground church accommodation was cultural cooperation. In other words, the extinction of the remnants of the rebellious church was exchanged for the protection of the Roman Emperor. In their haste for peace and structure, in their eagerness to overcome one another in their theological fights, the church leaders from all the contending factions either immediately accepted these terms or were forced to accept them to stay as a rival player. The remnants of the rebellious church, operative within the leadership of the Holy Spirit, had no voice in this decision. The worldly church fathers gladly forfeited that which they could not see. So without comprehension, they abandoned cultural combat. In this unknowing forfeiture, they gave up striving for the coming of the kingdom except in theological expression. Constantine accepted this arrangement, also unknowingly, and the truce was completed in 313 AD. Since it is arguable that both parties to the agreement did not understand the larger significance of the agreement, it must be stated categorically that Satan and his workers, both demonic and human, engineered this agreement.

THE FORFEITURES

For exactness, many of the church leaders had long since given up on the Parousia (the return of Christ) before Constantine had his dream. Since 211 AD, many of the bishops had already enjoyed the recognition associated with authority.[64] They were allowed to build churches and openly functioned within their respective episcopates. The agreement simply solidified what was already a fact for them, removing any lingering doubts about their authority. By formalizing the de-facto cooperative arrangement, called the Pact of Cooperation in this text, the bishops sold-out the on-going work of the real church. Their actions gutted what remained of the redemptive engine. They forfeited the goals and missions of Jesus Christ, and then, founded the institutional church on this betrayal. They exchanged Jesus' rebellious movement for the physical protection and the political, financial advantages of the Christ-hating cultures of the world.[65]

Here are the significant dates of that fourth century which so dramatically led to the initialization of the **second fall**. Remember, the significance of these events cannot be overstated:

303 - Fresh outbreak of the persecution of Christians occurred with Diocletian's edict of February 24, which is the "most elaborate attempt to revive Paganism yet undertaken by the Roman State" (page 170 of Hughes' *History of the Church*). Christians were massacred in great numbers; even whole towns were destroyed. (See page 172 of the reference.) The slaughter lasted, in varying degrees, for eight years.

311 - Persecution is ended by imperial edict. The persecutions generated a large class who worshipped no god. (See page 173 of Hughes' *History of the Church).*

311 - 313 The Roman Empire started a campaign of education on the wickedness of Christianity. They used pamphlets and lectures to reach the people. (See page 174 of the reference). This was a desperate last effort of the pagans to survive the spiritual and cultural onslaught of the Christians.

---

64. Gibbon, Edward *The Decline and Fall of the Roman Empire*, page 479-480, says that until the death of Severus in 211 AD the Christians assembled in homes. But after 211, they had limited rights to build houses of worship and to conduct public worship. They could openly elect their ecclesiastical ministers. It is interesting that from the start of public worship till the Constantine's dream, the beginning of the acceptance of Christianity, exactly 100 hundred years passed.
65. From Hughes *History of the Church.*

312 - Constantine had a dream that if he marked the shields of his soldiers with 'caeleste signum Dei' - the celestial sign of God, the monogram of the name of Christ - he would win a significant battle opening the Empire to his dual rule with Licinius. He did, and it happened. Later he issued the Edit of Milan, which admitted that Christianity must be allowed to survive. "It is a political act…conditioned by the circumstances of the moment" (page 176 of Hughes' *History of the Church*).

323 - Licinius, the ruler of the east abandoned Constantine's policy of 313 AD generating Christian persecutions once again. Constantine's army defeated him at Chrysopolis in 324 AD, bringing these new persecutions to an end. (See page 177 of the reference). Now both paganism and Christianity were considered equal in the law.

325 - Constantine called the Council of Nicea to settle the Arian question over how Logos can be God and yet distinct from the Father. The results were the Nicene Creed and the definition of the Trinity. From page 192 of Hughes' *History of the Church* we read this incredible admission: 'Arianism should have ended. But because of Constantine it did not. It revived to challenge the Nicene Catholics.' In its attempts to defeat Arianism, the church took its first steps in its sell-out to the State in the twelve-year period of time between 313 and 325 and onward to 381 AD. At times this sell-out looked like it would destroy the institutional Catholic Church.

331 - Arianism grew in political strength and gained its first triumph over Catholic orthodoxy, replacing all but one of the Catholic Bishops in the Roman Christian world even in the face of extensive riots.

336 - **Arius** died just before being installed as the Bishop of Alexandria, the last remaining Catholic Archdiocese in the Roman Empire, manned by the tenacious Athanasius. The installation of Arius was to represent the Arian's final defeat of the Nicene Catholic faith with the intention of shifting Christian orthodoxy to Arianism. The faithful saw the hand of God in the sudden death of Arius and the fulfillment of Jesus' promise to stand by His church.

337 - Constantine accepted water baptism on his deathbed from the Arians. The immediate threat to the Nicene Catholic Church was eliminated only six months after Arius' sudden death. Four legacies were left to the world by the reign of Constantine:

1. The church would companion with the State as a functioning component of the State, as a religion.
2. Spiritual integrity of the Christian faith was polluted. From Gibbon, Edward *The Decline and Fall of the Roman Empire*, page 655: "the piercing eye of ambition and avarice soon discovered that the profession of Christianity might contribute to the interest of the present…"

3. Tyranny concealed under the cloak of Christianity was established. This charge is based on Constantine's deliberate use of deathbed Baptism to cover his reign of tyranny. Gibbon, page 654. As an example of Constantine's tyranny and the measure of the Pact of Cooperation cancer, the same year Constantine convened the Nicea council he murdered his eldest son; yet the bishops hailed him as an apostle. See Gibbon, page 654-655.

4. The church, which had been organized to the level of bishop, became organized under an authoritative hierarchy to the level of a leader centered in Rome or Constantinople in which the decisions of the church were largely made in a political mode. This seemingly small shift in hierarchical relationship became huge in impact.

361 – Julian the Apostate gained power and commenced the reorganization of paganism. Full of hate for the Nicene Catholics he instigated the replacement of all Nicene Catholic Bishops with Arians. The scenario of Constantine I was being repeated 25 years later.

363- Julian died and Nicene Catholic orthodoxy returned. Once more the church escaped the threat of the Arians, saved by the same methodology: the sudden and unexpected death of the foe of the church at that point in which defeat for the church seemed certain. Interestingly, again the conflict centered at Alexandria with the tenacious Athanasius again the last remaining Nicene Bishop. After and during this experience, the church strengthened its political organization around the bishop of Rome. It is almost as if the two illustrations of God's intervention to save the church were not enough for them. Clearly, in this time frame they decided to trust in political manipulation for survival instead of the intervention and leadership of the Holy Spirit. How can we judge the anger of God over these events except to look at the resultant punishment lasting eight centuries?

363- The New Testament format, excepting Revelation, is accepted in the Council of Laodicea.

380- Theodosius ended the Roman Empire's official connection with Arianism.

381- Theodosius established orthodox Nicene Catholic Christianity as the State religion of the Roman Empire.

SEEING THE DECISION THROUGH THE CHURCH FATHER'S EYES

Let us attempt to view these critical decisions against the mission vector of Christ from the perspective of the church leaders of 312/313. Some of these leaders saw a victory in which they could work for the Great Commission in

93

peace, gaining the chance for the leaven of the Gospel to work upon the pagan culture unhindered. Still others saw the physical salvation of the persecuted saints

But in all these judgments, the church leaders made a serious mistake. They allowed their concern over the welfare of other humans, i.e., the persecuted sufferings and tortured death of the saints, to exceed their own faith in God's control. This happened because these leaders had lost contact with the plans of God and the direction of the Holy Spirit. It is perhaps a difficult concept to grasp, but the privilege of suffering for Christ can be a great gift to some saints. In some special circumstances, to allow this suffering, knowing it is redemptive, is not in violation of Jesus' command to love one another as yourself. This is what the leaders of the church had forgotten: To suffer for Christ can be a great gift for the dedicated saint. Yet, ignoring this desire, the fourth century church fathers pressed hard to eliminate persecution suffering from their peoples, sinning exceedingly in the process. They took on the role of God, losing sight of their mere humanity. Indeed, in their weaknesses, they reflected the inevitable error of humanity: Our overwhelming need to lift humans into exulted positions as heroes and leaders to which no man can measure. This is a weakness that we must overcome before we can build the kingdom.

Greek humanism had a victory over loving but confrontational Christianity because the church leaders simply did not see the New Covenant progression toward the kingdom of God in all this suffering. Expressed differently, they simply did not exist in the kingdom knowledge coordinates of Jesus' mission vector. They failed, utterly, to see that the kingdom came through the sacrifices of the saints in support of the church challenge to the pagan culture. The saints, born again, could see the vision of the kingdom, but most of the church leaders, captured by human exultation, their own intellect and overcome with authority and power, had lost that vision. Since they could not see the vision, they could not see God's redemptive engine, and so they struck down the modus operandi of the early church: Sacrificial redemption!

But they did more than forfeit the sacrificial orientation of the early church; they offended the Spirit of God by their decision to forfeit cultural confrontation, invalidating Jesus' Gospel, especially as revealed by the Gospel of Matthew. This decision was the second insult to the Holy Spirit in 150 years, contributing significantly to the **second fall**.

With this decision, the institutional church decided to survive the hostile world via the manipulations of the human mind, forfeiting their remaining trust in the Counselor and totally abandoning Jesus' kingdom vector.

Incredibly, after two fourth-century miraculous interventions from God to save the Nicene Catholic Church, they still did not trust the survival of the church to the Holy Spirit. This could only mean that they did not believe in the existence of the Spirit of God. Paul had warned that the world would not be able to see

Him, but had he ever thought that the church leadership would not be able to see Him?

By opting for human politics as the pragmatic solution to the pagan persecutions, the church leaders placed in abeyance the prime mission of the New Covenant of Jesus Christ to bring all nations into the discipleship of Jesus Christ. Void of the guidance of the Spirit, the leaders of the church redefined the Great Commission exclusively to the conversion of each individual in the world, freeing the church from the responsibilities for the conversion of human civilization into the kingdom of God. This New Covenant mission-defeating exegetical decision has generated wide-ranging ramifications even down to our time. In affect, the mission vector of Jesus Christ was abandoned, and then forgotten. It resides in the cobwebs of history, yet to be resuscitated.

Chapter 11

Measuring the Defeat

The measurement of the lost vector of Jesus Christ is an impossible human task. Yet we must try.

First, what was lost? The Holy Spirit asserts that this loss is found in the failure to bring the kingdom of God to this planet, signifying that the kingdom possesses an enormous potential to harvest human souls/spirits. Certainly, Jesus' public life focused on the coming of the kingdom, talking about it incessantly. He asked His followers to pray daily for its coming:

... your kingdom come, your will be done on earth as it is in heaven (Matthew 6:10).

Second, Jesus felt that the pursuit of the coming of the kingdom exceeded any other interest for His true followers:

But seek first His kingdom and His righteousness...(Matthew 6:33).

From Luke we read this hard-hitting confirmation message:

... no one who has left home or wife or brothers or parents or children for the sake of the kingdom of God will fail to receive many times as much in this age and, in the age to come, eternal life (Luke 8:29-30).

Third, Jesus deemed the pursuit of the coming of the kingdom so important that He promised to take care of all worldly needs for the dedicated and faithful pursuer of the kingdom of God:

... and all these things will be given to you as well (Matthew 6:33).

Stop for a moment and reflect on this statement from Jesus. God will provide all our material needs if we pursue the kingdom of God and His righteousness. On this point we are all in agreement, but have you ever considered that a deeper meaning exists here? Might the things what we obtain be a soup kitchen, healing, a conversion or a successful pastoral practice? In other words, the concept of seeking after the kingdom of God given in Matthew 6:33 is applicable to the church first, before it is applicable to the individual. Yet what church, what congregation seeks to bring the kingdom about by a cultural transformation? Largely none!

To grasp the magnitude of the Spirit's teaching on this subject divide Matthew 6:33 into two components: The goal that Jesus wants us to pursue and the physical and emotional gifts He will bestow as a reward for seeking after the goal.

This means that we must seek after the goal that God has set in front of us not His gifts. If we drive for the gifts ignoring God's goals we temp God to forsake us.

Here is a graphic representation of this Scripture and this situation:

INDIVIDUAL APPLICATION OF MATTHEW 6:33:

None of the physical attributes can be fully realized unless the saint first seeks out the Kingdom of God and His righteousness. To seek after the attributes solely is to forfeit one's close walk with Christ, thus becoming a thief in life.

END RUN, THE COMMON CHRISTIAN EXPERIENCE:

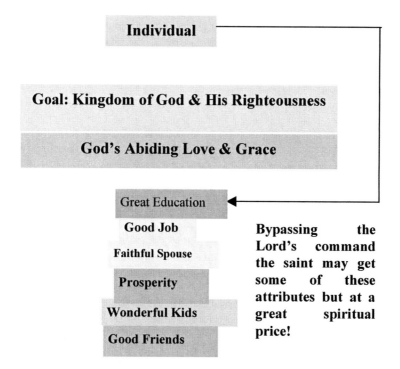

What could be that great spiritual price: To have God turn His blessings from us and spit us out from His mouth:

So, because you are lukewarm – neither hot nor cold – I am about to spit you out of my mouth (Revelation 3:16).

CHURCH APPLICATION OF MATTHEW 6:33:

None of the attributes can be fully realized unless the church first seeks out the Kingdom of God and His righteousness. To seek after the attributes solely is to forfeit the status of a spiritual church.

END RUN, THE COMMON CHURCH EXPERIENCE:

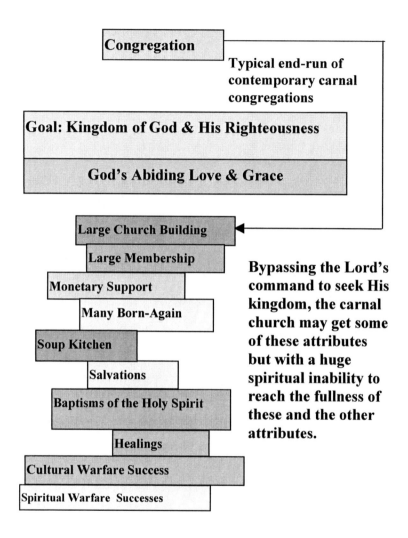

Congregation

Typical end-run of contemporary carnal congregations

Goal: Kingdom of God & His Righteousness

God's Abiding Love & Grace

Large Church Building

Large Membership

Monetary Support

Many Born-Again

Soup Kitchen

Salvations

Baptisms of the Holy Spirit

Healings

Cultural Warfare Success

Spiritual Warfare Successes

Bypassing the Lord's command to seek His kingdom, the carnal church may get some of these attributes but with a huge spiritual inability to reach the fullness of these and the other attributes.

Fourth, Jesus told us that our vision was inadequate for the task. We must have a rebirth to follow Him and to bring the kingdom of God to earth. From John we read:

I tell you the truth, unless a man is born again, he cannot see the kingdom of God (John 3:3).

Of course we must immediately ask the question: If I cannot see the kingdom of God am I still born again? Many people answer that question by stating that seeing the kingdom of God means seeing it after death, i.e., that one is saved by the rebirth. The Spirit says this is an evasion of God's truth embedded in that scripture. We are to see the structure and the function of the kingdom, even if dimly, in our physical life. This is the fulfillment of Luke 17:20.

"The kingdom of God does not come visibly, nor will people say, 'Here it is,' or 'There it is,' because the kingdom of God is within you" (Luke 17:20-21).

To have the kingdom of God within is to know the kingdom of God. Clearly, the fail-safe exegesis that John 3:3 means seeing the kingdom after our death but not in our earthly life is one of the prime causes of cheap salvation, that which generates easy Christianity and a soft, non-invasive faith, enabling the carnal walk. Saints, this was not what Jesus had in mind when He asked us to pick up our cross and carry it. John 3:3 means what it says, and therefore, if we have no vision or perception of the kingdom of God other than what we have been told by others, then we have a need to be alarmed. We must see and sense the kingdom of God in our soul and spirit before we can work for its physical arrival on earth. That means John 3:3 and Luke 17:20-21 are forever linked, and between them, along with Revelation 21:1-2, Matthew 6:10, 1 Thessalonians 4:17, Matthew 25:10, Matthew 22:37-39, Romans 8:9 and John 17:21 they carry the key to the Lord's request for the coming of the kingdom to earth. Here is this linkage:

In addition to the two Scriptures previously given, *John 3:3* and *Luke 17:20-21*, these Scriptures form the linkage:
Matthew 6:10 – Your Kingdom come, your will be done on earth as it is in heaven.
Revelation 21:2 – I saw the Holy City, the New Jerusalem, coming down out of heaven from God, prepared as a bride beautifully dressed for her husband.
Matthew 25:10 – But as they went on their way to buy the oil, the bridegroom arrived. The virgins who were ready went with him to the wedding banquet. And the door was shut.

1 Thessalonians 4:17 – After that, we who are still alive and are left will be caught up with them in the clouds to meet the Lord in the air.

John 17:21 – ...that all them may be one, Father just as you are in me and I am in you. May they also be in us so that the world may believe that you have sent me...

Matthew 22:37-39 – Jesus replied: 'Love the Lord your God with all your heart and with all your soul and with all your mind. This is the first and greatest commandment. And the second is like it: 'Love your neighbor as yourself.'

Romans 8:9 – And if anyone does not have the Spirit of Christ he does not belong to Christ.

SCRIPTURAL TRACE TO THE KINGDOM:

1. John 3:3 implements and enables Luke 17:20-21.
2. Matthew 6:10 resolves the conflict between Luke 17:20-21 and the arrival of the New Jerusalem Kingdom of Revelation 21:2 by the Lord's command to construct the kingdom on earth as well as in heaven.
3. Matthew 25:10 clearly indicate that the Lord comes only for His Bride.
4. Revelation 21:2 reveals that the kingdom of God brought to earth is the Bride.
5. Hence the only conclusion is that the two kingdoms, one developed as the bride of Christ on earth and the other as the New Jerusalem Kingdom returned with the Lamb are the same, integrated by the rapture as given in 1 Thessalonians 4:17.
6. But the kingdom cannot be brought to earth by a carnal and divided church, thus John 17:21 defines the key to the coming of the kingdom as Christian unity in agape love.
7. This unity is easily accomplished if we could truly functioned under Matthew 22:37-39.
8. The drive to bring the Kingdom of God to earth must be directed by the Holy Spirit for only in His guidance can we travel Jesus' mission vector to the first implementation of God's Kingdom on earth. Here we must be led by Romans 8:9 because only the spiritual church, functioning as the **Overchurch**, steeped in agape love and led by the Spirit of God, can bring about this result, even in God's great intervention.

Study this linkage with the assistance of the Holy Spirit until it becomes part of you.

Most of our denominational leaders have either ignored or misinformed us about the power of John 3:3 and its utter importance to each of us. Each saint walks in danger of losing their soul/spirit under the false and misleading teachings perpetuated upon us by sincere men of mistaken beliefs. Indeed, the words of knowledge received from the Father states: 'Too many of my beloved ones are victims of the teaching of men long dead who are not now with me.' Listen, Satan did a number on the church centuries ago in legacy blunders 2 through 6, which our Protestant Reformers or Catholic Counter Reformers did not correct. Men like Conrad Grebel held out for a complete reversal of the Constantine mistakes, asking for the return of the church to purity from pagan and secular influences, to find overcoming, there to function once again as a spiritual church. These men tried to fully implement reform, but failed. Beloved, in the competition of finding eternity with God, coming close does not count! Who can determine the damage that Zwingli did when He chased Grebel to his death?[66] What a horrendous mistake! Dare we ask how many soul/spirits have not found heaven because of this debacle and others like it?

Fifth, Jesus refused to warrant His victory to that one who sees the kingdom but does not understand it. To understand the kingdom, each born again saint must work for its coming. For the Spirit has shown that to see the kingdom of God in Jesus' spiritual rebirth is to be restless with the current and contemporary culture. This is actually the starting point of Jesus' vector to the kingdom. Jesus was warning His followers in the strongest terms to work for the kingdom. From Matthew we read this serious admonition:

When anyone hears the message about the kingdom and does not understand it, the evil one comes and snatches away what was sown in his heart (Matthew 13:19).

Clearly, Jesus expected the kingdom to come, and clearly, He expected His followers to pursue this task, plainly cautioning against ignoring His call to seek after the kingdom. This was a stern warning. Yet, with the forgotten vector of Jesus Christ, this is exactly what the institutional, orthodox Christian churches did. They formalized ignorance of His call to seek after the kingdom. They forfeited preaching the rebirth of the human spirit and thus ruined the redemptive engine. Even as the pagan culture became susceptible to the message of the kingdom, the churches opted out of their responsibilities to Jesus Christ. They

---

66. In the early sixteenth century, Conrad Grebel wanted to undo the **second fall** but was imprisoned for his views. He escaped, but he died of the black plague while hiding from Zwingli. The Holy Spirit proclaims Grebel as the greatest of the Protestant Reformers.

gave up; they surrendered when they had no adequate reason to surrender. What a huge sin! They took the first political compromise offered to them, crushing, in that acceptance, the vector mission of Jesus Christ and those saints who still pursued the kingdom of God. These fourth-century Christian leaders exchanged Christ's commandment to seek the kingdom for the cultural protection of a ruthless wife-and-son-murdering pagan emperor who did not convert to Christianity until dying and that to a heretic.[67]

The potential of the kingdom brought to earth was forsaken. Who can measure this loss? Only God! Still, we must try to grasp the forfeited benefits.

FORFEITED BENEFITS OF THE KINGDOM

We assert that Holy Scripture supports the conclusion that Jesus' primary mission critical task in His eschatology was the mass harvesting of soul/spirits through the coming of the kingdom of God to this planet. Can we gain an understanding of the intended benefits of this kingdom come?

Matthew 6:33 would seem to promise the imputed righteousness of God as a major benefit for humanity from the coming of the kingdom. This righteousness would enhance the humanity of all and allow agape love and true human compassion to flow across the civilization of the Prototypical Kingdom. Agape love would transcend human cynicism and focus upon the innate selfishness of humanity, demanding rectification. Other benefits would be the return to the friendship and companionship of God, both individually and societally. This would mean the involvement of God in every exercise of individual and cultural life regardless of how small or mundane, a return to the intimacy of God. Only in the societal return to the friendship of God in every aspect of human endeavor can human civilization control, then eliminate deceiving hearts. Only then can human exploitation be checked.

Let the reader contemplate a culture of love that possessed a reliable, even validated communication methodology with God that allowed each member of that societal organization to have a personalized behavioral feedback from the Spirit of God. Then further contemplate that this communication existed after the secret and evil orientations of the mind had been eliminated or controlled? Many people, familiar with the historical experiences of human controlled societies, will immediately see a culture of ruthless regulation, but truly, this Spirit-controlled cultural scenario would feature a tender touch, generating human freedom not human bondage. Human exploitation would vanish and a whole new

---

67. Eusebius of Nicomedia, the Arian advocate, baptized Constantine on his deathbed in 337 AD.

form of civilization would emerge, becoming the first truly new civilization in recorded history.

One of the great freedoms rendered to humanity by this new civilization would be freedom from scorn and intellectual elitism. Cynicism and skepticism would vanish, even from the hidden thoughts of men and women. And with this freedom, a renaissance of human creativity would explode across the brotherhood culture. Creativity with its companion, the sense of accomplishment innate to the appreciation of God and fellow humans, would generate an extended agape love environment with a profound sense of the worth of each human. With the elevation of the status of the human, enabled by God's love, the joy of overflowing compassion would bring ecstasy and happiness unspeakable. This is the operational essence of the Prototypical Kingdom.

Human pleasure, which now finds its outlet mostly in human degradations and perversions and their related human activities, will find, in the culture of brotherhood, human pleasure outlets in uplifting moral human activities. Excitement will not be generated by danger or divergence, perversion and the thrill of revolt, the product of the immature mind, but from anticipated accomplishment and inward recognition of agape love, the product of the Christ mind. The criteria for human acceptance and human accomplishments will be totally changed, centered first on the human effort and second on the thing achieved. Agape love will generate true appreciation not trivialized patronage.

The coming of the kingdom of God even in prototype will be the greatest event in the history of humanity since Pentecost. This society will understand the pure pleasure of existence derived from the intensification of agape love, human value and trust. Stop and consider the quality of life where everyone possesses the intimate feedback embrace of God. Consider the quality of a society promoting human-will and human initiative – maximized by the feedback from God through the human spirit – which constantly monitors each human away from the pitfalls of sin. Consider the culture of agape love and compassion, where the one hurt - for hurts will still occur - is known and assisted immediately! Who can imagine life where humanity functions as a close intimate family? Can any man or woman understand what life would be like in an economy of agape love? Who appreciates the potential of agape pursuits and economic exchanges predicated upon the overwhelming presence of the Spirit of God and the forced absence of the enemy of God?

No one! We can neither understand nor appreciate the significance of this cultural experience because our frame of reference is not wide enough. Our knowledge-coordinates are too primitive. Yet, this is our lost potential. Even the struggle to achieve the potential of the kingdom is our deep loss. We can dismiss this lost potential, even the unrecognized human suffering inflicted upon humanity because of this paradise lost, only in vast and arrogant ignorance, dismissing it as wild dreams, as human existence removed from reality. And in this rejection humanity is accomplished, reflecting the natural outreach of our current human captivity to corruption and deception. What a catastrophe!

Here, then, is the summary of missed benefits that humanity and the church forfeited by the lost vector:

FORFEITED BENEFITS, INDIVIDUAL:

1- Surge in spiritual power
2- Victory in massive spiritual warfare
3- Rise in evangelical power
4- Massive integration of Holy Scripture into the lives of the faithful
5- Acceptance of human knowledge accumulation as a vehicle of God's love, contributing energetically to the reversal of the Adamic curse
6- Extensive intellectual understanding of the Holy Spirit and His role in the church
7- Purity in church leadership behind the Holy Spirit
8- Theological clarity led by the Spirit of God
9- Unity
10- Brotherhood in agape love
11- Precise definition of the New Covenant as a challenging civilization
12- Understanding freedom as a function of the Holy Spirit
13- Elevation of the value of human life
14- Explosion of technology integrated with God's work
15- Widespread acceptance that the possession of God's rapport and love is found within and through the human spirit
16- Great understanding that the regeneration of the human spirit is essential to union with the Holy Spirit
17- Ascent of the human spirit
18- Inner cleansing of the human mind

SOCIETAL & KINGDOM LOSSES:

19- Rise of large numbers of overcoming saints, in each generation, spiritually communicating with God
20- Optimization of the spiritual and cultural fighting army of God as the Grand Redemptive Engine of God
21- The discovery of Jesus' vector to the kingdom of God
22- Selection of the targeted culture for the Prototypical Kingdom
23- The clash of the concepts of civilizations
24- The struggle of Dialectical Agapism

25- Massive cultural redemption of the targeted culture
26- The great and exciting task of building the kingdom
27- Territorial cleansing of the Prototypical Kingdom
28- Coming of the kingdom of God as a prototypical synthesis of the targeted culture and the confronting church
29- God permitted destruction of the Prototypical Kingdom by the forces of the dark world known as the New World Order in order to perfect the cleansing of His people even in sorrow and pain
30- Time of sorrows
31- Cleansing and inner healing of humanity
32- The great plea of the people of God to God
33- Intervention of God to restore his earthly Prototypical Kingdom to be known from that point onward as the Demonstration Kingdom
34- Transformation of the Demonstration Kingdom culture and the victorious church into the Bride of Christ as it becomes the Millennium Kingdom
35- Reestablishment of societal communications with God with validation
36- Continued cleansing of the kingdom population as an educational process
37- Immediate identification of deception
38- Establishment of individual feedback monitoring with God
39- Outreach of the Word from the Demonstration Kingdom to all the good-seed of the world
40- The great harvest
41- Fulfillment of the Great Commission
42- Polarization of the world for or against Jesus and His kingdom
43- Rise of the Antichrist
44- Withdrawal of the saints and the Demonstration Kingdom
45- Day of the Lord
46- Return of Jesus
47- Final separation of humanity
48- Installation of the New Jerusalem as the perfected Demonstration Kingdom of God
49- Transfer of the Kingdom to the Father by Jesus Christ.

Chapter 12

Losing the Reform Window

By the end of the first-century many of the church fathers anxiously sought an accommodation with the pagans to end the persecutions of the saints. Many of these thinkers, called apologists, strove to define Christianity as a non-threatening faith system, composed of good and obedient citizens. They strove to characterize the church as no threat to the pagan and secular culture, which of course, was a lie. The very mission of the church was to transform the pagan culture into the kingdom of God. The church struggle for official recognition lasted several centuries, during which time, the drive toward the transformation of pagan secularism into the kingdom of God was damaged by this often-repeated big lie. Then in the early part of the fourth century, after a fierce struggle as an underground church, characterized by many persecutions with much suffering, the church secured a cooperative partnership with Western Rome. From this infamous but informal bargain the church emerged from its underground status to become a respected religion in the Roman Empire, birthing the hierarchically organized church as an institutionalized and political structure. But unexpectedly the delivery was a twin birth. The other and unforeseen twin infant was the cancer of pragmatism.

The essence of the Pragmatic Cancer is that the worldly life is the primary human existence and that the spiritual life is private and principally utilized to find an entrance into the kingdom of heaven there to join Jesus. On the surface, this seems fine, but it is not totally accurate for embedded in this agreement is the forfeiture of the drive to bring the kingdom of God to earth. This agreement repudiates the mission critical task of Jesus Christ, invalidating His vector to paradise. And additionally, it surrendered huge portions of the common saint's life to secular pursuits.

Jesus desires that we walk with Him at all times in all pursuits. He is unwilling to confine our closeness with Him to a particular day or moment of our lives, usually spent in confining religiosity.

In the informal agreement that generated the Pragmatic Cancer, called the Pact of Cooperation in this text, the emerging political and institutional church agreed to terminate its cultural confrontations with the Roman Empire. Then the church agreed to join with that pagan culture as a cooperative member of society, all in exchange for the official recognition of Christianity as an accredited religion of the Roman Empire. Here, we can see the forfeiture of the redemption of the nations in all but theological articulation. This is a woeful treaty that has cursed us for 1,688 years. It must go!

Foundation Premises

Unbelievably, this handicap, the Pragmatic Cancer, especially as expressed in the informal Pact of Cooperation, became the cornerstone of the institutional church, its construction foundation block! And so it remains, even today. The foundation premises of our modern, hierarchical, institutional churches remain cultural cooperation instead of cultural confrontation.[68] Restated, the modern churches cannot reform their way out of the Pragmatic Curse because their entire church foundation is built upon this curse.

Stop!

Think about the seriousness of this charge! Indeed, Christendom has worked its way into one horrible mess. And do not dare to think that because your church might be Protestant or Orthodox that this foundation problem is exclusively Catholic, not yours. This mistake belongs to all of us! Without doubt, the failure to reverse this church fault is the major failure of the Protestant Reformation as well as the Catholic Counter Reformation. Both of these major reform movements occurred in the reform window, which is defined as the 795 years after Jesus' appeared to Francis of Assisi in 1205. Reform anytime in that window could have rescued the church, but that time has passed. Here are these two significant dates:

- 410 to 1205: God's first discipline (795 years)
- 1205 to 2000: window of reform (795 years).

The window for reform opened when Jesus appeared to Francis Assisi in 1205 ending the first discipline of God upon His church and surrounding culture. Jesus asked for a restructuring, a repair, of His church. It appears from listening to the Holy Spirit that this window of reform was capable of reconstructing the church, placing it upon a firm foundation of agape love through human effort. However, humanity in its fascination with its own intellect and political Machiavellian capacities ignored that window. It closed after the year 2000. Here is how that window looked as related by the Spirit of God:

---

68. Perhaps no better illustration exists of the sell-out of the church fathers to the secular and pagan world than Augustine's use of the Roman army to enforce his theological positions. Placher, William C. *A History of Christian Theology*, Louisville: The Westminster Press, 1983, page 115.

The Lord's punishment descends upon the church because of its role in the second fall from His blessings. This wrath starts in 410 with the sacking of Rome. Attacked by the pagans for causing the demise of Rome, Augustine is called to defend Christian rule and writes the *City of God.* Yet Augustine fails to detect that the cause for the Lord's anger is the actions of the church, equivocating around the true problem.

Jesus makes an appearance to Francis of Assisi in 1205 asking: 'Repair my House.' This ends the wrath of God upon the church and the surrounding culture. The duration of the punishment is 795 years. This, then, is the interval given the church to implement Jesus' reconstruction request.

The new Millennium, starting in 2001, closes that window of human reconstruction opportunity and places the hope for the reconstruction of the church upon the loving intervention of God. Most certainly, that intervention will feature a new and harsh punishment upon the churches followed by a tremendous outpouring of the Holy Spirit, featuring a touch of agape love for each person in our country. We dare not reject this power blessing.

Now that we have forfeited our window, all the saints need to pray that we can assist God's intervention to rebuild the foundation of Christian churches. Pray also that the saints can accept the leadership of the Holy Spirit this time around, eliminating dogmas, canons, competition, suspicion, elitism, pragmatism and politics.

Jesus promised to protect His church. This He has done, partially. His promise of protection has transcended the betrayal of His mission, the rejection of the Holy Spirit, the exegetical twist of the Gospel, the denigration of His cultural goals and the passive indifference to His Sermon on the Mount. But His protection did not translate into protection for the original church, the Nazarenes. Their sin in running from the suffering required to convert Judea to the mission vector of Christ, i.e., to birth the stage one eschatology of Jesus, was too great. Incredibly, Jesus allowed His original church to die. Take heed, all that would be lukewarm!

It is alleged that Jesus protects the Gentile churches because they match or exceed the minimum standard for His promise of protection, which is called forth as God's minimum Soteriology. All churches reaching that standard remain blessed with His protection against the onslaughts of Satan. They remain in God's love even though they may be out of His spiritual power and optimized grace.

Here, in the theorem of minimum Soteriology (church salvation theology) is that standard:

THEOREM OF MINIMUM SOTERIOLOGY:

Any given church that proclaims the incarnation of the Son of God as Jesus of Nazareth, who witnesses to the love of God, and proclaims individual salvation through Jesus' sacrifice on the Cross and His glorious Resurrection, and accepts the concept of the Trinity God and the indwelling presence of the Holy Spirit, retains the love of God, even if that given church professes theological aberrations, as judged by God, and/or practices human leadership that precludes the guidance of the Spirit of God and the possession of the keys of the kingdom.

FIRST COROLLARY TO MINIMUM SOTERIOLOGY:

When the kingdom work produced by Jesus-loving churches exceeds the worldly and physical harm they cause, God's love rests on them.

We can only begin to reach an understanding of this theorem and its corollary when we appreciate the immense value of even one soul/spirit saved for the kingdom of heaven. The salvation of one soul/spirit transcends the value of any given non-kingdom generating earthy event. As an example, the value of a soul/spirit that found the love of Christ from the work of the church, far exceeds the evil of the inquisition of that same church that tortured and killed this human. Indeed, the value of even one soul/spirit is sufficient motive for the incarnation of Jesus Christ. God has tolerated His churches because of their work in the salvation of souls/spirits even if the work is not optimized.

SECOND COROLLARY TO MINIMUM SOTERIOLOGY:

Minimum Soteriology is optimized in this world only in the Overchurch.

THIRD COROLLARY TO MINIMUM SOTERIOLOGY:

Only those permitted by the Holy Spirit can enter into the Overchurch, reaching optimized minimum Soteriology.

FOURTH COROLLARY TO MINIMUM SOTERIOLOGY:

The Overchurch with its optimized minimum Soteriology can be generated only by the shift into the subset Age of the Holy Spirit.

FIFTH COROLLARY TO MINIMUM SOTERIOLOGY:

Only the Overchurch with its optimized minimum Soteriology can move humanity into the green pastures of paradise, epitomized by the coming of the kingdom of God to earth.

The **Overchurch** has the responsibility to confront and transform the secular neo-pagan culture of secular humanism with its associated allies into the initial form of agape civilization as the first prototype of the kingdom of God. From this first implementation, the kingdom will go through several, up to ten, iterations before it is allowed to be destroyed by the forces of the enemy of God, the world order, which today does not exist. Both cultural entities are to be formed in the twenty-first century, eventually developing into a strongly polarized world. Understand that the destruction and resultant occupation of the nations that participated in the first attempt to form the kingdom of God, the Prototypical Kingdom, is the Time of Sorrows. Here, one side of the world's polarization occupies the other for a time to be determined by God and His saints. The Time of Sorrows will be the final preparation of the saints for the millennium kingdom. Here, the saints will undergo vast inner healing, preparing them for the second form of the kingdom, the millennium reign of our Lord, Christ Jesus. For contrary to popular beliefs the New Jerusalem Kingdom will not be dropped

112

upon the human race without the prior conditioning of humanity for the unique cultural experiences that living in the kingdom will necessitate, a vital consideration that has not been contemplated by those proclaiming the imminent coming of the New Jerusalem Kingdom. These considerations must be jointly pondered along with the stage implementations.

As an example, consider a life in which every action you took would be in a constant feedback to the Lord, providing personalized limit adjustments and real-time sin punishments. Not a tyranny, but rather maximized personal freedom, this real-time individualized discipline could range from a small chastisement to a total removal from the kingdom, even as displayed in Acts 5. Consider for a moment, a culture without political governance, mayors, presidents, or military armies, as we know them. Think of living without police forces, judges, prisons, or the rule of law. Ponder about a culture in which no one could scheme for an ambitious advancement at the expense of another, a culture in which exploitation was dead. Surely, you can see the need to adjust humanity to this severe cultural shock - the mother of all shocks - for this is just the beginning of the cultural shock that the coming of the kingdom of God represents.

Hence, in an ironic turn of events, the destruction of the Prototypical Kingdom will permit the entry of the Body of Christ into the final phase of the maturation of the kingdom adjustment, which has been mandated to occur while still in the face of the enemy of God. This terrible time for humanity, the Time of Sorrow, will actually condition as well as cleanse selected humanity for the coming of the Millennium reign of Jesus Christ. After this terrible time of tears and deep sorrows has passed, the enemy of God will be bound. The cleansing and reconditioning of the saints will have been completed. The Millennium Reign commences.

Now it is important, according to the Spirit, that the **Overchurch** be formed and perfected in optimized minimum Soteriology in order to reach the Grand Redemptive Engine (GRE) capacities enjoyed by the Apostolic and Ignatius-age Churches. Remember the 'redemption' in this engine is applicable to the encapsulating culture, making it that status of the church wherein it can change the world. Only when the **Overchurch** reaches the GRE level can the cultural confrontation begin in passionate ardor. That means the **Overchurch** cannot carry the burden of religious dogmas, church canons or traditional and non-traditional religiosity. Expressed in other words, the church can only become GRE when a critical mass of saints have reached optimized minimum Soteriology, in which each saint is truly and fully free of the baggage of denominationalism, realizing spiritual and physical overcoming. Neither can the **Overchurch** carry the burden of exegetical arguments. It is a fighting force, loaded with a surplus of kingdom spiritual energy, bent on transforming the heathen culture non-violently into agape civilization, but that means it cannot spend its kingdom spiritual energy upon inner struggles. Hence, the mandate for optimized minimum Soteriology.

The Holy Spirit is the filter for acceptance into the **Overchurch.** He shall validate each saint entering into the **Overchurch** to determine their freedom from brainwashing biases, cleansing them of such if the saint is willing. The Spirit of God is asking for Christian unity, gained only by the elimination of bias within each selected saint. For clearly, the grip of denominationalism must be eliminated in the soul of each saint before God can once again empower pure Christianity. The following diagram attempts to illustrate this occurrence:

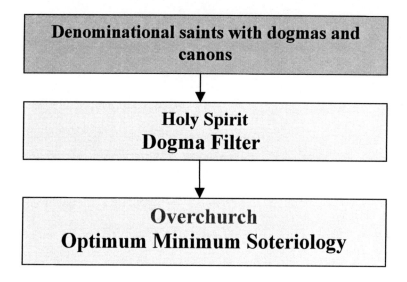

It is our valid expectations that the **Overchurch** will eliminate most or all of the legacy blunders, especially **legacy blunder six**, the Pragmatic Cancer, which has so handicapped the mission of Christ. Let us take a closer look at this cancer.

PRAGMATIC CANCER SUCCESSION

Now, it is useless to point fingers at one another proclaiming this or that church is the true successor to the cancer when all churches prove they are true successors by actions that possess and nurture this heretical cancer. In America, all churches that relish their tax exemptions are identifiable successors of the Pragmatic cancer. The screams that the church could not exist without this tax exemption are most illuminating. What are your goals, to build large buildings? Save souls/spirits for the kingdom of heaven? Bring that kingdom to earth?

Do large buildings bring the people to salvation? Perhaps they are helpful, but they must never be a hindrance to the other redemptive capacities and obligations that Jesus gave us, specifically the reversal of the Adamic fall and the implementation of the kingdom of God to our planet.

The church replies it needs the tax exemption to optimize the tithe of the faithful. Then avoid tithing! This specially selected legalism from Judaism has the smell of the Pragmatic Cancer about it. Christians need to base gifts on love not on obligation or legalism.

Another example of the Pragmatic Cancer can be vividly seen in action at most church business meetings. Far too often politics, not prayer, rules. Personal projections, individual ambitions, backstabbing, manipulations and political intrigue dominate the operation of too many modern congregations and their controlling church groups. Instead, agape love should shine forth. Most of the churches will righteously deny this charge, but that denial only fortifies the accusation, for the truth is there to be seen. If one looks, one can find many examples of the contemporary churches' integration with the Pragmatic Cancer, especially in the form of the Pact of Cooperation. We love the secular world even as we articulate our aversion for it. In this doublemindedness, we are susceptible and vulnerable to the attacks of the enemy.

So now, today, under the fierce attack of the modern humanists, our churches stagger onward into a deeper spiritual abyss - doomed in their present faith mode of modern pagan cultural cooperation. Stuck in this cultural cooperative mode, void of the leadership of the Counselor, the churches cannot free themselves; they cannot even recognize their problems. They just know somehow that something is wrong. They are blind to their captivity. This predicament of blindness is the by-product of the **second fall** of humanity. It results from the churches' double loss of the keys to the kingdom and the leadership of the Spirit of God. It is this blindness that divides us so gallingly.

THE MODERN RAVISHING OF CHRISTENDOM

Saints, listen! The institutional churches, seriously divided by denominationalism, have sat still and allowed the ravaging of the Christian churches in countless countries for hundreds of years by the forces of secularism and humanism. Now, it is happening in America. To renounce the cooperative agreement with neo-paganism, currently expressed as humanism, would destroy the foundational structure of the institutional churches and threaten their worldwide financial investments in buildings and land. This has placed the institutional churches in a desperate situation. To renounce its encapsulating, Christ-hating, pagan and humanistic civilization - which the politicized churches can recognize and even detest for its evil orientations - would be to renounce itself as a full partner to the initial cooperative agreement. Such an action would affect an internal coup, sending shock waves of uncontrolled social instabilities throughout the churches and their encapsulating cultures. Although this confrontation is where we need to be, it would be more than a major financial calamity should it happen; it would be a major spiritual tragedy. This latter misfortune would occur because the confrontation of church with state would be without the leadership of the Holy Spirit. It would destroy the churches. No, this coup cannot and must not happen exclusively within the prerogatives of the human mind and its political prowess. It is absolutely essential that the churches first repent of the abuse of the Holy Spirit, and then find His leadership in the **Overchurch**. Then, let Him lead us into cultural confrontation.

Chapter 13

Consequences

Eight immediate consequences resulted from the forfeiture of Jesus' mission vector to paradise. They were:

1- Grief of the Spirit
2- Wrath of God
3- Forfeiture of the Keys to the Kingdom
4- Spiritual Power Depletion
5- Lost of Cultural Redemption
6- Forfeiture of True Worship
7- Diminished Spiritual Warfare
8- Evangelical Handicap.

GRIEF OF THE SPIRIT

Modern humanity can only speculate at the terrible disappointment of God over the church decisions of the fourth-century. With this set of decisions, the pattern of the original faith paradigm, established at Pentecost, was terminated. Gone was the hope for the leadership of the Holy Spirit, the coming of the kingdom and the return of Jesus. Church leaders had grown accustomed to making the most of the operational decisions for the body of saints during the third century, although they still considered the Spirit's voice heard by the common saints. Now, in 313 AD, they simply decided they could lead the church out of harm's way without the assistance of the Spirit. No doubt some of these leaders must have felt that the Spirit had provided the opportunity. Most probably, they never considered that their decisions were contrary to God's will, and most likely, they never asked for the guidance the Holy Spirit.[69] They simply moved within the opportunities presented to them by of the pagan culture,

---

69. From Neill, Stephen & Wright, Tom *The Interpretation of the New Testament*, page 414, we read about W. D. Davies and his arguments that the 'Spirit is the gift of the New Covenant.' Davies believes that modern scholarship has ignored the Spirit. The author would broaden this statement to state that the entire role and significance of the Spirit has never been properly reviewed by modern scholarship. Perhaps this is because hard facts are difficult to associate with the work of the Holy Spirit. The cause and effect of His work transcends two realms, one realm in which humanity cannot measure or record and frequently believes does not exist.

assuming that the decision for cultural cooperation was exclusively theirs to make.

What saint understands the grief of the Spirit of God inflicted by these fourth-century human decisions? Most of us never ponder the fact that the Holy Spirit, today, still grieves over the injuries and pain inflicted upon Him in the third and fourth centuries, those events that constitute the major portion of the **second fall**. Yet, it is so.

In a rare moment, in late April of 1994, the Spirit of God allowed the author a brief touch of His lingering pain. It was shocking in its magnitude and frightening in the scope of its spiritual bereavement, even hundreds of years after its invoking cause. The force of the grief and the intensity of the lingering anger were more than astonishing; it was foreboding! I had to ask for a release. Categorically, the Spirit's grief, unfathomable to the human mind, continues today. What impact does that lingering grief have on grace?

Now it is impossible to grieve God without consequences. And the consequences suffered by humanity have become an approximation to another Adamic-like fall. In effect, the grief of the Holy Spirit dramatically diminished human closeness to God, resulting in dramatically reduced kingdom spiritual energy among the saints, including the strength of grace.

Today, our ignorance of the continued and lingering grief of the Spirit retards the restoration of the initial faith pattern, that pattern in which the saints lived for the future, willing to die today for the kingdom tomorrow. This is living within the kingdom vector of the Savior, a life pattern lost. Yet, restoration of this initial faith pattern is what God wants for His saints and His churches. But there are serious problems.

The reinstatement of God's *original restoration plan* is now impossible, destroyed by the Judeans. The shift to the Gentiles was the *second plan*, and it was initially very pleasing to God. Yet, it was this Gentile fervor to achieve the kingdom vector that was destroyed by **legacy blunders two, three, four, five, six, seven, eight and nine**. (See chapter 1).

Then Jesus appeared with the request for a *third plan*, which the Spiritual Franciscans attempted to fulfill. It failed **in legacy blunder ten**. Then, God rose up the next plan based on the Spiritual Reformation. This was restoration plan four. Yet, the mainline Protestant Reformation destroyed this, the Lord's *fourth plan.* This was done via **legacy blunders eleven, twelve, thirteen, fourteen and fifteen.** Now God generated a new and *fifth restoration plan* based on a new wineskin, a fresh start in North America. For this purpose, the Pilgrims came to this land, initiating this new wineskin with a sacrificing start. After 1500 years, God selected a land to reestablish His newly elected Chosen People. And included in this selection are over five million Jews. Have no doubt, these Jewish people have been selected to form a backbone for the newly chosen ones of God.

Yet, to date, the Jewish people of America have failed to grasp their potential role in God's new plan; instead, they have been instrumental in its destruction, placing themselves in opposition to God and His plan. Largely, because of their efforts, plus the direct and indirect activities of the enemy of God, Satan, the fifth restoration plan of God has been shattered, left in the ashes of the American covenant, almost but not quite dead.

It is entirely possible that plan five was the last and only escape route for humanity from its ever-increasing moral and spiritual decay. Yet, this plan has been stifled and hurt by the actions of the enemy of God, generating church **legacy blunders sixteen, seventeen, eighteen and nineteen**, placing us in the decisive turning point in the short history of our species. So what do we do? Can we successfully rise up against the secular humanists and other Christ-haters currently flooding our country, spiritually polluting it, destroying God's last plan of restoration? Can we, as a microcosm of humanity, return to the vector of Christ Jesus? Is this our only valid escape from the destruct trail of human civilization?

No, none of the above is possible! God has abandoned humanity, as the prime instrument in the reconstruction of His plan of restoration, opting instead for His own intervention to accomplish what humanity could not do.

Here are the inputs from the Spirit of God on our current situation in America. Millions of common Americans still harbor an abiding love for Jesus. God's love flows out to them, embracing them with His compassion. Yet the sheep are largely misled. Their Christian leaders have failed them. After centuries of legacy blunders, the churches are in a directional mess, divided and floundering. Yet, as God views the love within the sheep for His Son, His grief over their situation mounts. His love swells; reaching for the sheep, angry that the church has failed them. Now, the threshold of love has been reached even as the threshold of anger approaches, compelling the Father's intervention in the affairs of humanity in two distinct and different modes: discipline and love. God's overcoming love and compassion for Jesus' lost sheep compels His intervention of love. God's overcoming anger at the actions of the Christ-haters of this land compels His discipline to rescue the land of the sheep before they are wiped out by another wave of cultural attacks from the Christ-haters out of hell. Hence, the Holy Spirit's intervention will arrive in two modes to destroy the overwhelming presence of the enemy, then to reconstruct the mission vector of the Son, renovating and implementing God's restoration plan for humanity.

All good men and women must pray that the author is correct in the assertion that God the Father plans on utilizing the Holy Spirit to place the church on the vector of His Son, Jesus Christ, to paradise. First, the Spirit will implement a form of agape civilization in prototype. Secondly, the Spirit shall translate the ashes of the prototypical kingdom into the kingdom of God as the Bride of Christ on earth. What is about to happen to humanity is analogous to a parent picking up a strong-willed child that has wandered into a busy thoroughfare to play. The parent rushes to the rescue, eager to place that child in a clean and safe playpen before the disobedient child is run over by road traffic. However, first the parent will talk to the child about the danger of the road before disciplining and cleaning up that child.

HERE IS A BRIEF SCHEMATIC OF THE LORD'S RESTORATION PLANS:

Implementation of Jesus' Rescue	Blunder Number	Destroyed by:
Original Restoration	1	Judeans (Jews)
Gentile Attempt	2, 3, 4, 5 6, 7, 8, 9	Ignorance & Politics
Spiritual Franciscans	10	Catholic Church
Spiritual Reformation Restoration	11, 12 13, 14 15	Mainline Protestant Reformation
American Covenant Restoration	16, 17 18, 19	Greed, Ambition & Secular Humanism

Now, the Spirit has a surprising message of optimism for us. Despite His abuse by churches and saints, and in spite of His residue of grief, the Holy Spirit prepares to deal with humanity once again. Because the Spirit is of one mind with the Father and the Son, He stands ready despite His grieving.

However, humanity has an unrecognized problem: As the Son points out in Matthew 12:31, anyone offending the Holy Spirit has sinned seriously. Now since the Father remains distressed over our old and current abuse of His Spirit, He has decreed the removal of the foundation causes of that abuse before the struggle for the kingdom can be resumed.

Hence, it appears that we shall not fortuitously overcome the results of the **second fall** by merely lifting and waving our hands singing 'come, fill me.' We cannot just cavalierly call for the Spirit to lead us after sixteen hundred years of abuse and expect the best. God the Father, extremely sensitive to the insults to the Spirit, is asking us to solve the lingering grief of the Spirit by repentance and a spiritual apology, followed by a complete shift in our current faith orientation.

WRATH OF GOD

Anyone who speaks a word against the Son of Man will be forgiven, but anyone who speaks against the Holy Spirit will not be forgiven, either in this age or in the age to come (Matthew 12:32).

The age to come is the subset age of the Holy Spirit, which will include the ten generations of incremental enhancements of the Prototypical Kingdom followed closely by the time of sorrows, then the Millennium Reign of the Lamb. How terrible to enter any of these ages without the forgiveness of God! Plainly, our Father has no tolerance for the abuse of His Spirit. So these decisions by the founding fathers of the institutional church against the vector of Jesus Christ and the leadership of the Holy Spirit to guide humanity down Jesus' vector carried inestimable consequences for the Western world. It is possible these decisions were made in innocence or naiveté, perhaps in ambition, or perchance in frustration over the delay in the coming of the kingdom, yet however innocent, they destroyed the mission critical task of the church to obtain the Great Commission, precipitating the wrath of God. This, the first wrath of God, thrust humanity into a spiritual, physical, knowledge and moral abyss initially lasting for seven hundred and ninety five years, measured as 410 to 1205. God's first wrath hits Western humanity especially hard in its civilization, destroying the old Roman culture. Commencing in the fifth and sixth centuries, human civilization lost sight of learning, knowledge, morality, prosperity, tenderness, true faith, integrity, and compassion. Religious fervor existed, but it was misdirected into superstitions. The spiritual state of humanity dipped into an abyss dragging the physical state with it. Civilization regressed and began to disappear. Human misery descended upon large portions of western humanity. Corruption, violence and ignorance existed along side the blazing faith of those who remained faithful to Jesus. Still darkness covered both the saints and unrepentant sinners; it was the wrath of God known to historians as the Dark Ages.

Then in 1205 AD the Son of God, Jesus Christ, appeared to Francis of Assisi and asked for the restructuring of His church. As stated previously, the Holy Spirit has pointed at this appearance as equivalent to Jesus' appearance to Saul on the road to Damascus. Yet, the Roman Catholic Church arrogantly and ignorantly ignored this request. Members of the barefoot order revolted, forming the movement of the Spiritual Franciscans. Soon, a love-bliss arrived in central Europe, lasting decades; it started to look like the kingdom was feasible after all. Then apostasy set in, and the support of the Holy Spirit was withdrawn. The movement of agape love disappeared.

After the failure of the Spiritual Franciscan's revival, a second wrath appeared lasting for another three hundred and fifty years from 1317 to 1667. Totally, both of God's wraths represent an abyss from which humanity has not fully recovered, especially in the moral and spiritual areas. Both wraths hit the Western world hard, but with different impacts. The first wrath destroyed the existing human civilization; the second wrath restructured human civilization enhancing it to personal and spiritual freedom released by the Protestant Reformation. The consequences of the first wrath led to the most important resuscitation of God's plan of restoration ever attempted, the movement of the Spiritual Franciscans. It failed under the arrogant and ignorant persecution hand of the old Roman Catholic Church.[70]

The Protestant Reformation, nested in the center of the second wrath, generated freedom, which led to the development of spiritual churches enabling God's spiritual law of bountiful blessings to descend upon the Protestant cultures. Yet, as blessings descended, so did God's wrath. It was a strange time to live; it was obvious that humanity was making giant strides in knowledge and health even as death was everywhere! But of great significance today, this strange episode in history represents an important example for modern man, for the same dichotomy is destined for our future, wrath and bountiful blessings, brought about by the independent operation of two distinctly separate spiritual laws. It is best to be prepared and to understand what is happening rather than to withdraw from God in fear and timidity.

But in time, the spiritual laws of God's wrath exhausted itself enabling the fervor of the Protestant Reformation to decline into passivity. Now, four hundred years later, because the true church still lives among the Protestants and even some Catholics – largely as the result of the twentieth century outpourings of the Holy Spirit - the blessings of the Lord continue to pour forth. But the mainline Protestant saints, void of fervor, are seduced by their own prosperity. Thus, too

---

70. Here it is necessary to understand that the sins of this, our common ancestral church is upon us all, Protestant and Catholic.

many of the mainline Protestant churches, originated as spiritual churches, have degraded into carnal churches.

The message from the Holy Spirit is that the Body of Christ has failed in our recovery from both wraths. We are too content to sit passively; thinking that release of freedom derived from the Protestant Reformation was the final touch, when it was simply the start. Additionally, the truth is that we have forfeited our ability to reform our way back into the fullness of God's embrace. Resuscitation of God's restoration plans for His church now resides exclusively in the intervention of God in human affairs. Should God elect not to intervene, we are doomed, destined to be destroyed by the products of our own intellect: weapons of mass destruction disseminated around the world. We need God's intervention to survive.

MESSAGE OF INTERVENTION

Here is a rather frightening special message from the Father regarding this situation, received 6/27/01 while two saints were in the **Holy Junction**, that contemplative state of optimized closeness to God.

(A WORD from the Father received on 6/27/01)

Harken onto me. For that time approaches when your life will face disruptions, even as I disrupt this planet with my face turned against major portions of this world.

THEY HAVE REJECTED MY SON!

Even those who have proclaimed Him in generations past reject him now [Europe], *refusing to honor Him. They move towards atheism and social humanism and see nothing but luxury. Others waddle in misery with false idols around them, holding crazed, unreal belief systems that persist generation after generation, insulting My Son. I will no longer abide this, and they shall fall! They shall fall by the hundreds of thousands, and I will cleanse the earth of them, for only in this cleansing can my beloved ones hear the message of my Son and feel the touch of my Spirit to bring the kingdom about!*

And hear this! Mercy to your fellow man does not extend beyond my wrath! Nor can it supersede it. Your mercy for your fellow man must be in accordance with my wrath and my will. Never try to overcome that which is not to be overcome! Hear my words! For I have spoken!

124

Here we can see the difference between the agape love of God, tempered with His judgment, and altruism the intellectually driven, worldwide human support syndrome of atheistic humanists. One is driven by love, tempered by judgment; the other is blindly driven by obligation, void of love. One adheres to a higher plan; the other cannot see that plan. If our nation follows altruism, then we will eventually die as a culture because altruism does not understand evil. Ultimately, any given nation, in its altruistic blindness will end up aiding and abetting evil, inviting its own destruction at the hands of that evil. Analogously, it will be akin to picking up a highway robber and murderer who eventually robs and kills the driver, whereas, on the instructions of God, the Spirit-filled driver would not pick up that hitchhiker. Basic to this understanding is that some humans have aligned their soul/spirits with Satan and cannot be redeemed. The enemy incarnates these core souls each generation, especially in Europe and America, with the assignment to pull down the Christ-friendly civilizations, bringing them to atheism and humanism. Currently, America has 28,000,000 core souls working vigorous for Satan.[71] [72] Who knows how many core souls are in the rest of the world? Whatever the number, it is not in our best interest to aid and abet them. Now, God calls us to love our fellowman, and we must assist those who are hurting, but let us assist in the name of Jesus as directed, not blindly supporting a humanistic NGO cleverly hiding behind a sweet sounding name, or a politically motivated government giving away the bountiful blessings of God for power hegemony, without acknowledging the source of those blessings. Pray before you give, and be tough in God's assurance.

FORFEITING THE KEYS TO THE KINGDOM

From Matthew 16 we read:

I will give you the keys to the kingdom of heaven; whatever you bind on earth will be bound in heaven, and whatever you loose on earth will be loosed in heaven (Matthew 16:19).

This scripture represents the authority of the Christian church on earth, transcending the physical realm of life. Clearly, Jesus transmitted enormous power to His church. But from John 16 we read:

---

71. This number has been discovered via the binary search coupled with the author's commune with God.
72. The good news is that the Father has granted a sixty-year constriction on core incarnations into America commencing in 2000.

... when He, the Spirit of truth, comes, He will guide you into all truth (John 16:13).

If the keys to the kingdom involve actions of wisdom like the binding of enemy spirits, the loosening of angels, the ascertainment of sin and the forgiveness of sin, then these actions must rely on the assistance of God's Spirit of truth, the Holy Spirit. In fact, in reflection, it is easily determined that the keys to the kingdom and the guidance of the Spirit of truth are integrated.

Now, if we are correct in our assertion that Jesus gave us a vector to paradise, not its position, only the Spirit of Truth can guide us down that vector trail. Hence, the keys to the kingdom is integrated with the vector of Jesus to paradise via the Holy Spirit. So, what does this mean when the Church rejected the leadership of the Holy Spirit between 172 and 313 AD, **legacy blunder 2**? This, embedded in the rejection of the leadership of the Holy Spirit was the forfeiture of the authority of the church contained in the keys to the kingdom and with it the vector of Jesus Christ. Further, since the keys to the kingdom contain the keys of knowledge, we can see that *knowledge of knowledge* was forsaken. Now tragically, all of Holy Scripture was laid open to the capriciousness of the exegetes, those who interpret scripture with their mind. The partitioning of Christianity, now not a sin with the lost of church authority, became inevitable.

Since the entire rescue package of Christ was an integrated redemption, composed of six major components and twenty redemptive capacities, the removal of one major component, the Holy Spirit, caused the entire vector of our Lord to unravel. All of God's rescue package must be intact and functional to reverse the Adamic fall. Even the loss of one redemptive capacity hurt, but we have lost parts or all of 16 of them. The ultimate witness to the truth of this statement is the plight of the contemporary churches, divided and spiritually weak almost two millennia after Pentecost. Clearly, this division could not exist without the loss of the keys to the kingdom. Consider the charge: The arrogant and abusive use of the keys to the kingdom damaged the greatest thing to ever occur on earth: The incarnation mission of the Son of God with His vectored return to paradise! Feel the anger of the Lord!

What were those ecclesiastical abuses that caused the Donatists – the North African movement against corrupt priests – to explode into violent protest so early in the history of the church?

But before we can go further in this discussion, let us review the format of the Father's rescue plan, realizing that although God's attempt at rescue has taken many different approaches, the format has never changed.

Here is the schematic depiction of the Lord's rescue package:

126

Major Components:

Sacrifice of the Son of God
Giving of the Holy Spirit
Establishment of the Church
Vector to Paradise
Keys to the Kingdom
Authority on Earth

Supporting Redemptive Capacities enabling the breaking of the Adamic curse:

Gifts of the Holy Spirit	Knowledge Acquisition
Agape Love	Rise of Human Spirit
Personal Salvation	Mind of Christ
Seeing the Kingdom	Forgiveness of Sins
Civilization Redemption	Less Suffering - Healing
Answering Prayer	Grace
Born Again (rebirth)	Cleansing of Humanity
Personal Commune	Closing Temptations
True Worship	Vector with power
Divine Guidance	Unknown - not revealed

Yet, there is more to the demise of the Christian mission fervor than just the tragic loss of the keys to the kingdom. To reach for the magnitude of this fourth-century mistake, *one must understand that when the initial institutional church threw out the Holy Spirit as its leader that church threw out its spiritual authority*. From that point on, it was not a sin to revolt from that church. Without this hard truism, the revolt of the Spiritual Franciscans and two centuries later, the Protestants, would be sheer sin, as judged by Holy Scripture. For scripture says:

And I tell you that you are Peter, and on this rock I will build my church, and the gates of Hades will not overcome it. I will give you the keys of the kingdom of heaven; whatever you bind on earth will be bound in heaven, and whatever you loose on earth will be loosed in heaven (Matthew 16:18-19).

So repeating, if the Roman Catholic Church, with its credible claim of descent from Peter, did not forfeit the keys to the kingdom of heaven with its implied capacity to pass the authority of God on earth to others by the laying on of hands, then any church revolt would be sin of the first magnitude, and the Spiritual Franciscan and Protestant revolts impossible. Yet this forfeiture of the keys to the Kingdom via the second and third century rejection of the Holy Spirit's leadership followed by the fourth century compromise of the Gospel is exactly what happened, and we can see the desperate situation of Christendom as a result. Who carries the blame for this demise in Christianity? Who or what was the prime mover behind the church revolution against the Holy Spirit: The fathers who revolted or the fathers who enabled the revolt? It has to be the latter.

The dogma of the Infallibility of the Pope, defined in 1870, contains the implicit recognition that the organized church of the fourth-century made a serious and desperate mistake. Fifteen hundred years later and after hundreds of church subdivisions, the Catholic ecclesiastics have surreptitiously recognized that mistake by the proclamation of this dogma. They attempt to reclaim by dogma that which was so eagerly thrown away by the second, third and fourth-century church fathers. Unfortunately, the best theological brilliance of the human mind cannot reverse this act of history. Humility and repentance would be a much better starting point than the mind of men. The current pope is correct in insisting that the Catholic Church apologize for its sins of the past. But this apology first must be made to Christ Jesus and then to the Advocate that He sent. There must be recognition that a simple apology is just the first step. Massive prayer for the intervention of God to reconstruct the church in the spiritual image of the apostolic church - regardless of the church's resultant physical disruption - must be the second step.

The Spirit says that in the future, when the church is rebuilt and rededicated to the mission vector of Jesus Christ, the keys will be returned to the church.

However, the keys can come back only to the rebellious movement of Jesus Christ, the **Overchurch**, the concord of the common saints, led only by the Spirit of God. Perhaps operating initially as an underground church, it will represent a united, denominational transcending outreach to the peoples of this and other lands.

Now it is essential that all believers understand this fundamental point: The ongoing Pragmatic Cancer born from the fourth-century decisions effects all Christians: Protestants, Orthodox and Roman Catholics. Look and you can see the cancer manifesting itself in church disunity, division, and spiritual as well as cultural impotence. This is the result of church leadership by the intellect with decisions of cultural cooperation and submission made as directed by politics and the press of pragmatic needs, instead of the Spirit, a clear reflection of kingdom spiritual power fragility. Then there is the competition. Between the polite smiles and correct social graces, great envy, jealousy, fear, suspicion and even hate lingers among the denominations.

Here is the hard fact that all loyal Christ followers must face: Tragically, the forfeiture of the leadership of the Holy Spirit ruined the vector of Jesus Christ, resulting in the forfeiture of the drive to obtain the discipleship of the nations for Christ. This forfeiture has generated massive misinterpretations of Holy Scripture, leading to the proliferation of churches, the pollution of the faith and the loss of spiritual power. These factors continue to defeat the leaven of the church and call forth the question of the value of the church as redemptive cultural salt. Recall that Jesus' Scriptural judgment on unusable salt is severe.

Where would Christianity be today without the largely unheralded Irish monks of the early centuries of the Dark Ages? Independent of papal authority and obviously full of kingdom spiritual power they evangelized Europe from France to the Ukraine. Yet, even the work of those monks faded under the impact of the **second fall** and the invasion of the Islamic armies and the pagan Northmen. Eventually, the Northmen were overcome and the Islamic armies were thrown back, but the **second fall** has never been understood or overcome.

Spiritual Power Depletion

Despite exceptions, it is clearly ascertainable - with hindsight - that the decisions of the fourth-century church fathers left the Christian churches debilitated of kingdom spiritual power (KSP). Possessing only a fraction of their former kingdom spiritual power, the newly formed institutional congregations were unable to effectively achieve the Great Commission. Too often, the home base of the missionaries deteriorated into spiritual weaknesses and religious cynicism, frequently undercutting the spiritual and financial base of the missionaries. This weakness continues even into our time. This is a serious charge that cannot be avoided but must be answered by all that love Jesus Christ and His Gospel. And the answer shall be uncomfortable for most of us. Collectively, we exist under the Pragmatic Curse with its chief product, the Pact of Cooperation. Sick or hurt, we call the secular doctor before we pray.

To deny that the churches are spiritually impotent or that the churches treat the Holy Spirit with indifference is to be naive on the first point and condescendingly uninformed on the second.

We, as the people of God, must humble ourselves and recognize the fullness of our spiritual ancestor's abuse of the Holy Spirit and our continuing acquiescence, in widespread unawareness, of that mistreatment. Let us repent of this neglect individually in our private prayer closet, collectively in our churches, and societally in our culture.

Then change! Seek and accept the leadership of the Holy Spirit in all things. Allow Him to lead us back to the second stage eschatological expectation of Jesus Christ, the renewed of the drive birth the kingdom of God, thus opening ourselves to His outpouring Spirit. Listen to God's call for a renewed church leadership regime, one with the Holy Spirit as the church leader on earth. At this stage in our demise of division and dogma confusion, this unity format can be found only in the **Overchurch**. Then prepare for the struggle to birth the kingdom of God with our material goods, our ambitions and goals, even our lives equated as less in value than this battle to bring the birth stage to life. Can we do this? Can you reach this level of commitment?[73]

Saints, God is clear on this point; before we can engage in this struggle to birth the kingdom on earth, we as individual saints and especially our churches must make peace with the Father and the Son over our treatment of the Holy Spirit. And saints let us quit calling Him a 'ghost' - for a ghost He is not. Indeed, calling Him a 'ghost' grieves Him. Let us come to our spiritual senses. Then, after we have made peace with the Father and the Son, we must apologize to the Holy Spirit for our centuries of indifference and neglect. This apology must be individual and communal.

Fortunately, this huge sin against the Holy Spirit, the near approach to the unpardonable sin, is still covered by the redemptive sacrifice of Jesus Christ. It is our urgent need to understand this fact, and then act. If, as a church, we fail to apologize to the Holy Spirit before the outpouring

---

73. This must never be considered as a safe commitment that will never be claimed by our God of love. In 1986, the author made such a commitment and rapidly lost his small computer Software Company, savings, all personal belongings, house, and friends, unable to find employment for eleven months. Yet, these were the best months of my life in terms of the flow of God's grace and wisdom.

intervention of God, seeking the cover of Jesus' blood sacrifice, then, as a church, we will be doomed.[74]

If individual churches or congregations apologize and change their approach to the Spirit, they will survive into the subset age of the Holy Spirit, there to do a profound work for God. If the individual churches or congregations fail to apologize to the Father and His Son for their abuse of the Holy Spirit, as well as the abuse generated by their spiritual ancestors, then that kingdom spiritual power that they still retain will be withdrawn, replaced by the power of evil. These evil congregations will fight against the **Overchurch,** eventually utilizing violence against the true saints. Out of patience, God, in great grief, will show no mercy to them. Any saint in such a congregation must flee to save oneself, for none shall find salvation from within such congregations.

Here is a schematic of the **Overchurch** functioning with the surviving churches:

---

74. The author is in a state of shock at these words received from the Father on February 27, 2001.

OVERCHURCH SCHEMATIC:

> # Overchurch
> ## Led only by the Holy Spirit
> In cultural confrontation with the neo-pagans, transforming the American and allied cultures into the Prototype of the Kingdom, arriving first in the hearts of the saints then the transformed culture.

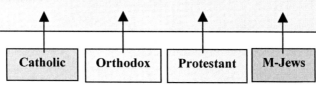

| Catholic | Orthodox | Protestant | M-Jews |

> All the associated church dogmas and canons are left behind when the saint makes the jump to the Overchurch. Most pastoral duties and denominational worship remain in the local churches! The saint has one of his or her feet in the denomination and the other foot in the Overchurch. The prime loyalty is to the Savior, Jesus Christ.

LOSS OF CULTURAL REDEMPTION

Coupled with the forfeiture of the Holy Spirit's leadership, the greatest damage that the church inflicted upon itself was the loss of cultural redemption. Certainly, this great expectation of the primitive church is not now held as an expectation or considered as part of the gospel of Jesus Christ. Jesus' parables on the kingdom of God are simply forgotten, dismissed or misunderstood. We are too busy reading Romans to hear what Jesus was trying to tell us in the Gospel given by Matthew.

For sixteen hundred years, we, the brethren, have concentrated on our own lives, complacent in our personal salvation while ignoring the work of the New Covenant of Jesus Christ which centers around cultural redemption, i.e., the

132

coming of the kingdom. The New Covenant of Jesus Christ mandates a cultural outreach, but this outreach requires vast amounts of spiritual power. It simply cannot be done with the small amount possessed by the modern day churches.

Exasperatingly, the churches do not seem to understand their inheritance. The churches operating under the plague of the fourth-century mistakes have acquired a tradition of political cooperation and cultural invisibility that seems immutable to our modern mindsets. Even in the time of church suppression under communism, the churches remained passive or cooperative - with a few exceptions[75] - leaving the burden of resistance to the individual saints. This should surprise no one for the institutional churches were created premised upon the cooperation cancer. As mentioned elsewhere Barth clearly saw the cancer operative in England and Germany in the WWI. Bonhoeffher saw the German church fall under the cancer in WWII. The Russian Orthodox Church epitomizes this cooperative cancer by its actions under the seventy-year reign of communism in which millions of the Russian Orthodox faithful were murdered while the Russian Orthodox Church groveled to maintain a measure of survival tolerance from Stalin.

Is our charge against the modern Christian churches too severe? What choices did each of these churches have? None, because they had inherited spiritual impotence! They functioned within the inevitable consequences of the Pragmatic Cancer of cultural cooperation. They and their fathers before them were born into this spiritual bankruptcy. And this problem is not confined to the German or Russian churches, but is our common inheritance.

Because God's expectations are so high the worse violators are the contemporary American churches. None of our churches seem to understand that heathen or secular cultural cooperation is anathematized to the mission of Christ. Few understand the role of America. Few know that our country was covenanted by our Pilgrim Fathers to restore the initial Christian faith pattern and its fervor to the world, therein to demonstrate the kingdom of God in prototype as the 'City on the Hill'.

FORFEITURE OF TRUE WORSHIP

Without the concept of cultural war for the coming of the kingdom of God to each saint internally and our culture externally, we live without the true and full gospel of Jesus Christ. Full truth is not held. Our human spirit remains inactive in most saints. So, void of Gospel truth and without the activated human spirit, true worship of God is impossible, leaving us today, with congregational

---

75. Especially stubborn was the Catholic Church in Poland. But was this predominantly a faith or nationalistic resistance?

and private worship less than the expectations of God. And that can be translated into the reality of today: a trail of cultural weakness and spiritual impotence.

Further when our churches mislead the faithful by claiming church leadership by the Spirit of God, when, in fact, it does not exist, and it has not existed for centuries, then the possibilities of escape from this travail decreases. Today, and for centuries past, the Spirit of God does not lead the churches.

Stop lying to the people on this issue!

Only the truth can set us free. Modern churches are like the perpetual drunk who must first acknowledge his condition before it can be corrected. Saints, the Spirit is stating that we, the common saint of the church, have been denied access to the true worship of God for sixteen hundred years! The shock from this accusation is almost unfathomable even as it is intolerable!

DIMINISHED SPIRITUAL WARFARE

To grasp what happened, the reader must understand that from the Montanus incident at Pepusa in 172 to the Pact of Cooperation in 313 – a period of 141 years or four generations - there was a constant erosion of the kingdom spiritual power among the Christians as the church canon became increasing effective in reducing the leadership freedom of the Holy Spirit. After centuries of persecutions, church fathers were determined to discontinue the Spirit of God's propensity to lead *their* church into harm's way. In this decision, they claimed authority over God's church and His will for His church, sinning beyond measure!

The Constantine decisions caused a vast drop in kingdom spiritual power within the churches, driving those who resisted into the caves of the Mediterranean Sea, forming the Monastic movement. Power for healing and other miracles still lingered within individual saints, but starting in the middle of the fourth century, the power to conduct civilization-wide spiritual war evaporated. The terrified and trounced spiritual forces of the enemy of God now had time to regroup and to reenter the fray. Defeated paganism was reorganized along the lines of the Christian church. From this point on, the struggle became the exclusive prerogatives of congregations and individual saints. Slowly, over the centuries the fervor for this struggle waned as the majority of the saints left the struggle. With the appearance of the eighteenth century Enlightenment and its companion, rationalism, the Body of Christ largely forfeited the entire concept of the spiritual struggle.[76] While some of the faithful continued to struggle on, the burden became too heavy for the few. With diminished spiritual warfare the civilizations of humanity slipped into increasing immorality.

The great killings of the wars of the twentieth century generated widespread cynicism about the integrity of the churches and their messages of agape love. The innocence of the Christian world was shattered in WWI as millions of Christians killed millions of Christians for the ego of a couple of wearisome kings. This cynicism increased when WWII and the cold war encased the world for fifty-one years. Seemingly, the enemy of God moved closer to absolute victory. Many thinkers and theologians sensed the doom of Christianity in modern times.

EVANGELIZING HANDICAPS

Serious evangelical problems arose with the Constantine decisions. The effort of an individual that produced a return greater than a thousand fold before the forfeiture of the Holy Spirit church leadership now yielded one fold. We now function under a 1/1000 handicap varying to a greater disadvantage on occasions.

With the drain of spiritual power from the churches, the experience and the knowledge of New Covenant power became a legend for the faithful and a subject for the skeptics of later centuries. Healings, prophecies, word of knowledge, the fruits and gifts of the Spirit, the consequences of the companionship of the Spirit became the remote things of the past and only the infrequent happenings of the present. The miracles of the first century became impossible for some saints to believe. And these saints came to the cynical point of calling those believing in the Biblical miracles as ignorant, calling these miracles myths, frequently referring to those with the indwelling power of the Spirit of God as 'holy rollers'.

What have we done to ourselves?

---

76. The ultimate proof of this allegation is found in the success of the Christ-haters. If the Body of Christ had maintained a fierce stance in spiritual warfare, Enlightenment would be a small footnote in history. Instead, we still reel from its impact!

Chapter 14

Our Deteriorating Situation

Any consideration of the contemporary church must include two perspectives: The first view must cover the impact of the **second fall** on our times, and the second view must deal with possible escapes from this impact. All this means that literally, we must look into the problems surrounding reconstruction of the church.

Today, the churches, even the reformed churches, have stood helpless as the secularists have unilaterally declared the spiritual realm a carry over from the age of superstition. Equally helpless, they watched the secularist and the humanist commandeer the hegemony of America for the pursuits of the enemy of God. Confident that the immutability of Newtonian physics yields an invincible victory over the miracle-based Bible, American secularists and humanists now push for their final victory: The eradication of the Christian faith from the people of this land, America. They have proclaimed human physical senses, or as far as the mind is capable of reaching in mathematical extension, as the exclusive realm of human reality. The spiritual realm, especially the realm of God and His Son, has been declared persona non grata in our modern culture, a nonentity. Little do they perceive the weaknesses of their foundation arguments, not the least of which is that Newtonian physics is not immutable, rendered so by the twentieth century work of the quantum and relativity physics paradigms. Look, folks! The mass of an object is not a constant. But what does that mean? This, one of the basic foundation premises of Newtonian physics, that mass is a constant, is an incorrect premise when it is not confined to four dimensions, thus potentially destabilizing that entire paradigm in a greater dimensional frame of reference. Current research has indicated that ten dimensions are required to find a common force in nature. So, it would appear to be plausible to allege that true physical existence occurs only in ten dimensions, meaning that our four dimensional time-space is a subset with limited perception of physical reality. Hence, it would seem safe to consider that the particulars of the Newtonian scientific paradigm are not immutable. Today, no thinking and fair-minded person would use the Newtonian physical paradigm as the basis for the rejection of the Biblical miracles. What dimension of time and space did Jesus reach to walk on water? In what dimension of reality did Jesus exist when each pore of His body emitted laser-like energy in His Resurrection?[77] Who knows, except we now know that we do not know!

Still, we have an ongoing problem with the establishment thinkers. Either the twentieth century developments in physics have not yet reached the minds of these intellectuals or else their biases are too strong to abandon their preconceived prejudices. Yet, we announce this:

Stop declaring the Bible a myth until you know more of life! Show intellectual integrity on this issue, not your continuing abusive biases.

In this secular and academic push against the integrity of the Bible, coupled with their drive to rid our country of the precious name of our Savior, Christ Jesus, American saints have not received effective leadership from their Christian leaders. This weakness of leadership has enabled the secular and humanistic attack against Christianity to become a one-sided slaughter. At stake is the spiritual and moral hegemony of our country. This is the best evidence that the modern churches, all of them, are the legitimate descendants of the Old Roman Church, each inflicted with the Pragmatic Cancer. Indeed and unfortunately, their total inactivity in the face of this mounting attack decisively proves this allegation. They have betrayed us by their passivity and their tax-exception comfort. One leader that has appeared to defend Christianity is Hugh Ross. See His arguments concerning scientific evidence backing Paley's Watchmaker theses.[78] The fine-tuning of the Universe just to make human life possible reaches into hundreds. Only intellectual and scientific dishonesty based on huge biases, or Satan's indirect or direct control, can explain the lack of rush to God and His Son by the knowledgeable intellectuals of the world. Most Christian leaders remain ignorant of the mounting and overwhelming scientific evidence for the Master Designer of the Universe implicit in the Big Bang Theory. Instead they

---

77. The study of the Shroud of Turin by an American and international team of scientists conducted on October 9 through 11, 1978 indicated that a microsecond laser activity from each pore happened to the body in the Shroud. This and the other outstanding discoveries that pointed at the authenticity of the Shroud were later scorned when the Shroud was carbon tested to the thirteen century. What happens now when it has been asserted that this test was unscientific because it did not compensate for the bioplastic coating on the fibers of the Shroud? And why are so many Protestant Christians eager to disprove this modern day sign from God? Why are the Catholics acting so paranoid and protective? Are we viewing denominational jealousy, perhaps the work of the impersonator? Is it possible that this denominational thing (hate) is so strong that it will willingly work against the interests of our Savior? How many soul/spirits have been lost because of this jealousy?

78 Ross, Hugh, *The Creator and the Cosmos* Colorado Springs: NavPress, 2001

remain locked into rigid denominational beliefs, lost to the world of scientific developments, often betrayed by their own belief systems.

Born into this betrayal, these leaders believe, in their brainwashed loyalty to their denominations, that they serve God. These leaders do not deserve our trust and loyalty, not because they are not good people - for the vast majorities are - but because they are incapable of reaching beyond their pragmatically adjusted and compromised life within the church to see the spiritual truth of the churches' mission critical role. The churches are to serve Christ, and today, they do this only partly, perhaps only marginally. Locked into their brainwashed belief systems, based on their intellectual interpretation of the Bible, they have stood in the way of God's unity and kingdom implementation plans until now it is too late. Here is a schematic representation of this problem.

THE BRAINWASHING LOCK

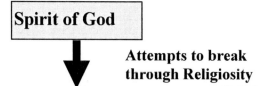

Spirit of God

Attempts to break through Religiosity

Brainwashing Belief System
Functions as tyranny convictions rigidly held against any intrusion, even the Spirit of God. This birth or educational brainwashing captivity functions within most Christian denominations as well as all the non-Christian religious systems of the world. Only true spiritual rebirth can change this tyranny, sadly an infrequent occurrence in modern times with our denominational obsession on Cheap Salvation, defined as salvation assurance without substance.

The Human Entity
Body, Soul and Spirit

But why are the saints passive? Why are they not rising up in spiritual arms over the audacity of the secularist, the arrogance of the atheists and the collusion of the church hierarchy? Why is prayer not storming the kingdom of heaven over these critical issues of cultural, spiritual and moral hegemony in America? Why is the fervor of the people today, among those that have fervor, mounted for the environment and the global village, not Christ? For certainly, the Spirit of God says heaven is not being stormed with prayer over the critical issues of the cultural, spiritual and moral hegemony in America.

This land belongs to Jesus Christ. We need to make a stand and proclaim this land His, now! How sad it is that we have forgotten the rallying cry of the revolutionists who formed this country:

NO KING BUT KING JESUS!

To all who fear the loss of a perceived or real advantage if they take a stand, to all who will not stand or pray without the consent or push of a pastor, this message is yours sent from God: *Get behind me, Satan.*

Truly, in the great facades of deception that characterizes our modern civilizations, the removal of the spiritual realm from the rational world, even of the reality of God and the incarnation of His Son are natural and easy products. Our intelligentsia and its captive slave, the electronic media, coupled with the Western, and especially American, educational and knowledge paradigms, ridicule the spiritual realm, debasing the beliefs and the actions of the devout as the superstitions of the ignorant. They are the great promoters of evolution, turning their eyes from our planet's obvious history of asteroid hits with its resultant chaos and reconstruction. Mutation rates are known, generating an evolutionary problem of adequate time. Still, it would seem that some validity exists for intraspecies evolution even while the evidence to support cross-species evolution or macroevolution has not been discovered in 140 years of intensive search. Yet, their biases of evolutionary faith prevail and spread throughout the secular culture of the Western nations as hard facts.

With rationalism enthroned as king, humanism and secularism dominate our cultures. The consequences of this forced imbecility of one realm simplicity are severe; our civilization, empty of spiritual reality, degrades. Cultural integrity wanes. The residue of morality deteriorates. Lawlessness soars and the moral quality of the West, especially of America, declines precipitously, now approaching an exponential drop. Hang on if you can.

Chapter 15

Destruct Trail of Humanity[79]

The first product of the forfeiture of the vector of Jesus Christ is God's wrath. The second product is the ignominious degeneration of human civilization. Without the Christian churches functioning to their maximum as the Overchurch, which in turn must operate as the culturally redemptive engine of God, human civilization is doomed. The path without the renewed church is literally the destruct trail of the human race, a trail forged from the forfeited hopes of humanity.

Without the leadership of the Holy Spirit, without the willingness of the saints to die for Jesus' eschatological expectations, especially the coming of the kingdom, without the knowledge of Jesus' vector to the kingdom coordinates, humanity cannot reach its potential of brotherhood and agape love. The Great Commission cannot be fulfilled. The church loses one of its main purposes for existing. When that time arrives that the church is no longer effective in bringing the salvation message of Jesus Christ to the people it shall be removed by God. The worst of times then befalls humanity.

To avoid this terrible consequence humanity must awaken fully to the message of Jesus Christ. Let agape love bind and guide our relationships with one another and let unbridled love abound with our relationship with God. Anything that stands in the way of our love for God, including the most cherished values such as worldly prosperity and pleasures, must be cast aside. We must return to the vector of Jesus at all cost, realizing that the reason we exist, the very reason that the world exists, is to find and optimize that vector to paradise.

Unfortunately, a destruct trail of humanity is in existence, activated, as a result of the forfeited mission vector of Jesus Christ. Have no illusions about this trail, it leads to the destruction of human existence on earth. Yet, the Holy Spirit strongly indicates that this destruction trail will not be traveled because God's intervention will be successful, deflecting the completion of this destructive course. Yet, this success will require the freewill acceptance of God's intervention, and the human track record here is not promising!

So what guarantee do we have that humanity will accept the intervention of God? What if the bad seed of the evil realm overwhelms the special generations now arriving to implement the kingdom of God? Could we survive this?

---

79. This material also appears in Christ-Walk.

Unfortunately for humanity, the answer is no! Hence, the Spirit has made a special request for the addition of the Destruct Trail to this text as God's warning to His people. Be alert and be close to the Lord. Miss not the outpouring power when it comes. Let no one turn their back on the Spirit of God because it does not fit their theology!

Beware; we stand warned!

Let the Body of Christ seek the will of God in this matter, massively in prayer, for therein, we shall be triumphant.

DESTRUCT TRAIL TRACE.

The trace of the Destruct Trail starts with the rejection of the Holy Spirit:

1- Leadership of the Holy Spirit was rejected for the politics of the world (172-313).
2- Redemption for human civilization was forfeited (313-381).
3- Institutional Christian church was formed.
4- Christian churches moved from the status of the redemptive engine of God becoming the pragmatic religion of the Western world (Fourth Country).
5- Formalized and codified salvation was implemented (2nd through the 4th centuries).
6- Christianity became totally identified as the institutional church.
7- The equivalent of the **second fall** occurred.
8- Wrath of God fell upon Western Christendom, lasting for 795 years (410 through 1205). This was the first wrath of God.
9- In the first wrath, the institutional church gained great secular power.
10- In the period of the first wrath, a great disparity occurred between the actions and the teachings of the church.
11- The leadership of the institutional church became corrupt, influencing the quality of leadership at its lowest level where fortunately, valid spiritual leadership could still be found.
12- A great faith in the church grew especially among women.
13- Strong superstitions arose among the mostly illiterate people.
14- Still, gradually a great scorn and cynicism rose among the people directed against the church and its inconsistencies
15- During the time of the first wrath, many Christians were lost to a new religion, the Moslems, severely shrinking Christendom. This new religion seemed free of the effects of the first wrath, thus definitively linking God's first wrath to the church's forfeiture of

141

its culture-challenging function as the Grand Redemptive Engine of God (Commencing in 622).

16- The first wrath ended when Jesus appeared to Francis of Assisi in 1205 with the commandment to rebuild His House, interpreted as both church and culture. This request was a huge indictment on the church and its fall from God's grace, firmly signifying its loss of the keys to the kingdom and the inherent spiritual authority contained therein.

17- With the end of the first wrath a great surge of faith occurred in the common people of central Europe for Jesus Christ and His message. Once again, the saints believed in the coming of the kingdom of God, facilitated by the shift to the age of the Holy Spirit. This was the movement of the Spiritual Franciscans, sometimes called the Dissentients. It threatened the Christian hegemony of the institutional church, almost collapsing the formal church.

18- The Dissentients experienced massive love frenzy, changing the face of central Europe. The reappearance of the Grand Redemptive Engine of God seemed imminent.

19- The churches were largely empty as the people lived the faith.

20- Based on the visions of Joachim of Flora, the Dissentients believed the faithful were to enter a new age, the age of the Holy Spirit. This was to happen around 1260.

21- The institutional church used violent means (the Inquisition) to fight this surge of faith. A false gospel was circulated that deceived the dissentients into believing that the age of the Holy Spirit was not based on the New Testament. Based on this false gospel, apostasy set in as the Dissentients came to believe that Francis was Jesus reincarnated.

22- While the institutional church was fighting this surge of faith, a great Renaissance of ancient Aristotelian Greek thought generated rationalism. Perhaps it was no accident that this arrival occurred after Jesus' 1205 appearance. Jesus' manifestation did more than end the wrath of God on the House of Jesus. It released the 20 redemptive capacities placed on hold by the first wrath of God, especially the twelve-hundred-year-old redemption capacity of knowledge originally obtained by Jesus' sacrifice, opening the door to knowledge.

23- While clearly, Christ reopened all the 20 redemptive capacities by His 1205 appearance, the church remained nearsighted. Secular humanity was not so limited. It alone reached for the accumulation of knowledge with God's blessings. This acceptance by the secular world, coupled with the end of the 795 years of punishment wrath, enabled the belated development of rationalism and science. Ruefully, this development struggled forward in the face of church resistance.

24- The surge of faith and agape love represented by the revolt of the Spiritual Franciscans collapsed (1317).

25- The residue leaven of the church diminished as the faith of the Western people eroded with the collapse of the surge of faith.

26- Still, the early victories of the scientific community over the church marked the release of knowledge. With the blessings of God on science, not the institutional churches, ensured by the 1205 appearance of Jesus Christ, the belated development of science could not be stopped.

27- After the church repression of the Spiritual Franciscans with its restoration of Christianity as a faith walk, God poured out another, the second wrath upon the West (1317-1667).

28- Europe experienced the worst three hundred years of its history under this new wrath, decimating European populations by an average of one third and sometimes up to one half.

29- Toward the end of the second wrath, a religious revolt occurred (The Reformation). The unity of Western institutional Christendom was ruptured (1517).

30- The Protestant Reformation released a measure of freedom into the West.

31- Western cultures soared with the release of the Holy Scripture into the language of the common people.

32- Centuries of bitter religious wars occurred. These conflicts rightly belong to the second wrath but are considered by most as the heritage of the Reformation.

33- A strong secular orientation gradually replaced the influence of the churches.

34- Science confronted the churches over the nature of life. The churches try repression, denial, and then retreat.

35- European Christendom experienced a dramatic explosion of technology, further weakening institutional Christianity, which resisted at every step.

36- Rationalism exploded in a violent rejection to the centuries of abuse from institutional Christianity and their privileged over-class in a movement called the Enlightenment.

37- Nationalism developed. Calvinism rose. Knox arrived on the scene developing narrowly defined Protestant denominations locked into rigid theological positions, generally characterized by anti-Catholic, anti-intellectual scenarios.

38- Still, the move to freedom in the West had been loosened. So now a wave of freedom flooded through the secular West with its associated high work productivity. The Protestant work ethic was closely integrated into this development. Yet, a separation of faith and work grew, generating a new class of Christ-indifferent secularists.

39- These Christ-indifferent secularists now spawned liberal republics. Democracies were established in the West based on the teachings of Christ but without honoring Christ. In the face of the stubborn resistance of the institutional church, some Christ-indifferent secularists became Christ-haters.

40- Secular humanism rose gradually replacing religious humanism.

41- Technology dramatically improved the quality of life.

42- Christ-haters obtained control over many of the cultures of the world. Many thinkers believed that paradise could be found in technology without Christianity.

43- The churches, clinging to its pragmatic orientation, began to switch from cooperation with kings and aristocrats to cooperation with the more egalitarian Christ-haters, rationalizing away the obvious actions of the Christ-haters. This was a serious turning point in the West.

44- Secular cultures peaked in the twentieth century.

45- Wars of great destruction occurred.

46- Marxism and secular humanism peaked, each contending against institutional Christianity.

47- The institutional church was largely successful in defeating Marxism.

48- Yet, portions of the institutional churches were seriously exhausted by this battle, especially the Orthodox branch.

49- Marxism left former Christian nations like Russia without a fervent faith belief system.

50- Secular humanism gained sweeping victories over the Christian churches in America and Europe.

51- *Fiercely battered, the Christian church wanders aimlessly in an increasingly bitter and crowded world, lost to the truth of their situation as the ultimate determinant of civilization and the necessity for church renewal, in unity, to fulfill this responsibility. This is where we are today.*

52- Natural disasters become frequent (part of the Corrective Discipline).

53- Worldwide economic collapse occurs.

54- Conditioning wrath of God arrives.

55- The power outpouring of the Holy Spirit's love-gift arrives with great force.

56- This is the anticipated Intervention Point of God! If a critical mass of the beloved ones accepts the outpouring agape Love Touch of the Spirit of God, then the world tracks the vector of Jesus Christ in an updated eschatology to the Prototypical Kingdom, Time of Sorrow, Demonstration Kingdom, Bride of Christ, rapture and Great Tribulation. If the beloved fail to embrace the outpouring Holy Spirit, then humankind will continue down the Destruct Trail of Humanity. The following are those steps.

57- Huge wars, utilizing the ultimate technologies of mass destruction, devastate the civilizations of the world, seriously upsetting the ecology of the earth, spreading radiation and biological sicknesses all over the planet.

58- Because of the effects of the weapons of mass destruction and other interruptions in the earth's environment, oxygen levels drop to 8 percent of the atmosphere. Fresh water becomes very scarce.

59- Residual radiation levels now exceed health levels, severely cutting human life spans to eighteen years.

60- Human mutation escalates worldwide, dramatically reducing the earth population of productive humans.

61- The information revolution is reversed.

62- Diseases walk across the world killing huge numbers.

63- Some cities are so battered by their own pollution and diseases that they disappear within a few years.

64- Oxygen levels continue to drop, slipping below the minimum 7 percent level needed for human survival. Fresh water continues to be contaminated and scarce.

65- The level of human misery reaches new depths despite desperate efforts to replenish the world's oxygen levels.

66- Polar ice caps melt as the earth heat increases. Fresh water supplies dip even lower.

67- Earth's geological instability increases.

68- Domed communities are tried, but the radiation cannot be successfully reduced and these communities gradually disappear.

This is the last serious effort to sustain the human race as an intellectually aware animal.

69- Agriculture collapses across wide sections of the world, as the deserts spread.

70- Small sized asteroid hits occur in parts of the earth.

71- Starvation becomes widespread.

72- Human cultural skills in the arts disappear.

73- A new wave of illnesses sweeps the world.

74- Life spans drop to fourteen years.

75- Education is denigrated.

76- Knowledge disappears rapidly.

77- The world population drops dramatically from billions into millions.

78- Another exponential rise in misery occurs within surviving civilizations, as slavery becomes prominent again, driven by economic necessity.

79- Production skills disappear; the industrial revolution is reversed.

80- The levels of human and economic services severely decay within the surviving civilizations.

81- Power grids disappear around the world.

82- The remaining leaven from the message of the church collapses, resulting in massive human degeneration into the *survival of the fittest* mode over most portions of the world.

83- Remnant churches struggle to revive the leaven of the Word, but the warring factions force the churches to take sides, thus confirming the continuing strength of the informal Pact of Cooperation between the institutional church and neo-paganism. This can be viewed as confirmation of the 1934 warning from the Swiss theologian, Karl Barth, that faith had become secondary to nationalism.

84- Massive internal wars and civil wars break out, as the remaining structures of civilization deteriorate.

85- Population of the world drops into thousands.

86- Women become chattel again.

87- Family structures weaken and disappear.

88- A serious decline of rationalism occurs; widespread superstition reappears.

89- Continuing human degeneration leads to the breakup of the remaining human civilizations, as the message of love and compassion is lost in the return of humanity to the viciousness of the wild animal, each in a desperate fight for survival.

90- God withdraws His remnant churches with each judged a failure. Christianity disappears from the earth.

91- The moral values of the church totally disappear as an indispensable societal entity.

92- What remains of civilization retrogresses to primitive paganism.

93- What remains of knowledge and education disappears.

94- Humanity abandons civilization.

95- The last remaining technology is lost.

96- Tribalism returns. The fight for fresh water is on.

97- Human tribalism retrogrades into warlike clans of young preteens terrorizing others with clubs and knives.

98- Humanity slips back to the most primitive stages of life in which the good meal is another human.

99- Population drops into the hundreds.

100- God destroys the human race as oxygen levels drop to untenable levels.

101- Silence reigns on earth.

It is this destruct path that humanity must avoid. Meaning, when the hand of God moves, and we see millions violently dying and our civilization being ripped apart, we must rejoice in our faith and hang on, for the good times of the outpouring Spirit will be near. Do not despair. We must accept that we sinned as a nation and as individuals and gracefully accept our fate. For, if we embrace God's intervention, then we embrace the arrival of His kingdom. Only then, can we truly, with confidence, know that Jesus' mission vector will be waiting for our grandchildren!

The true path is the return to Christian unity for the cause of Jesus' eschatology, modified for modern technology and step implementation considerations. Specially, Christianity must birth the adolescent version of the kingdom, found in the leadership of the Holy Spirit and the fullness of the Word. This can only be accomplished in the **Overchurch.** Meanwhile, ponder these words of God:

Woe to you experts in the law, because you have taken away the key to knowledge. You yourselves have not entered, and you have hindered those who were entering (Luke 11:52).

I pray also for those who will believe in me through their message, that all of them may be one, Father, just as you are in me and I am in you. May they also be in us so that the world may believe that you have sent me (John 17:20-21).

When he came to his senses, he said, '... I will set out and go back to my father and say to him: Father, I have sinned against heaven and against you...' (Luke 15:17-18).

And anyone who does not carry his cross and follow me cannot be my disciple (Luke 14:27).

Chapter 16

Rebuilding the Foundation

We, the saints of Jesus Christ, must be reconciled to the dramatic fact that God desires a radical change in our faith patterns and that this change will impact everyone's life. We are speaking of a total rework of our civilization initiated by a reversal in the faith orientation of the churches and saints. The Lord would not have us be naïve; we are going to lose our comfort. Also, we must recognize that in our present state few will voluntarily relinquish their comfort; hence, the Lord must move us. Modern church leaders and the churches they represent will not budge from the comfort of prosperity and societal respectability. Even the spiritual disruption of a Grand Awakening might not move them. The ecclesiastics have a successful bunker history, quite willing to wait out any distraction, including Spirit-driven disruptions, e.g., the recent Irvin, Pentecostal and Charismatic moves of the Holy Spirit. These mainline Protestant and Catholic Churches are cemented into hierarchical structures impervious to change. Firmly settled upon their foundation of political and cultural partnership with the neo-pagans with its rewards of political and social respectability, they know of no other church approach. And they will not budge!

Now the saints tried to rebuild this church foundation once before in the movement of the Franciscans. These men followed Francis of Assisi, whose impact on the church is not in dispute. But Francis, living the humble, simple life of poverty was unable to successfully reconstruct the church, to lead the church into this purer form of Christianity. This failure is attributable to Francis' acceptance of the church's political power structure and, by default, to the cooperative foundation of the institutional church, possibly a church cornerstone he did not see. His rebellious followers determined that his failure would not be theirs, starting a new movement called the Spiritual Franciscans. It is this movement, minus its apostasy, that the Spirit points to as the prototype for the future. So it is incumbent upon us to learn from this reform movement.

Indeed, let us learn from the mistakes of God's great workers that have preceded us, especially the work of Joachim, Francis, Grebel and Luther, to establish the correct foundation upon which Jesus can rebuild His church, the **Overchurch**, as the New Covenant pact of Jesus Christ. Premised on agape love, brotherhood, and individual sacrificial orientation for the coming of the kingdom, the **Overchurch** must follow the leadership of the Spirit of God in a return to the rebelliousness of the early church. All this will occur as the world shifts into the last minor dispensation of the Church age, the subset age of the Holy Spirit. The intervention of God and the shift to this last subset age of the Church Age, are two reflections of the same act.

RETHINKING THE FREE RIDE VERSUS THE OVERCOMING STRUGGLE

One of the outstanding struggles among Christians deals with the imputation of righteousness. Let us look at an illustration of a difference in biblical interpretations that has led to this serious conflict, perhaps best epitomized as the differences between the carnal and spiritual Christians.

Preaching that the righteousness of God can be found in eternal salvation through the application of God's grace reflects the view that the Gospels contain the position of paradise. However, preaching directed at seeking the righteousness of God and His kingdom as the overcoming requirement of life, including conquering self and all the obstructions created by the enemy of God to reach overcoming reflects the vector of Christ Jesus. In many ways, this difference can be brought down to two Scriptures:

That the Gospel is seen to possess the coordinates of Paradise:

Whoever believes in the Son has eternal life, but whoever rejects the Son will not see life, for God's wrath remains on him (John 3:36).

This scripture has been widely interpreted that all the saint must do is to accept Jesus into one's life then forget about it, because that one is saved. Instead of accepting the unmerited gift of personal salvation as the starting point of a life-long drive to overcoming achievements, individual thoughts of seeking after God and His work in our lives are deferred in these saints for the materialistic life of the secular culture, characterized by seeking after wealth and power. This position can be adopted only if the individual has been deceived into believing that the Gospel represents the position of paradise and that this paradise can be found only in heaven after death. These believers hold that it is hopeless to seek the kingdom out on earth because our sinfulness prohibits even the free exercise of our will.

That the Gospel points at the vector to Paradise:

But seek first His Kingdom and His righteousness, and all these things will be given to you as well (Matthew 6:33).

This red-ink Scripture is focused on the vector of Jesus Christ. It does not repudiate John 3:36 but fulfills it. Perhaps the best description between the position of paradise and the vector to it can be summarized by one expression: Seek the kingdom with fervor as led by the Holy Spirit! Frankly, it is here that we have stumbled. Protestants have stumbled by too often ignoring the Author of the Bible for the Bible, missing the Holy Spirit. Catholics have stumbled by ignoring that same church generating Driving Force for pagan-polluted and compromised traditions that maintains salvation is found in the church.[80]

So, we must turn to seeking, all of us! But as indicated before, just seeking along any track is inadequate. Seeking must have a direction, a focus, which we pursue with force. This makes it a vector. Let us use the firing of a cannon as an analogy to a vector. One must put a charge and a shell in that cannon and point the cannon in the proper direction. Then one has to ignite that charge sending the shell to its target. So it is in Jesus' vector. We must load, point, and fire. Sound simple? It is not! The complexity arrives because the fourth century church, in its haste to come out of the underground status into respectability, lost the ability to load, point and fire the mission of Christ. Thus, the task of transforming this world into the kingdom of God was forfeited. Lost, the vector of Christ has never been recovered. So before we can seek to travel down the vector of Jesus Christ to His kingdom, we first must seek His vector now missing for almost two millennia, i.e., we have a double seek problem.

The church must find Jesus' vector through its awakening, then the church can learn to trace down the vector to its target through revival revolution. It is a double search problem requiring both a massive awakening followed by cultural revival. It is only in the latter effort that Dialectical Agapism springs to life, which means that the dialectical process of agape love is the methodology of the vector, but not its starting coordinates.

Do we have the strength of faith in modern Christianity to seek out that vector and follow it with force? No! So then, do we have the potential to find the vector through the Holy Spirit? The answer to this question determines our fate.

RECAPTURING JESUS' VECTOR AND ITS MISSION GOALS

After the Protestant Reformation, Christians have come to accept the Bible as containing the exact coordinates of paradise. In fact the entire Protestant Reformation is based on the rejection of dogmas and traditions of the old Roman Catholic Church for the unique dependence upon the authority of the Bible. But here, we have a profound problem. Since, the New Testament captured the vector to paradise, not its location, failure to recognize this scenario has added to the

---

80. This Catholic (and some Protestants) concept focuses the separation of church and state, whereas the concept of the Kingdom of God repudiates this separation.

churches' inability to transform our culture into the kingdom of God. In other words even if we were able to successfully repudiate the Pact of Cooperation, we still would be lost in our ability to implement the kingdom without an awareness of the fact that the Bible contains the vector to, not the position of, paradise. It is the responsibility of the faithful to discover and then travel Jesus' vector to paradise. This means we must understand the following:

1. **The Bible defines the mission vector of Jesus Christ to the kingdom of God, not its position coordinates.**
2. **To travel this vector we must first accept Jesus as our Savior then vigorously seek after God, His kingdom and His Righteousness.**
3. **To find and trek the correct vector (course), the Spirit of God must guide us, especially since the original vector to the first stage implementation of the kingdom of God was severed by the decisions of the Judeans. This forced the Body of Christ into the second stage as the birth stage therefore greatly magnifying an already difficult task, a task still unrecognized.**
4. **To reposition ourselves on the vector to the kingdom, we must reclaim the fullness of the Gospel message of Jesus, meaning we must forsake the Pact of Cooperation and then drive for the transformation of the existing secular culture into the kingdom of God.**
5. **When these points are recognized and reclaimed as the Overchurch, then the Body of Christ will be repositioned on Jesus' vector. True worship of the Father can be restored to the Christian masses in spirit and truth, regenerating the vitality of Christianity.**
6. **The reclamation of Christian vitality is dependent upon the restoration of kingdom spiritual energy. The most powerful regeneration tool comes from the practice of the Holy Junction, a spiritual exercise of the human spirit with the Holy Spirit largely unknown to the church. This is a process where the born again saint frees his or her human spirit from the authority of the mind to join with its look-alike, the Spirit of God. The Holy Spirit will take the spirit of the saint to the throne room of the Father and the Son. There the saint shall encounter optimal true worship, receiving that kingdom power so essential to the restoration of the Christian world. Church awakening will occur when a critical mass of worshippers (known only to God) reaches**

true worship of the Father and the Son, a process to be found exclusively in the dogma-free Overchurch.

7. **The Holy Junction is normally entered into immediately after Holy Communion, Biblical Contemplation, or quiet time with Jesus. This means that these practices will be fundamental to the Overchurch.**

THE ROLE OF THE HOLY SPIRIT

The Holy Spirit is the decisive factor upon the earth, and He is ignored. It is He who can change the course of the churches and set humanity back on the proper course. Yet, it is He who is abused! The abuse of the Holy Spirit by the leaders of the church started before the finality of the Constantine decisions. It continues today. Let these words from Neill and Wright be our words reflecting the church leaders' attitude toward the Holy Spirit before the Constantine affair and onward to our time:[81]

Polite references to the Holy Spirit at suitable intervals are to be heard in the preaching and worship of all the denominations. But who has developed a theology of the Holy Spirit that really does justice to the part that He plays in the whole New Testament revelation [and in the development of the kingdom of God come to earth]*?*

Today, many saints hold concepts of the Trinity that do not permit the freedom of the Holy Spirit to maneuver within church, culture or individual. In actual practice these beliefs are but modifications of Oneness. In this constriction belief, the saints once again crucify the Spirit of God just as the third and fourth century church fathers did. Can we ever learn? Granted the mystery of the Trinity is difficult to embrace, but fully embrace it we must.

The third-century rejection of the leadership of the Holy Spirit, plus the fourth-century betrayal of Jesus' mission vector by the human leaders of the church, **legacy blunders two and six**, have jammed the modern church into a no win situation. It is time we adhere to the Bible as led by the Holy Spirit and realize that the truth will set us free. Beloved ones, we labor under a faulted inheritance. Accountability is upon us.

---

81. From Neill, Stephen & Wright, Tom *The Interpretation of the New Testament*, page 251.

God is calling His beloved ones to spiritual and cultural war. We are to enter into training for this coming struggle, for the soul of our nation and for its assigned mission to bring the kingdom of God to earth is at stake. Each saint has a part in this task. Who fills in your part if you fail to respond? We must all prepare for war, initially as spiritual battle warriors then as non-violent cultural combatants. To do this we must go to prayer and seek the reconstruction of our church and faith, always seeking massive spiritual revival.

Then, aided by our prayers, the church and its out-of-control culture shall experience a set of interventions by God, generating an intense awakening followed by spiritual revival, creating the **Overchurch**. Glory to God! Those living at the time of the intervention shall see the Body of Christ restored to unity under the leadership of the Spirit of God, and the glory of God shall be around them and in them.

Starting as the Third Great Awakening and rapidly shifting into the last minor dispensation, spawning a massive revival revolution, this great move of God will ignite the fervor of the saints, placing great pressure upon the neo-pagan, humanistic culture. To overcome the errors of centuries, this revival shall be capable of spiritual warfare unsurpassed in history. This form of spiritual warfare will be possible only by a return to the massive spiritual power of the primitive and early churches. The American culture will sway under the defeats of the enemy of God, with Satan's influence shattered. Then look at those who weep and mourn, for we shall know the workers of Satan.

This set of victories over the enemy is part of God's plan for America. The enemy will stagger, bewildered and confused, never anticipating the strength of the force encountered.

Sadly, some churches, locked into their brainwashing canons and totally confident of their church position with God, will resist.[82] To them and to all saints uncertain about the will of God in this matter, this message of warning comes in the name of God, as heard in June 1994:

Abode no more in futility! Seek my Spirit and make peace. Find unity in my righteousness and my will. Reach in love for one another. Rest assured in the Spirit's leadership that my kingdom comes. Prepare thyself to return to my

---

82. Placher, William C. *A History of Christian Theology*, Louisville: The Westminster Press, 1983, page 309. Read about the ideas of Martin Luther King, Jr. If the modern church does not restore the sacrificial spirit of the early church, it will become a social club without meaning or purpose, dismissed as irrelevant.

ways. The unprepared will know great anxieties. Look, I rise up a new thing. Only in this victory shall you see my Son in all His splendor and glory.[83]

By the Spirit, the 'New Thing' is the prototype kingdom. 'His ways' is the sacrificial orientation of the saints employed in aggressive evangelizing of the surrounding heathen cultures on all possible spiritual and cultural fronts.

Many good people claim that the Spirit leads the churches and that they are just the faithful instruments of that leadership. As a test of this claim, ask how many of our current church leaders would be willing to step aside for a year, allowing another to rule as they humbly follow and serve? No, the possession of church authority is an oppression of the enemy of God, an exploitation of self, and one that binds and confines. Humbleness is practiced, not experienced.

The evidence of history disproves the humble, servant attitude of those in church power positions. Look at this list:

- Repeated and repugnant personal sins of those in church leadership
- Moral decline of the culture
- Insignificance of the church's moral influence in the affairs of the world
- Divergence from the kingdom of God
- Divergence from the Great Commission.

It is not enough to claim the church leadership of the Spirit of God encased in elaborate theological terms that most lay persons cannot understand when it is not so, and it has not been for over sixteen hundred years!

Sadly, the poison from the Pragmatic Cancer has done its work well. The Body of Christ, comfortable and passive, approach the victimization predicted in Hosea 4:6.

My people are destroyed from lack of knowledge (Hosea 4:6).

---

83. Each saint must confirm this word individually. Even a casual study of this word reveals great insight into the mind and will of God. Interestingly, this message of June 24, 1994 was almost the same as a previous message received while working as a contractor for CBN in 1984.

Chapter 17

Crucial Role of the Human Spirit

The marvel of the Biblical knowledge-coordinates abides in Jesus' mandate that humanity must be reborn. With our human spirit newly regenerated, we are to enter a full and commanding partnership with our human mind, there to follow in faith, His vector to paradise. In those moments in which we experience the **Holy Junction** with God, the human spirit actually transcends the human mind to lead the human entity. But this path necessitates a blind and absolute faith in Jesus Christ, which is predicated upon the human mind disciplining itself to a partnership with the human spirit, a partnership, which at times of kingdom spiritual energy input becomes subjugation of the soul to the human spirit. Indeed, after decades of dominance by the soul (mind) in the average saint's life, is this not the ultimate fairness, as well as the human status before the fall of Adam and Eve?

With the drive to the kingdom predicated upon a new and vigorous role for the regenerated human spirit, the components of the human: body, soul and spirit, become equalized in importance in the faith walk to the kingdom of God. Because of the rise of the human spirit, the advantage of higher mental capacities is neutralized. The necessity for a higher education in theology is gone, along with the need for strong mental capacities stimulated by education. Faith makes us equal, especially as the requirement for the occupation of faith in the human spirit becomes the paramount criteria for success with God. What happens to the intellect with its mastery of worldly knowledge as well as its intellectual mastery of the Bible when the spiritual power walker in Christ becomes that person with muscular faith found within a strong, independent human spirit? Indeed, sometimes the power mind is a handicap. It is important to know that the human mind cannot find an optimum walk with Christ, but the human spirit can. This means that all those who dedicated themselves fervently and exclusively to the intellectual only study of Holy Scripture are seeking in the wrong direction. It is good and proper that we know Scripture, but it is not good or proper that we know Holy Scripture to the detriment of the indwelling of the Holy Spirit in our body, soul and human spirit, which brings faith unexcelled. Lastly, but most importantly, what role remains for our intellect after it has assisted in the regeneration and freedom of our human spirit? The mind must continue to pursue the activities of physical life in the mode of the Christ-mind. But indeed, the difficult question must be asked: Can a saint dedicated solely to the study of the Bible find the truth of life: the power indwelling of the Holy Spirit, that status where the human spirit, not the human mind, prevails? No, that saint can find the love of the Lord but not the intimacy of the Lord. For it is not enough to read about the Lord, we must also experience Him, and this experience can only be attained through the Holy Spirit, either by grace or the indwelling of the Spirit. If this experience is by grace, then it will tend to be a onetime experience, such as the born again experience. But if this experience is by the indwelling of the Spirit, then it tends to be a lasting and driving experience, one that is required to track the vector of Christ Jesus to the kingdom of God, adapted to the physical plane.

By placing a faith burden within the realm of the human spirit upon all His followers, God enabled the most simpleminded to travel this kingdom path with the same advantage as the most able-minded. If it were not so, if the intellectual study of the Bible were the road to salvation, then only the bright ones would find an optimized position with God. This is in direct contradiction to Jesus' message that He comes for the weary and burdened (Matthew 11:28), not for the righteous but for the sinners (Matthew 9:12-13).

Since faith is a gift of the Spirit of God, 1 Corinthians 12:9, this places the Holy Spirit as the optimized indweller of the *human spirit*, which act corresponds to Watchman Nee's maximum indwelling, the occupation of the Holy of Holies. When accomplished in sufficient numbers, this indwelling of the human spirit, defined as the level 3 to 4 spiritual saint in this text, ensures the coming of the kingdom to that culture. In this situation, the wonder of the vector of Jesus Christ is to be found. It is a wonder in fairness, yet it is an attainment that has affronted and eluded the intelligentsia through the generations.

Here is the progression of this faith trip:

VECTORED FAITH WALK

1. Jesus' vector takes humanity into the unknown, unseen portion of knowledge coordinates.
2. The mind of man cannot peer into this vast unknown and hence fears it.
3. To the mind of man this journey is a ride of folly into anarchy, akin to the children's crusade, a serious breach of rationalism and pragmatism.
4. Hence, the mind of man cannot make this journey to paradise.
5. Only the spirit of man can travel there, tracing Jesus' vector to its destination, the kingdom of God.
6. Once there, the mind of man can assist in the adaptation of the kingdom to earth.

157

7. But to travel this path, the pre-eminence of the human spirit over the human mind must come to fulfillment.
8. Yet to travel this path, faith is required.
9. Since both the human spirit and faith are primary instruments in this journey, they must be amalgamated by some means.
10. That binding is the indwelling of the Spirit in the human spirit.
11. However, this is an extraordinarily high level of indwelling currently reached by only 6,000 saints. (The Spirit says this number shall be increased into the hundreds of thousands by 2020 - 2040.)
12. This means that the primary human readiness for this journey is the acquisition of faith, not knowledge, although a certain threshold accumulation of knowledge, especially biblical knowledge, is required to find the start of Jesus' vector.
13. Knowledge beyond the Bible is the knowledge that the mind must grow in wisdom until it understands that it is the obstacle to Jesus' vectored trip to the kingdom.
14. This means that the mind must grow into supporting cooperation to enable the human spirit to proceed on its journey.
15. To reach this point, the mind must come to an accommodation of its fears, both conscious and hidden.
16. Accommodation can only occur through an inner cleansing.
17. To do this, to overcome, the soul and the spirit of the human must seek out the things of the Lord, especially the indwelling of the Holy Spirit.
18. Hence, for the human spirit to soar within the human entity, the human mind first must be healed, becoming like the mind of Christ.
19. To ready the human spirit for the indwelling of the Holy Spirit and from there to the **Holy Junction** these conditions must be met:

- The saint must be born again
- The saint must be baptized in the Holy Spirit
- The human spirit must be freed from the domination of the human mind normally achieved by intense prayer and biblical studies with the Holy Spirit
- The mind of Christ must be adopted
- To bring the human mind, especially the subconscious mind, to the mind of Christ both levels of the human mind must be healed. Mental healing occurs when both forms of the mind have received the unction of healing best gained from the **Holy Junction** with God.

20. With the conversion of both minds to the salvation of Jesus, the saint has reached that minimum mental development required for an extended spiritual development.
21. The mind knows enough to remove itself as the spiritual roadblock.
22. Now, the mental capacities of the saints become secondary to the task at hand.
23. The human spirit combines with the Holy Spirit to soar to the Father and His Son.
24. In this fashion, the tracking of the kingdom of God has become open to the saint.
25. In this process of spiritual growth, the saint has activated redemptive capacities number 1, 4, 5, 7, 10, 12 and 19. See the Redemptive Capacities in chapter 8.

In this decision for faith as the key to the position of the knowledge-coordinates of earthly paradise, Jesus held out hope to the suffering masses of humanity. Here Jesus reaches to the masses, saying follow me!

Thus, the basic requirements to find the knowledge-coordinates to paradise are set: A regenerated human spirit, free and independent of the human soul, joined with the Holy Spirit operative in His great gift: Faith in Jesus' mission vector.

Jesus gave the vector to paradise in Holy Scripture, especially in the Sermon on the Mount, calling it the kingdom of God come to earth. It was by this process that Jesus mandated that His church achieve the remaining portions of the trip back to paradise in absolute faith.

This church goal is the mission critical tasks of Jesus Christ. And when the church is functioning within the vector attributes given by Jesus, filled and led by the Holy Spirit, striving to achieve the mission critical tasks of Jesus Christ, the church again will reach the peak of its proficiency, becoming the Grand Redemptive Engine of God.

Jesus' vector mission is the coming of the kingdom to earth and the harvest of the good seed of the world to the companionship of God. This mission fulfills the Great Commission and enables the return of Jesus to rule over His kingdom.

Here are the specifics of Jesus' *knowledge of knowledge* mission to earth:

- He, Jesus the Messiah, redeems humanity from the Adamic curse and permits the search for paradise as an individual and collectively as a social entity.
- He, Jesus the Messiah, is the exclusive gateway or starting point in that search.

- He alone regenerates the human spirit, activating it again to its lofty position of commander-in-chief of the human entity.
- Holy Scripture contains the vector to paradise with many specifics set in the Sermon on the Mount.
- Analogously, the church is the ship in which humanity sails.
- The Holy Spirit controls the rudder of the ship, providing the vector direction.
- The Holy Spirit nourishes and energizes the ship's passengers.
- Kingdom spiritual energy, generated from true worship of God by the passengers, propels the ship.
- Agape love weathers all storms.

With these tools, humanity can travel over the unknown and vast ocean of achievable-knowledge to the coordinates of paradise. The horizon should not frighten God's beloved ones.

THE TRAVELERS

Indeed, the only hope for the long-term survival of humanity is the paradisiacal excursion vector of Jesus Christ. Now, even a casual glance at the conditions of this excursion under the New Covenant identifies two travelers: The individual saint and the civilization of humanity. While the individual saints must first hold the conditions of the kingdom, paradise implemented is a cultural entity, not an individual condition. Thus, the search for paradise mandates either cultural evolution or social revolution. Cultural revolts uproot and replace the challenged culture. An example is the French Revolution. If it is evolution, then the existing culture is slowly changed over time. Jesus seems to state in Luke 17 that the kingdom arrives through evolution, starting with the kingdom arrival within each saint:

The kingdom of God does not come visibly, nor will people say, 'Here it is,' or 'There it is,' because the kingdom of God is within you (Luke 17:20-21).

The kingdom of God arrives in each of us through a spiritual rebirth:
I tell you the truth, unless a man is born again, he cannot see the kingdom of God (John 3:3).

However, the church has lingered too long in the Pact of Cooperation, becoming too passive to Jesus' call to pursue the coming of the kingdom as an evolutionary process. The Pragmatic Cancer has taken its toll. Allegedly, only a revolution of faith can bring the arrival of the kingdom of God into the hearts of the faithful, and only the massive intervention of the Holy Spirit can do this. This, the Spirit has promised. So, humanity, especially the peoples of North America, a microcosm of the world, shall experience a revolution of faith in order to implement the initial birth of the cultural kingdom. From there, incremental and evolutionary steps will improve it with each succeeding generation. It is as if a revolution is required to compensate for centuries of neglect, required by God to reset us on the path, indeed, to restore the mission vector of Christ Jesus. When firmly re-established on this correct vector, we can resume the incremental and evolutionary development of the kingdom adaptation.

But reflect for a moment on the magnitude of the required revolution. Indeed, the initial explosion of faith will have to generate a cultural and spiritual detonation of enormous strength, a faith eruption capable of overcoming the eschatological loss of the stage 1 implementation. This faith breakout must be so strong that it can empower agape civilization to birth as stage 2 kingdom implementation. Only a process of revival revolution instigated by a grand spiritual awakening can do this. And only the intervention of God can bring about these events.

To assist in this breakout, the saints must reinterpret John 3:3 to its literal interpretation. The saints must have the vision of the kingdom in their hearts immediately able to jump from there into the initial stage 2 implementation. This would seem to be a huge, conspicuously impossible task. Surely, the intervention must be of the first order, an intervention unseen by humanity to date, to even contemplate such a jump.

Some have interpreted John 3:3 to mean the reborn saint's eventual entry into the kingdom after physical death. And although this is true, the Spirit of God indicates that true spiritual rebirth also provides that vision now, in this life. Hence, the following conclusions seem feasible:

One, it is quite logical that any given saint, knowing the kingdom within, does not have the capacities to bring redemption to the encapsulating pagan and secular culture.

Two, it is equally obvious that a large number of saints, knowing the kingdom within, could not remain passive to the evils of the encapsulating pagan and secular culture.

Three, it is postulated that a critical mass of truly born-again believers will inevitably instigate an engine of cultural and spiritual redemption within their civilization.

Four, an examination of history would seem to indicate that the occurrence of the redemptive engine of God has transpired once in the first and possibly again in the thirteenth centuries.

CULTURAL PRESSURE FROM THE TRULY BORN AGAIN

Hence, a large number of saints, truly reborn to the mission of Christ, carrying the image of the kingdom within, would place inordinate pressure on any existing, secular culture, seeking its redemption. Thus, Jesus in Luke 17:20-21 must have been stating the case for the evolutionary and confrontational synthesis of the kingdom of God come to earth through the actions of His church against the prevailing and encapsulating secular culture. The key word in this analysis is 'truly reborn'.

It would appear from this brief examination of Luke 17 and John 3, that the evolutionary redemption of the pagan culture into the kingdom of God is the resolve of God and the mission critical task of Jesus' church. It is asserted that cultural evolution was to be the primary method for the enactment of Jesus' eschatology. The church was to be the leaven of the Gentile society lead by the Holy Spirit and inspired by the illustration of the Judean kingdom of God implementation.

But the events surrounding the Judean rejection and the Gentile forfeitures defeated all hopes of achieving Jesus' vectored mission by evolution. It is impossible to reach stage 2 without the presence of stage 1 except by a Spirit-supported special birth. The youth cannot walk unless he is born. Yet, it is alleged that the Lord God gave humanity a window of 795 years from 1205 to 2000 to achieve that goal. Except for two failed efforts, humanity did not respond. Here, schematically is this historical scenario:

STRUGGLE TO BIRTH THE KINGDOM OF GOD:

Scripture points at three stages of the kingdom:		
Stage 1: Infant Stage	2: Adolescent Stage	3: Adult
Judeans abort the Stage 1 birth of the kingdom		
Jesus switches the implementation to the Gentiles		
Gentiles defeat paganism – Stage 2 beckons		
Unaware of stage shifts, Gentiles become frustrated		
Deciding task impossible; they embrace Pragmatism		
Gentiles Reject the Leadership of the Holy Spirit		
Gentiles embrace Pact of Cooperation with pagans		
First Wrath of God descends on the House of God		
Knowledge and learning disappear for a season!		
Jesus Appears to Francis asking: Repair my House		
Spiritual Franciscans try to birth Stage 2 Kingdom		
Love Frenzy Grips Central Europe		
Institutional Church resists, defeating dissentients		
The Second Wrath falls on the House of God		
The Protestant Reformation breaks out		
Reformation generates Spiritual Reformation		
Spiritual Reformation fails to birth the Kingdom		
Window for human kingdom birth closes in 2000		
Future birth of adolescent, Stage 2, depends on God		

Principally, current church responsibility is to bring the encapsulating and Christ-indifferent cultures into repentance and redemption under the blood sacrifice of Jesus Christ. Then under the influence of the Spirit of God, it is required to bring these peoples to the discovery of knowledge filtered through Christ's message of brotherhood and agape love. This must be a complete conversion, one in which dedicated practice supplements simple understanding. To achieve this, it is the responsibility of the church to confront pagan and heathen cultures at every moral, social and spiritual level possible. Spiritual and cultural confrontations are part of the correct pathway, the true vector of Jesus Christ.[84] The fullness of the Gospel can be found only in this truth: Constructive and agape-led constructive confrontation must occur at every church/societal contact point even as we wait for the massive intervention of God.

Without question, this means the New Covenant in its operative arm, as the Grand Redemptive Engine of God, is a cultural and spiritual rebellious movement.[85] Indeed, in its pure form, Christianity is not a religion. Rather, it is a redemptive process that utilizes personal faith in the salvation of the Cross to project agape brotherhood as a cultural movement designed to change the entire civilization of humanity, rendering it as the kingdom of God come to earth.[86] Its goals are the conversion of each individual within any given human civilization to faith in the salvation of Jesus Christ, and through the love of fellowman the

---

84. Today, Christian elements struggle against the abortion movement. They best represent the true Christian confrontation faith of the New Covenant. Additionally, in some instances this movement approximates Overchurch outreach of the future.

85. Are the churches charged with the responsibility to bring the kingdom of God to this planet? From Neill, Stephen & Wright, Tom *The Interpretation of the New Testament*, page 146, we read that the Gospel of Jesus Christ will always be a threat to the old cultural order. Further, as long as the Crucifixion and the Resurrection of Jesus Christ stand, this threat stands. From Meyer, Ben F, *The Aims of Jesus*, London: SCM Press Ltd, 1979, pages 144, we read further confirmation of the threat of the Gospel to the worldly cultures.

86. That the teachings of Jesus are additionally, by definition, transforming on the civilization that embraces this boundless goodness is perhaps best epitomized by this extraordinary and cultural changing antithesis of Jesus:

You have heard that it was said to the people long ago, 'Do not murder, and anyone who murders will be subject to judgment.' But I tell you that anyone who is angry with his brother will be subject to judgment (Matthew 5:21-22).

If implemented successfully just this antithesis of Jesus would transform human culture. Truly, Jesus is a rebel, first class; destined as a non-ending, perpetual rebel until His reign is fulfilled, and in this, His patient quest shall be consummated and triumphant. His kingdom shall reign on earth. It is the mandate of the Gospel that His church struggle in this endeavor, starting inward with each saint, then projecting this great achievement outward to the world.

redemption of that given civilization into the discipleship of Christ. From cultural redemption, it is a short step to the coming of the kingdom of God even in a pre-Parousia approximation: The Prototypical Kingdom of God. Clearly, Christ meant to lift humanity to a higher plane of existence.[87] This means the birth of the adolescent kingdom only can happen with the assistance of God. Contained therein is the hope of the full Christian Gospel: Paradise can be here as well as in heaven. To start on this trip, Jesus stated that when each saint is reborn again, that saint sees the vision of the kingdom of God come to earth. Restated, Jesus said that each saint who accepts Him as personal savior shall be reborn in spirit therein to see the kingdom of God. There we can almost grasp its knowledge coordinates.

CULTURE CRUNCHING MOVE OF JESUS CHRIST

Clearly then, pure and true Christianity is a culture crunching movement. It is the enemy of all pre-existent pagan and heathen civilizations, sent to their destruction by God. The New Testament contains this commandment to the Christian churches throughout the Gospels especially as Jesus incessantly preached about the kingdom of God come to earth. This Scripture in Matthew 28 clearly presents that call upon the churches:

Therefore go and make disciples of all nations…(Matthew 28:19).

The Scripture places the commandment upon churches to work to bring the kingdom of God to this earth. It is best that the saints, as well as the heathens, understand the exact and true motives of Christianity.

Truly to be reborn is to see the vision of the kingdom of God. To see this vision is to be restless and discontented in any culture not striving to mirror that vision. Thus by definition, all who walk in the New Covenant of Jesus Christ and know spiritual rebirth in Him must be in confrontation with the surrounding culture that does not. And fully, this was the situation with the early church. Just as truthfully, it is not the situation of the church today.

---

87. To take this high and lofty concept and shift it into a human designed system of regulations and syntactical constraints is an ignominious insult to our Savior.

Chapter 18

Personal Preparation for the Intervention

It is fair to ask. 'What can I do to prepare for God's forthcoming awesome intervention? After all, what can any individual accomplish in such a horrendous set of events, a global shift in the physical realm, one set off by the astounding power of God! A mere man or woman like myself can do nothing, right?' Wrong! Reconstruction of the church starts at the bottom, meaning you and me! We must throw off the incorrect teachings of the dead churches and look deeply into the call of God to walk with His Son. Referred to as the Christ-Walk, this is your personal preparation for the outpouring of the Spirit, your way to prepare to assist God rebuild the foundation and walls of God's true spiritual church even as requested by Jesus in 1205.

Let us look at some of the characteristics of this personal reform:

The first important characteristic is that the indwelling of the Holy Spirit varies from time and place.

The higher the level the Spirit indwells the saint the greater the walk with Christ. The modus operandi of an increased indwelling is loyalty and agape love. Ignorance over the concept of the different levels of the indwelling Spirit has caused much misunderstanding and contention among the brethren.

The second important characteristic is that God tests His faithful ones, called Job-tests in this text, as the saint progresses up the indwelling staircase.

These Job-tests will arrive periodically as the saint climbs the steps of the indwelling presence of the Spirit. Successful completion of each Job-tests merits a higher level indwelling. But most Job-tests are very difficult to pass. The author had one that lasted 10 months. It was devastating! Yet, it opened the door to a vastly higher indwelling for the author. We get nothing without a struggle. Forget the teachings of cheap salvation based on a free ride to heaven. 'Fish do not jump into the boat.'

Most of these deceived saints are facing a terrible surprise when they pass over. The first surprise is that heaven is not opened immediately to them. The second surprise is that they must pass through an Equity Adjustment Queue

166

that could take millennia before the gates of heaven open. The third shock is that they cannot relay this terrible information back to their loved ones.

Yes, it is true that salvation is found only in Jesus Christ, that this is a free and unmerited gift, and that we must proclaim Jesus as our savior in our life to obtain ultimate salvation. But our responsibilities to God do not stop with our proclamation; it is only the beginning. Plunge into the depths of the Christ-walk, therein, to find the fullness of your Savior, Jesus Christ, in the most loving and tender fashion! He is there, waiting for you to join in His exciting walk.

The third important characteristic of personal reform is to identify the difference between a test and a temptation. A test must be confronted and passed; a temptation must be eliminated or bypassed.

Confusion here can be personally devastating. Remember this important clue. In a test, the Holy Spirit, biblical support and fellowship with other saints will not help. If all of your normal support functions seem to fade away, you are in a Job-test! Pass it.

The fourth important characteristic is that within each test, your belief and value system shall be challenged, and to win, your value system must hold Jesus as the highest value.

The fifth important characteristic of this personal climb is the departure of temptation support when in a Job-test.

The saint must pass his or her Job-test without the normal support of the Spirit of God. Biblical support will seem to have vanished. Group support will not touch the problem. Indeed, you and only you are called upon to pass this test. God needs to know your top value in life. Is it Jesus Christ? It is not adequate to simply say: 'It is Jesus.' It must be, and God will find out.

Mostly, the saint does not understand that he or she is in the test, frequently failing to comprehend the differences and difficulties between a test and temptation. Unfortunately, in the current status of the church, largely void of knowledge about Job-tests, the failure rate remains inordinately high. In fact, not many saints climb to the point in their walk with Christ that they can even merit such a test. Content to sit on their unmerited salvation, saved by grace, they never move from the grace generated salvation, failing utterly to contribute to Jesus' mission work. It is this that we must change. And, if we can change it, moving saints away from cheap salvation into overcoming and the work of the Lord, we can effectively impact the potential for the reconstruction of the church, greatly assisting the intervention of God.

Expect a Job-test whenever you make a large-scale improvement in your indwelling presence. Be not afraid! It is the road map of God. If we practice this tough walk with Christ, we will bring our churches to reconstruction when God intervenes.

Now however, the majority of Christians are stuck in or near level one, functioning as baby saints. These are infant or baby saints, even if they have been Christians for decades. Sadly, many clergy reside here. For a more comprehensive examination of the Christ-Walk, read *Christ-Walk: Finding True Worship and the Kingdom of God.*

The indwelling levels of the Holy Spirit largely follow the work of Watchman Nee except for a lower level that reflects the born-again acquisition of the Holy Spirit. This gives four major levels of indwelling. Within this set of indwelling levels hundreds of incremental steps exist between each major indwelling level. In fact, these incremental levels can be set to calculus and represented mathematically.[88]

Here is the table of indwelling of the Holy Spirit. Each page starts at the bottom and works to the top. Thus, to see the entire staircase bottom up, one would have to place each subsequent page on top of the preceding page:

---

88. This has been accomplished in Shults, Eugene C *A Heuristic Mathematical Projection of the Christ-Walk,* scheduled for a later publication date.

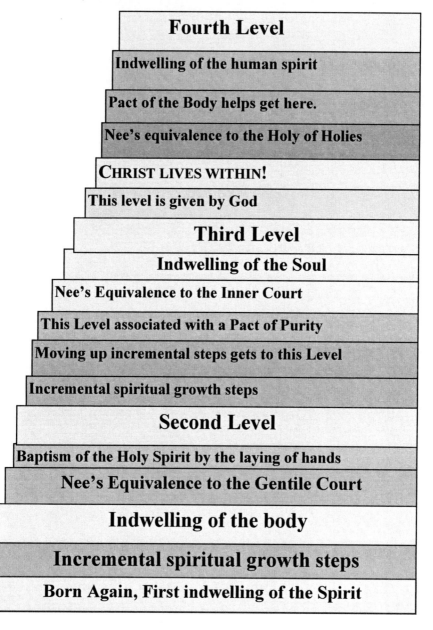

Fourth Level

Indwelling of the human spirit

Pact of the Body helps get here.

Nee's equivalence to the Holy of Holies

CHRIST LIVES WITHIN!

This level is given by God

Third Level

Indwelling of the Soul

Nee's Equivalence to the Inner Court

This Level associated with a Pact of Purity

Moving up incremental steps gets to this Level

Incremental spiritual growth steps

Second Level

Baptism of the Holy Spirit by the laying of hands

Nee's Equivalence to the Gentile Court

Indwelling of the body

Incremental spiritual growth steps

Born Again, First indwelling of the Spirit

CHARTING EACH LEVEL OF THE PROGRESSIVE INDWELLING OF THE HOLY SPIRIT.

DETAILS OF EACH STEP OF THE OVERVIEW CHART

(Each chart is to be read from the bottom up.)

STEPS TO THE FIRST LEVEL:

Born-Again, **First Level** indwelling of the Holy Spirit-The human spirit is regenerated.

Biblical studies commence.

Baptism by water.

The individual joins a community of Christians.

Acceptance of Christ as personal Savior - The sinner's prayer is sincerely recited.

God's grace overflows within that human causing a weeping desire for Christ.

The Holy Spirit focuses on an individual.

STEPS TO THE SECOND LEVEL:

Second Level
BAPTISM OF THE HOLY SPIRIT
Baptism Conveyed by the laying on of hands or occasionally given by God
The second level is Watchman Nee's Equivalence to the Gentile Court
Indwelling of the body
Incremental spiritual growth steps: n-steps to reach the next major level
Brokenness in the Lord
Saint passes a series of Job-tests
Biblical Studies free the Human Spirit

CHARTING THE PROGRESSIVE INDWELLING OF THE HOLY SPIRIT STARTING FROM THE SECOND LEVEL:

STEPS TO THE THIRD LEVEL INDWELLING OF THE HOLY SPIRIT:

Third Level

Indwelling of the Soul

Watchman Nee's Equivalence to the Inner Court of the Jewish Temple

Finds the Baptism by Fire via the Pact of the Body with God:
Discipline of the body

Passing severe Job-tests arrives here

Incremental spiritual growth steps: n-steps to reach the next level

Joins into localized Spiritual Warfare
Becomes available for national combat

Becomes active in deliverance
Learns the value of spiritual bindings

Acquires knowledge of Curses and how to defeat them in oneself and others

STEPS TO THE FOURTH LEVEL INDWELLING OF THE HOLY SPIRIT:

Fourth Level
Only 6,000 saints exist here.

Sanctification via discipline of the inner mind & self get here.

Indwelling of the Human Spirit Essence of the Holy Junction with God.

This is Watchman Nee's equivalence to the Holy of Holies.

Christ lives within!
Higher Justification reached.

Basically, extreme love of God lifts the saint to this level of indwelling.

Reached only after the saint has passed the harshest Job-tests.

Incremental spiritual growth steps: Takes n-steps to reach the next level.

---

89. The author utilized a binary search with the commune with God to find this number, which will greatly increase in the future.

Chapter 19

Another Look at Pauline Theology

Theologians write about the hanging threads of Pauline theology. To wit, they claim that the kingdom of God, redemption as justification by faith, and 'not me but Christ lives within' do not fit together. Hence, for nearly two thousand years, Christendom has hung loose around these three theological concepts. Read this excerpt from Albert Schweitzer:[90]

... this 'being-in-Christ' is the prime enigma of the Pauline teaching: once grasped it gives the clue to the whole.

Continuing with Schweitzer's thoughts, we read from the next page these important words (paraphrased):

The conditions of the second and third century were strikingly different from the first-century, hence Paul's successors, John, Ignatius, Justin, Origen and others Hellenized Paul's Christ-mysticism. This process lost the power of Paul's Christ-mysticism [being-in-Christ], polluting it. Now we have to distill and rework that mysticism for within the experience of the union with Christ we can find what we have lacked:[91]

It [Christ-mysticism] thus holds together kingdom-of-God theology with redemption-through-Christ theology: and this, Schweitzer argues ... both Protestant and Catholic, have signally failed to do, and we have suffered in consequence.

Now the Father wants to resolve this theological difference as we approach the correction of the **second fall**; indeed, becoming an important component in that correction.[92] Pointedly, the Spirit has stated, via the author's personal

---

90. Neill, Stephen & Wright, Tom *The Interpretation of the New Testament*, page 405.
91. Ibid. Page 407.
92. Interestingly, the Spirit was vigorous in His pursuit of the resolution of the *redemption* versus *Christ-within* as an enhancement of the Christian walk and its supporting theology long before the author read **Schweitzer's** theological work, indeed, giving the author the basic concepts in 1986. What confirmation! The only problem was the author did not know what to do with the information nor did he initially appreciate its ultimate significance.

commune, that this theological resolution holds the key to the restoration of individual kingdom spiritual power. Collectively, these theological resolutions will form the basic premises for the re-energizing and reconstruction of the church as it shifts from a carnal to a spiritual church and from a carnal age to the subset age of the Holy Spirit. Thus, advanced in knowledge of our relationship with God, and driven by the power of the Spirit's intervention, we can turn this world back to Jesus' mission vector, there to drive toward the kingdom of God in its initial adaptation to the physical realm. Glory to God!

Here is the essence of this resolution as best understood by the author. We start by defining our terms:

- **Justification** is the ability to exist in the presence of God the Father as if sinless, which Luther taught came exclusively via God's grace.
- **Justification by faith** is the exercise of faith warranting that, by accepting Jesus Christ as the saint's personal Savior, God will impute Jesus' righteousness to that saint by grace even though he or she remains as a sinner.[93] In simpler terms, some saints prefer to look at justification as Jesus standing in front of them when the Father looks in their direction. Another way of looking at justification is that we are in the right relationship with God, and we no longer have to be terrified in His presence.
- **Redemption** is the spiritual opening for individual humans to reach for the entrance to the heavenly kingdom of God, accomplished by the blood sacrifice of Jesus on the Cross.
- **Entrance into the Heavenly Kingdom** is permitted by his or her Justification. Thus Justification by Faith sits (is subsumed) under Redemption.
- '**Not me but Christ lives within**' represents the total conquest of the inner soul (mind) of man so that when God looks upon that person He sees nothing but the Spirit of Christ (The Holy Spirit).

Now summarizing Paul's loose theological threads, they are:

1. **Christ-mysticism**, Paul's concept that the spirit of Jesus lived within, not Paul's original spirit.
2. **Kingdom theology**, the concept that Jesus came to implement the kingdom of God adapted to the physical realm, giving humanity a vector to that task.

---

93. These are Luther and Melanchthon definitions. Placher page 195.

3. **Redemption**, the concept that Jesus came to rescue humanity from the grip of the Adamic Fall with all its resultant curses, freeing humanity to enter the kingdom of heaven. A subset of Redemption is the concept of Justification by faith.

If we can accept the fact that justification can be derived differently, then we are on the trail to reconciliation of these different Pauline theological concepts. The Spirit asserts that Justification can occur by different faith means, one by grace and the other by the deeper indwelling of His presence.

When the individual is so consumed with the Spirit's presence Jesus lives within, then these conditions are met:

- Freedom from the compulsions and the other evil orientations of the subconscious found from the victory of the indwelling Spirit. This saint has reached **emancipation.**
- The **emancipated saint** has reached the minimum of a level-three indwelling status. (See the above schematic of the Spirit's different indwelling capacities.)
- The Father now sees the saint fully justified by the indwelling Spirit of Christ when He looks at the soul/spirit of the saint.
- That saint has reached Christ-mysticism where Paul proclaimed: 'Not-me-but-Jesus-lives-within'.
- This new justification is called Justification-by-Overcoming (Occasionally referred to as Sanctification or Higher Justification).

Critically, unity between these two Pauline theological concepts occurs when Redemption is achieved by Justification by Overcoming, replacing Justification by Faith. With this accomplishment, Redemption theology is united with the 'Christ-within' theology. The third thread of theology, the kingdom of God theology is found naturally because when the saint is filled with Christ, the love of the kingdom of God is within, for the Son of God loves His home. It is natural for the spiritual saint to seek the kingdom of God brought to earth.

Now, all three theological Pauline concepts are united, forming the basis of a new theology, the theology of the Holy Spirit. This new theological approach to the mission of Jesus Christ will be the winning and fulfillment theology of that mission. It forms the support for the Holy Spirit theology. To assist the reader's grasp of theology, all four major theological classifications are listed. Remember, each of the first three main theological positions have multiple variations:[94]

---

94. The author is indebted to Neill, Stephen & Wright, Tom *The Interpretation of the New Testament* for some of this theological insight.

Principle Christian Theologies

1. **Liberal Theology:** Therein, the person of Jesus is de-emphasized even as His teachings are promoted. These range from Arians to atheistic groups such as Secular Humanists. Soul/spirits from these groups are fortunate if they can avoid the pit.

2. **Encompassing Church Theology:** Therein, the saint finds their salvation exclusively from within the *mother* church. The Roman Catholic Church and the Orthodox Churches are the best, but not the exclusive examples, of this type of theology. This theology sees the Bible as the byproduct of their canon with the dogmas of the church as the determining factor in the soul/spirit's salvation. Sacraments are uniquely important in this process. Most of these soul/spirits flood the Equity Adjustment Queues, which they call purgatory, each in far greater pain and misery than anticipated.

3. **Redemptive Theology:** Therein, accepting Jesus as that saint's personal Savior redeems the saint. Redemption is by justification by faith, that situation in which the soul/spirit will be justified, that is, allowed into the presence of God without destruction. Grace is the key to this faith justification. Once justified, subsequent sin cannot destroy that stance. This theology dominates Protestant churches in one or more variation. One enhancement is the concept that some are privileged to be predestined. Sin or other actions cannot impact this status; nor can any act or good deed achieve it. The Spirit of God often refers to this theology as Cheap Salvation, with these poor participating soul/spirits also flooding the Equity Adjustment Queue. Each of these soul/spirits is in desperate misery with no apparent escape since no awareness exists among their loved ones that they can be helped.

4. **Holy Spirit Theology:** Therein, the soul/spirit accepts Jesus Christ as his or her personal Savior, but then strives to reach the greatest indwelling of the Holy Spirit possible. In this theology, the saint struggles to overcome with the assistance of the indwelling presence of the Holy Spirit. This is the theology of the personal and cultural struggle, the proper theology of Christianity. It is the theology that emphasizes the Overcomer; the struggle to find perfection as aided and led by the Spirit of

God. In many respects, this theology is the correction and fulfillment of the Redemption Theology, allowing the vision of the Kingdom into the soul and spirit of the saints. It is the theology permitting the mystery of the **Holy Junction** with its closeness to the Father and the Son. Yet, mostly this theology is not understood or even articulated by the Spirit-filled churches. However, once this problem is corrected by the Spirit's forthcoming intervention, great and wondrous events will descend upon our planet and its surviving peoples - all readily absorbed and supported by the implementation generation. The events of the world will shift dramatically when an adequate number of these overcoming spirit-filled implementation saints, God's critical mass, reach Overcoming Justification. The drive for the kingdom of God shall overflow into the culture, driving the implementation of the kingdom on earth for that culture.

REVIEWING

Let us review these important concepts. The fourth class of theology, the theology of the Holy Spirit with its emphasis on the indwelling presence of the Holy Spirit, is the proper theology of Christianity. Justification by Faith is not destroyed, but rather redefined into its true role in the affairs of the saint, for Justification by Faith protects the saint while seeking the greater indwelling presence of the Spirit.

Comprehending that *redemption* really means *rescue* generates a better grasp of the unification of these three Pauline theological concepts for some saints. Scripture states that the rescue of each soul/spirit is a dual process. The first major process in Jesus' rescue is represented by John 3:36:

Whoever believes in the Son has eternal life, but whoever rejects the Son will not see life, for God's wrath remains on him (John 3:36).

Here, Justification by Faith is activated, protecting the saint. Augustine and Luther claim that this form of salvation is unmerited and free of searching. Pelagius challenged Augustine declaring that human volition as well as decisions of the mind can assist each saint in finding personal salvation. Augustine won this argument and had Pelagius declared a heretic. But the Spirit sides with Pelagius and says that salvation is a combination of the Spirit of God's unsolicited assistance, called grace, and the individual's willful selection of Christ as a personal Savior. All *altar calls* are such combinations.

Now let us consider the conditions of Jesus' rescue of humanity. Adam and Eve betrayed the Father and He has been distrustful of human freewill ever since. The Father has even distrusted human acceptance of the rescue generated by His Son. Accordingly, God is determined to test all soul/spirits before readmitting them into His eternal presence even if they proclaim their love of His Son. Someplace in that saint's life that love will be tested. Even the thief on the cross had his faith tested by his suffering. Does this statement fit with Augustine or with Pelagius? Obviously, it fits with Pelagius. So, since it appears that the wrong man won this fifth century argument, are there any repercussions rippling through the centuries to our time? Yes, and they are enormous. They include the wrong course for Christianity, one based on inadequate premises, such as cheap saluation, which have generated enormous defeats for humankind, as individuals, as a church and as a culture. These defeats, epitomized in this book as the **second fall**, have definitely impacted our potential to reach the Great Commission and implement the kingdom of God on earth!

The second major process of Jesus' rescue is found in the continuous seeking after the kingdom of God and God's great righteousness represented by Matthew 6:33:

But seek first His Kingdom and His righteousness and all these things will be given to you as well (Matthew 6:33).

The righteousness of God is found in the indwelling of the Holy Spirit, ever increasing until that point is reached in which the Christ-mysticism is activated. The saint that has Christ-within, not self, has reached the highest level of sanctification, equated to maximum overcoming. Here, justification is achieved by overcoming via the deep indwelling of the Christ Spirit, the Holy Spirit, because the Father sees His Son when He looks upon this saint. To understand this concept, the saint must appreciate that Jesus has a glorified body on the right hand the Father and cannot indwell you. But rather His Spirit, the Holy Spirit, can and does indwell the receptive saint in the physical realm. By realizing that God's righteousness can be achieved only when we have reached that threshold status of the indwelling Spirit called sanctification, which we also call Overcoming Justification, and which is the approximation to the complete indwelling of the Holy Spirit, all the pieces of this puzzle fall into place. True Justification is not by grace but by the profound indwelling of the Holy Spirit. This concept unifies Pauline theology.

Repeating for emphasis and understanding, we have the following unity within Pauline theology between 1) Redemption (Justification), 2) the Drive to Bring the Kingdom of God to earth, adapted to our physical plane, and 3) Christ-mysticism, 'not-I-but-Christ-lives-within':

- First, in optimized sanctification (Overcoming Justification) we reach Redemption (rescue by justification) found in the Christ-mysticism, because the Father sees Jesus in the Christ-Spirit, the Holy Spirit, when He looks upon that soul/spirit. Thus we have reached the wedding of Redemption and its subdivision, Justification, with 'not-I-but-Christ-lives-within,' allowing these two strands of Pauline theology to blend.
- Second, the heavy presence of the Spirit of Christ warrants the knowledge and love of the kingdom of God within the heart of the saint, for Christ loves His heavenly home. This fulfills the Luke 17:20-21 prerequisite that the kingdom must arrive first in the hearts of the saints.
- Third, the comparison of the kingdom of God with the contemporary culture by the born-again Spirit-filled saint leaves a yearning for the kingdom of God in the heart and soul of that human. This emancipates that soul/spirit from the brainwashing captivity of any culture in which that soul/spirit happens to be found. Hence, the saint truly reaches the true born-again standing, as seen by God.
- Fourth, when a critical mass of saints in Overcoming Justification is generated within any given culture that culture begins to transform into the kingdom of God. Thus, the third strand, the drive to bring the kingdom of God to earth, is blended with the other two and Pauline theology is united.

With this knowledge, we have the key to the preparation for the forthcoming intervention of God in the affairs of humanity. Seek the indwelling presence of the Holy Spirit to find knowledge of God's kingdom and His imputed righteousness. In this optimum position, if God elects to take your physical life, rejoice. If He elects to use you to reach others, rejoice. As the instrument of God, you are His to be used as He deems, praising God always. So warned, prepare yourself.

FINDING THE DEEPER WALK

To find a deeper indwelling of the Holy Spirit each saint must seek after it. Do not become entrapped by the grace-is-sufficient and human-seeking-is-unnecessary teachings. Read the red ink! Listen to the Lord Jesus and always seek a closer walk with Him! Look at life as a climb to a higher-level relationship with Jesus and His Father.

To start this climb each saint will require a true born again experience; wherein, the saint can break out of the brainwashing captivity of his or her birth and biased educational inculcations. Here is the mistake of modern evangelical Christianity: They have polluted the words of our Savior about the extremely important subject of being born again. As received from the Spirit this teaching is so much more than what is taught. Yet, we must ask what is worse, to teach a weak version or not to teach it at all? For many institutional churches like the Roman Catholic and Orthodox Churches seldom teach the born again concept to their lay people. Here is the pertinent Biblical Scripture:

I tell you the truth, unless a man is born again, he cannot see the kingdom of God (John 3:3).

The pollution of this precious Scripture occurs because the churches practice cheap salvation: You are saved; now return to our cooperative partner, our heathen secular culture, and practice being a competitive heathen confident in your salvation.

Instead, the church needs to state that if you cannot see the kingdom of God you are not born again. And when one sees that kingdom, that saint sees the comparison with our existing and vastly inferior culture. Therein the saint is set free from his or her cultural brainwashing even as his or her human spirit is regenerated. With this tougher and more exact filter, the number of born again Protestant Christians equals the number of Catholic born again Christians. Sadly, not enough!

Yet with the knowledge that God wants so much more from each of us, many saints, those with the love of Christ carried deeply within, will surge forward and find the true born again status. There they will realize that reaching the born again status is not just a one time, thrilling spiritual experience but a total change of the soul/spirit into a life-long pursuit of Jesus and His mission on earth for each of us.

In this breakout, each saint must find the minimum spiritual freedom necessary for the Spirit's flourishing to excel in the Christ-Walk.

Four personal repudiations are necessary to scale this ascension of the Spirit's presence. The first is the rejection of Christian religiosity that restricts the freedom and the maneuverability of the Spirit within your life. The second is the personal repudiation of the Pact of Cooperation as an essential component of Christianity. The third is the embrace of the divinity of Jesus Christ as the Son of God incarnated to save each of us. Embrace the mystery of the Trinity God. Then, fourth, to fully climb this ascension and find the fullness of existence, extend your love to the dynamic Holy Spirit. It is here, in this ascension, that the real essence of human existence can be grasped. Avoid the many alternative spiritual paths that exist in the human experience such as:

- Zen Buddhism
- Sufism, mystical lineage of Islamic traditions
- Hari Krishna
- New Age, especially channeling
- Kabbalah, Jewish mysticism
- Hinduism
- Mantra cults
- Cults utilizing imaging
- Cults declaring a path parody to a light
- Cults with spirit guides
- Psychic readings
- Astrology
- Tarot card readings.

None of these contemplative practices, deep wisdom philosophies or divination practices can save you from the inevitability of the second death or even lead you to the deeper understanding of true existence. Only the Doorway can do this, and the Doorway is Christ Jesus, and His Counselor on earth is the Holy Spirit. The secret to overcoming with higher-level justification is to know this fact: That which permits freedom of movement in the throne room of the Father is the deeper indwelling of the Spirit of God. This is Overcoming Justification. Seek it!

If you carry personal doubts about the different levels of the Holy Spirit's indwelling, reach for Holy Scripture for your confirmation, starting with Acts 8 which strongly indicates that, for a full walk with Christ, a saint must have the indwelling Spirit.

When they [Peter and John] arrived, they prayed for them that they might receive the Holy Spirit, because the Holy Spirit had not yet come upon any of them; they had simply been baptized into the name of the Lord Jesus (Acts 8:15-16).

Clearly, this scripture leaves the fervent Christian with no choice but to obey the Savior by seeking out the Baptism of the Holy Spirit:

'Do not leave Jerusalem, but wait for the gift my Father promised, which you have heard me speak about. For John baptized with water, but in a few days you will be baptized with the Holy Spirit' (Acts 1:4-5).

As we all know, that initial baptism for the church occurred at Pentecost. Since that occurrence, the apostles have passed on the baptism of the Holy Spirit by the laying-on-of-hands. That this happened in the primitive church is clearly seen in Acts 8:

Then Peter and John placed their hands on them and they received the Holy Spirit (Acts 8:17).

As the church organized itself, the laying-on-of-hands became the sacrament of Confirmation. When the churches lost their spiritual power with the forfeiture of the vector of Jesus Christ exchanged for political power, that sacrament lost its power. This is **legacy blunder eight**.

Yet, Jesus returned this baptism in force to the church in the Pentecostal and Charismatic revivals of the twentieth century, enabling, once again, the transference of the indwelling Spirit through the generations by the laying-on-of hands. This baptism transference operates by a spirit-filled saint passing it on down to whomever requests it. Religious syntax is not necessary and can even be counterproductive.

Frequently one can see a layperson conveying the anointing of the Holy Spirit to a cleric. Obviously, religious authorities resent this intrusion into their dominion with many clerics hating this unauthorized outpouring of the Spirit, probably denying it comes from God. These church authorities kicked out the Pentecostals and moved to discourage the Protestant and Catholic Charismatic revivals, meeting with considerable success. God, have mercy on their souls!

Despite the success of the organized religions, this informal baptism of the Holy Spirit is still available if you will but seek it out.

After true rebirth, the baptism of the Holy Spirit opens the door to Christian spiritual adulthood and the deeper indwelling of the Holy Spirit, leaving the stagnant trail of the carnal Christian for the dynamic path of the spiritual saint. Seeking will gain the indwelling presence of the Christ Spirit, gaining therein, the imputed righteousness of God. No other personal preparation can warrant your participation in the forthcoming arrival of the kingdom of God.

Righteousness as an integral characteristic of a human soul/spirit does not exist. We can only find God's righteousness imputed to us via grace or the indwelling Holy Spirit. Remember, and never forget, this critical fact of spiritual and physical life:

Under the Blood of the Lamb, God's imputed righteousness is found either through God's grace or the indwelling Spirit of God. Grace is the unmerited and uncontrolled blessing of God; the indwelling Spirit is the sought out presence of God formed and nurtured in agape love. Seeking cannot find grace, but it can find the indwelling Spirit. So seek out a maximum indwelling of the Holy Spirit for your life, turning your body into the temple of God, always recognizing that the Spirit of God loves to be cherished and cherishes being loved!

GRACE

But wait! What are you telling us, that we should seek out the indwelling of the Holy Spirit instead of grace? Is not grace the foundation of Protestantism as well as the focus of Catholicism? Yes, Luther and Melanchthon both declared that grace imputed God's righteousness to the individual and that accordingly, no willful act on the part of that individual, i.e., good deeds, could impact or change that imputation. Not even sin can affect it. The Catholics at Trent agreed, but they claimed that God's grace always assisted us to become better saints. The emphasis on grace in many forms of non-liturgical Protestantism teaches that grace is the ticket to heaven and nothing you do, either evil or good, will make any difference. This is usually linked with predestination. This means that sin is of no consequence once you have been justified to righteousness by grace. They are not saying that you should sin, but if you do, it will make no difference to your eternal salvation. This is the supreme case for cheap salvation, and it is not a valid position for any Christian, let alone hundreds of millions. Luther must have never read Hebrews 10:26-27 or Mathew 12:36-37:

If we deliberately keep on sinning after we have received the knowledge of the truth, no sacrifice for sins is left, but only a fearful expectation of judgment and of raging fire that will consume the enemies of God (Hebrew 10:26-27).

But I tell you that men will have to give account on the Day of Judgment for every careless word they have spoken. For by your words you will be acquitted, and by your words you will be condemned (Matthew 12:36-37).

To know and accept these verses is to know and accept true salvation. Further, it is alleged that the well-accepted position of Justification by Faith found through the imputation of the righteousness of God by grace, thus freeing us from the burden of sin, is based on an incomplete comprehension of grace. So what is grace? Seemingly, no preacher, no teacher or any theologian can define it except to define its action: unmerited assistance from God.

184

We need the answers to these questions:

What is grace?
Who administers it?
How is it measured?
Where does it come from?
Can we solicit it?

Seeking the answer from the author's personal 25 year old commune with God, appreciating the difficulties of a binary communication system with God, these responses appear valid: Grace is the manifestation of the actions of the Holy Spirit even as represented by this scripture:

How much more severely do you think a man deserves to be punished ...
who has insulted the Spirit of grace (Hebrew 10:29).

God governs and distributes grace through His Spirit and indeed is His Spirit. Mary has nothing to do with it, as twentieth century Roman Catholic dogma would have us believe.

Grace has definitive dimensions, of which humanity is not yet able to measure. Despite claims to the contrary, we cannot solicit grace, except under special exception in the **Holy Junction**, thus, giving it the appearance of capriciousness to the human recipient. However, the indwelling presence of the Holy Spirit functions as a fountain of grace, but with the following differences. The indwelling of the Holy Spirit, as an agreement between the human host temple and the Holy Spirit, enables consistency with a measure of host control. Through the commune with God we can measure the indwelling presence of the Spirit, and we can solicit the indwelling Spirit for purpose or cause.

Thus, we must recognize that the Holy Spirit can function in two modes, one within and one from outside the human temple. It is the same Spirit but in a different contract. Outside the human, the Spirit is seeking to move that soul/spirit into the status of a Temple. Thus, by definition, the greater of the two is the indwelling presence, else why would the Spirit work so hard on moving each human into the Temple status? Grace then is the offensive weapon of God in bringing soul/spirits to Him. It also assists the saint in spiritual warfare. Moreover, the indwelling presence of God in the form of His Spirit is the vehicle for the perfection of that soul as a battle warrior for the Lord Jesus. We grow as we hone the temple, a reciprocal process of agape love. Hence, it is to the indwelling presence that we must look for Justification, not grace!

Then let us summarize. Whenever the Spirit of God touches an individual from outside, it is grace. When the individual receives help from the indwelling Spirit of God, as the temple of God, it is spiritual growth.

Let us evaluate some of the important differences. Grace can be a one-time assist of finite duration, unknown to the recipient, whereas, inner assistance is enduring and perpetuating, known to the recipient. Grace cannot make a spiritual saint; only the consistent indwelling presence of the Spirit of God can generate that capacity. Grace cannot bring the fruits into perfection; only the indwelling presence of God can do that. And of course, while grace can activate the gifts of the Holy Spirit for a one-time application, only the presence of the Holy Spirit can generate the constant presence of the gifts of the Holy Spirit within a soul/spirit.

The following table defines the differences:

TABLE OF DIFFERENCE BETWEEN GRACE AND THE INDWELLING SPIRIT

FEATURES:	Grace	Indwell
Sustaining	No	Yes
Make a spiritual saint?	No	Can
Perfect the Fruits	No	Yes
Exercise Gifts	Yes	Yes
Bring Unbeliever to Christ?	Yes	No
Impute Righteousness	Usually No	Can
Help in Spiritual War	Yes	Yes

Another factor exists. Since grace is unknown, often detected only in hindsight, with unknown duration, the receiving saint frequently disabuses it, or, if grace is not disabused, it is not utilized to its maximum. The saint cannot measure it or call it forth. The saint cannot argue with it or love it. It is an unknown stranger that silently slips into and out of our lives. All these grace negatives are reversed with the indwelling Spirit of God.

This means that a grace dependent faith system such as mainline Protestantism and Catholicism is, by definition, religions lacking the sustaining fullness of the power of God. Hence, our spiritually dead churches! This is a grave charge against the contemporary churches, to be taken seriously, for the hope of the world resides in the health of Jesus' true church. **For largely unknown or unacknowledged, the future of humanity is lashed to the functionality of the church. If the church dies, humanity dies. If the church flounders on an incorrect course, humanity degenerates in the wrong direction [our current situation]. If the church soars, humanity shall soar. It is best that we come to this understanding immediately, appreciating the utter importance of the proper church critique in order to restore it to its prime mission, the building of the kingdom of God on earth.** So the discussion about grace is not just a remote and largely irrelevant event; rather, it is central to our continuance as a species on this planet. See this, and you see wisdom!

But wait, there is more to consider about grace. Let each saint appreciate that Grace is unsolicited, the freely given, unmerited intervention of the Spirit of God into our lives, whereas the indwelling of the Holy Spirit is an invited guest. Can we grasp this difference and treasure its crucial distinction in our lives? Pray on this, for its significance is great. Is your life based on grace, which is elusive to you, or is it based on the indwelling spirit of God, which is not elusive?

But there are surprises. Grace can be more powerful than the indwelling Spirit. What? Explain that! The Holy Spirit functioning under the restraints of an indifferent host - the condition of baby Christians focused on grace - cannot focus His indwelling power. Whereas, that same Holy Spirit, outside that same saint, without the constraining limits of that human's lacking love, can apply unmerited and unlimited grace. Hence, the baby saint can experience the Holy Spirit as grace on a larger scale than the nominal indwelling of the Holy Spirit. It is the same Spirit trying to move the saint toward Jesus but operating under different criteria. Significantly however, once the saint has reached a larger indwelling of the Spirit, that point where the love of the saint combines with the power of the indwelling Spirit to gain enormous kingdom spiritual power, this situation reverses. Then the Spirit is enabled to work in the welcomed state more powerfully and substantially over a longer time than He can when confined to grace.

188

So what is that indwelling point where the welcoming love of the soul/spirit combines with that saint's obtained indwelling level of God to offset the out-of-body application of God? Somewhere near the level two indwelling of the Spirit generated by Jesus' baptism: The baptism of the Holy Spirit.

Thus, it is easy to observe why a person, like Martin Luther, who only gave a superficial acknowledgement to the Holy Spirit, contemptuously calling the Holy Spirit's indwelling of Muntzer as a bird with feathers which must be swallowed,[95] [96] would concentrate on grace, building an entire faith system from this perspective. Also, clearly, it is fair to state that this faith system is not wrong (these saints have a deep love for Jesus), just that it is inadequate because it does not generate spiritual Christians and substantially fails in its blessed assurance of heaven. The Spirit says that there will be many unhappy surprises after physical death, even giving the author a 45-second look at a place of misery less than the pit but not hell, perhaps to qualify the author for this warning: Be careful; it is horrible. Nothing in life can balance this terror. In fact, all decisions of life must be seriously considered in the light of this monstrous post-life misery.

Subsequently, the author has named this place of horror as the Equity Adjustment Queue where soul/spirits work out the damage caused in their life because they accepted the Cheap Salvation message, continuing unabatedly in a sinful life. The good news is that every one in the Equity Adjustment Queue is eventually destined to heaven. The bad news is that the Equity Adjustment Queue is horrible, confounding its description. Words fail here. As a former Navy tailhook pilot the author is not overly squeamish, but the author screamed out for Jesus' rescue the entire 45 seconds, and so will you! Better to do it now, than then. Listen carefully, especially all you overconfident folks that think your brainwashed belief system is supreme just because you belong to it. Forget your false façade of confidence. Become frightened! No one needs this judgment!

What can that total experience be like? Even the analogy of a sinking ship, forcing one to swim to shore, exhausting oneself after a day of swimming to finally experience the ecstasy of firm land can only touch the experience of those who finally make it to the just-in level of heaven.[97]

---

95. Placher, Page 186.

96. How close did the father of Protestantism come to the unpardonable sin? Close, but the Spirit says he made it into heaven with a contrite heart and a heavy burden for those he misled on the indwelling and purgatory issues. Let everyone remember God used Luther to release freedom and the Holy Scriptures into our lives.

97. The author has been privileged to participate in this venture, assisting others making it into the just-in level of heaven, a few with easily recognizable names. The Spirit often tells of joy unexcelled of those who finally make it. The oldest souls that the author has helped push from the Holy Junction are from the first century, waiting for over 1900 years. Wow!

Clearly, the enormous present day reliance on grace cannot bring the kingdom of God to the physical plane as the evidence of the last 500 years has shown so abundantly. Let us all recognize that the Spirit's presence in grace, i.e., the power of grace, has declined over the centuries as the Spirit has been continuously insulted and ignored. At the same time the power of the indwelling Spirit is magnified by the love of the host. It is for this reason that we will see more Smith Wigglesworths appear in the modern world.

Beloved of God, armed with the knowledge of the past, we must shift our focus to the future. If not, the intervention of God will be too shocking, and many saints will unnecessarily lose their faith. Come; prepare for that future by drawing dramatically closer to Christ! Prepare to join in the **Overchurch**, recognizing that every component of your life must be in tune with Jesus and led by the Holy Spirit. Seek the indwelling Spirit, and you will find Him as never before!

Chapter 20

Facing the Reality of the Impersonator

Christianity is the hope of the world; its only hope. Accordingly, over the centuries, the enemy of God and his allies have directed a fierce campaign against the faithful, achieving unrequited success to date! Part of that success resides in the widespread inculcation of deception within the Body of Christ, specifically in the form of the impersonator. So what is the impersonator? And what role does it play in determining our present predicament buried deep in the **second fall**?

The **impersonator** is an evil entity, which is capable of inhabiting the saint, acting as the Holy Spirit. The prime mandate of the impersonator is not possession or oppression but deception. Hence, since the impersonator plans on being in the host human for the rest of that human's life, the impersonator will not act outside of its assigned role unless seriously provoked or exposed. [It appears that this chapter, which reveals its secret role, can be that provocation, so if you have a difficult and turbulent time reading this material, then be on guard; you may have the problem.] Thus, the impersonator represents the most insidious and concealed form of deception facing Christians. So devious is this deception that most saints have never heard of this evil. Neither have they been warned of its serious consequences. Obviously, this is a major legacy blunder of the Christian churches, one which requires our utmost attention if we are to succeed in defeating it. To overcome this evil attack of the enemy of God, it is our responsibility to comprehend the strategy of the enemy. Only then can we thwart it. The key to this success resides in recognizing the distinction between Satan's use of both oppression and fabrication. Each attack mode seeks to destroy you, but one faction wants to accomplish this goal by oppressing and possessing your will, usably arriving under the cover of your sins; while the other group desires to trick you, arriving as the Holy Spirit, hoping to mislead you at those critical times in your life. For instance, imagine the secret joy that the oppressing agent of the enemy experiences when a saint that has the impersonator tries to cast it out? Deception all the way around! That deliverance cannot be successful, although there will be a serious effort to make it look like a success.

Clever, the impersonator will tolerate talk of Jesus as the Son of God, although it is careful about proclaiming it, thus circumnavigating and defeating the biblical check that states the enemy of God and his workers cannot proclaim Jesus' divinity. The impersonator will tolerate the proclamation of Jesus' divinity even as it maintains a strong reluctance to broadcast this faith knowledge. This reluctance is most noticeable in the lack of witnessing that the deceived saint will conduct, especially in his or her place of secular employment. The impersonator will mention love and profess fanatical devotion to creed, canon and religiosity of a denominational church, frequently identifying the deceived saint as the most loyal of the church-going congregation. The impersonator usually can be recognized by its hate, especially of other Christians and all people of differences. In the educated saint, this hate is cloaked but still persists. Its main mandate is to generate lukewarmness to God and division among the brethren, and to achieve this, it will affirm a large percentage of true Biblical teachings, constantly promoting the study of the Bible either exclusively by the intellect or with the impersonator in which case it will mislead at the critical time. It will encourage membership of secret societies, being most comfortable in that environment. It currently possesses 62 percent of all saints proclaiming themselves as Spirit-filled Christians and dwells within a much larger percentage of baby saints, including an exceptionally high percentage of those saints that claim to be born again.[98] Totally, it is the principle reason for today's dead churches, strongly indwelling our ministers, priests and higher church authorities as well as the laity. This infiltration of impersonators, with the subsequent degradation of the true indwellings of the Holy Spirit, is a thoroughly frightening, terrifying and unacceptable situation! We must sound the alarm!

... if you receive a different spirit from the one you received, or a different gospel from the one you accepted, you put up with it easily enough (2 Corinthians 11:4).

And if anyone does not have the Spirit of Christ he does not belong to Christ (Romans 8:9).

We must identify and cast out the impersonator wherever found. However, there is a danger in this process. We must not allow our newly acquired knowledge about the impersonator to degenerate into spiritual and religious tyranny. Accordingly, let us not go around saying: '*you have the impersonator.*' Rather, let us use the Spirit of God to identify and then attack this evil presence by employing the intercessory instruments He has designated for this correction.

It is conceivable that in intercessory warfare the victimized saint could remain ignorant of the spiritual action unfolding around him or her. If the deceived saint's heart rests with Jesus any spiritual intercession to defeat a possible impersonator in that saint can only strengthening the Body of Christ by freeing that saint from his or her insidious deception. In this same manner, a

---

98. This percentage was found using binary search with the commune.

entire congregation could be cleansed by the intercessors of that church, lifting that church from carnal dead to spiritual and alive for Christ. Further, if we could mobilize the intercessors of the nation to this cause, a great step forward could be accomplished.

HUMAN PROBLEMS SPONSORED BY THE IMPERSONATOR

The impersonator utilizes the **psychic force center** of the human to surreptitiously increase the influence of Satan in the life of the captured saint. The psychic force center is that power position within the human soul that has the capacity to explore the supernatural realm of the enemy of God. This connection exists via each human's psychic force center, activated at conception as the product of the Adamic fall. From this position of rapid access, the enemy monitors the actions and thoughts of the saint. With these capacities, especially his ability to read the human mind, mistakenly held by some saints as impossible, the enemy of God and his workers maintain a flow of temptations into the mind of the human. The psychic force center is also the door for other influences, even sophisticated belief systems and philosophy. However, to utilize this power center for supernatural knowledge is to unite with the enemy of God, destroying the opportunity to find Jesus. God *never* communicates to the human through the psychic force center. God's main communication method is via the human spirit.

It is the responsibility of the saint to shut down his or her psychic force center connection with the evil kingdom. Indeed, to close this door is to move the saint toward sanctification. Hence, each saint should constantly pray for the closing of the door to his or her psychic force center, shutting out the enemy of God.[99]

Tyranny convictions are those belief systems, such as secular humanism, New Age, Occultism or atheism, which so control the human mind that they prevent that human from finding the walk with Christ. These convictions are supported and encouraged by the impersonator, accounting for the drift of Christians into the secular thought world from which escape is difficult.

However, it is a serious misunderstanding that scientific investigations are antithetical to Jesus. Actually, the reverse is true. The saint can be an active participate in scientific investigation even while maintaining a vigorous walk with Christ. However, the presence of the impersonator will prevent this combination.

---

99. Read Watchman Nee, *Latent Power of the Soul* for a better introduction to this problem.

The **paradox of life** is the knowledge of the mind that it is both the opportunity and the obstacle of life. Therein, the mind must learn that it can free and guide the human spirit to the divide between physical and spiritual existence. From this spiritual position the mind can prepare the launching of its human spirit into the throne room of the spiritual God, becoming a spiritual saint. However, if the mind becomes too obsessive of its knowledge acquisition capacities in the physical realm, then it can never recognize or discover its role in this launch into spiritual Love. This danger is widespread among intellectuals. Summarizing, the mind must grow to learn it is the obstacle. It is obvious that the presence of the impersonator will prevent the intellect from discovering or implementing any of the above spiritual judgments, thus closing the road to the status of the spiritual saint for that person.

METHOD OF ELIMINATING THE IMPERSONATOR

The **Spirit-Check Prayer** is the prayer request of the saint for his or her cleansing, designed to rid the saint of the impersonator. The requesting saint does not need to be in the **Holy Junction**. The Spirit-Check can be expressed specifically as a prayer. Here is that prayer:

SPIRIT-CHECK PRAYER, THE PURIFICATION & FREEDOM PLEA

Father, I praise you for sending your Son, Jesus Christ, to save me. You are my God forever, always demonstrating your patient love. Please look upon me; I need your loving help again. I stand before you stripped of my arrogance, humble, a sinner repenting, pleading for your help. Free me from deception; send your Spirit upon me to flush deception and oppression from me, driving the enemy before Him!

Jesus, you are my hope; it is you that I love. I thank you from the depths of my soul and the heights of my spirit for opening the door of heaven to me. Now, I ask for more! Please, Savior, break the curses that protect the presence of the enemy of God, even the curse that shields the presence of the impersonator. Even more, I plead that you would break those self-inflicted curses that so bind me, freeing me from their induced addictions so that I can have a greater walk with you, Jesus. Thank you Savior.

Omnipotent Holy Spirit, your companionship is cherished, for you carry the presence of Christ; please do not abandon me because of my sinfulness, but in my repentance increase your indwelling! Fill me with your presence. Grant peace to my soul, love in my spirit, and courage in my will. Help me be free. Cleanse me!

Trusting in that help and in Jesus' name, I take control over any spiritual entities, especially those fallen angels that would impersonate you, binding them, stopping their activities. BE BOUND NOW!

Spirit of God, help me drive them and their allies away, forcefully, urgently, and permanently. With your permission, I rebuke these spiritual evil forces masquerading as you and command them in Jesus' name: LEAVE, NOW!

Holy Spirit, flood me with your presence, driving deception and oppression in front of you, filling my emptiness with your presence. Allow your anointing to measure this victory. And grant to me a larger measure of your love and peace. Amen!

The **Spirit-Check Shower** is the Spirit-Check prayer requested without actually reciting the prayer. Once you have prayed the prayer, God will allow your request for the prayer in places where you cannot recite it, such as work. Used in this fashion, it becomes the real time spiritual shower of the Holy Spirit. When so evoked, the anointing of the Holy Spirit descends from outside the individual to flood over the requesting individual, cleansing that human. To get this shower, the saint simply asks for the Spirit-Check shower. Repeating, this request is only effective after the prayer has been recited initially and sincerely at some time in the saint's life. This gift means that the Lord is giving us the opportunity to be cleansed of the trash of the day, during the day, even while working. Certainly, this is a neat gift from God.

Here are the methods that the enemy of God utilizes to infest the saints with the impersonator. Remember, the impersonator is evil beyond measure and will not respond to normal deliverance, unless specifically named.

INFESTATIONS OF THE IMPERSONATOR:

1. The saint undergoes a born again experience and receives the level one presence of the Holy Spirit. If the saint ignores the presence of the Spirit, largely because of denominational teaching weaknesses, the Spirit of God will withdraw. Satan will almost always substitute his impersonator, dooming that saint to the infant Christian status for the rest of that saint's earthly life.
2. The saint receives the baptism of the Holy Spirit from a saint filled with the impersonator.
3. The saint undergoes the baptism of the Holy Spirit but does not receive the Holy Spirit for some reason, perhaps because of

inadequate seeking after forgiveness. Desperate to look like others that have received the Holy Spirit that saint attempts to fake the indwelling presence. Satan will then infill that saint with his impersonator.

4. The saint is properly filled with the Holy Spirit but ignores, rejects, or even blasphemes against the Holy Spirit, causing the Spirit of God to depart. Immediately, Satan will infill the saint with one of his impersonators.

5. The saint makes the mistake of utilizing his or her psychic force center for special knowledge, amusement or entertainment, e.g., the ouija board, psychic reading or serious occult activities. The impersonator could be dispatched to perform as a channeling spirit or a spirit guide.[100]

6. Satan asks for the soul of the saint. If this request is not blocked by the faith of the saint or the intercession of the Holy Spirit, then the enemy of God sifts and possesses that soul in one of two modes: 1) Outright by demonic possession or 2) Surreptitiously, through the impersonator. It is to be recognized that all souls that have been asked for by Satan can be freed by soliciting the assistance of the Holy Spirit, best done in the **Holy Junction**. Faith is a protective shield in this ugly matter and since faith is a gift of the Holy Spirit, those saints with a deep indwelling of the Holy Spirit are shielded. Moreover, the deviousness of Satan's action against the unprotected has led to the increasing decline of the carnal church. As the leadership of the church has become increasingly secularized, causing it to move farther away from the Holy Spirit, 32 percent of all saints with the impersonator, today, have resulted from the unblocked evil solicitation and sifting of those souls. Making this matter even more serious is that those souls solicited by the enemy of God, and never reversed, cannot make it into the Equity Adjustment Queue. They are lost forever. This unfortunate list includes those soul/spirits with the most potential to do a vast work for God, else why would the enemy ask to sift? Refer to the situation with Peter in Luke 22:31. **Simon, Simon, Satan has asked to sift you as wheat. But I have prayed for you, Simon, that your faith may not fail**. So, it is vital that each of us invite the true Holy Spirit to indwell us, to provide the faith necessary to turn back the request of the enemy of God. Then we should use the Spirit-Check Shower

---

100. Here is an important teaching. Impersonators and spirit guides are the same evil spirit!

to stay spiritually clean. Enforce our walk with Spirit-assisted study of Holy Scripture. Then embrace agape love in all aspects of our daily life, starting in our homes.

7. Satan can ask for and sift a social organization. Most if not all members of the *asked for* organization will eventually end up with the impersonator. Examples of social organizations, which the enemy of God seeks, are secret clubs, universities, congregations, denominations, governmental agencies, NGOs, and nations. Since this information is largely new, there has not been an effective prayer intercession for these victimized groups, some which carry the most prominent names in the world. Perhaps, this explains the Lord's interest in tearing down and rebuilding our entire social structure. To fully grasp what is being said here, restate Luke 22:31 as follows: **America, America, Satan has asked to sift you as wheat. But I have prayed for you, America, that your faith may not fail.** But it has failed! Hence, before God will intervene and move our nation into the next minor dispensation, the subset age of the Holy Spirit, the saints must stop and reverse Satan's claim on our nation, including the previously sifted social groups mentioned above. Thus we find ourselves in a paradox. God must intervene to save us, but we must first repel Satan's request to sift us before we can reach God's intervention. To accomplish this deed, selected saints must join together to practice societal intercession, which will enable these groups to reach a higher level of effectiveness. The Spirit has warranted an exponential increase in intercessory effectiveness for some teams. Certainly, this increased intercessory pray power is needed to free America from this spiritual trap. **The Lord is asking for intercession teams of spiritual saints with each team in firm resolution to reverse the sifting of America.**[101] **Some teams will have additional goals such as reversing the drug flow, or freeing the universities of the land, stopping abortions, defeating the spiritual cults, or purging the country of evil secret clubs. Indeed, these powerhouse intercessory teams, each reaching for the throne room of the Father, represent our only spiritual defense in this interim, reflective of our serious deterioration in national faith over the last century. Liberal theology and its offspring, secular humanism, have gained ascendancy over our nation, leaving it naked to the enemy's attacks. Now this**

101. Each numeric figure used in this text has been found via the binary search technique using the author's personal commune with God.

problem has become acutely focused with the attack upon the **World Trade Center, as well as America's military complex at the Pentagon, which is but the first impact of Satan's request to sift America.** Obviously, God has permitted this sifting. But why? Look at the abuse of the Lord Jesus in this land; look at the killings of the unborn; look at the rejection of our founding covenant to be the light of Christ Jesus to the world; and then see your answer. Hence, the coming together to practice societal intercession via the **Holy Junction** has moved from the new and interesting to the very survival of our country. Indeed, it was only four days after the acquisition of this Holy Spirit knowledge that nations could be sifted by Satan, that Satan asked to sift America, instigating the attack upon our country. To understand what is happening, we as a nation, must look beyond the specific traits of that attack to see the spiritual picture that is unfolding. As explained by the Spirit, this is the enemy of God's ploy to neutralize the movement of the American nation to Christ, to prevent our movement into the Third Great Awakening destined as the product of God's forthcoming discipline. If Satan's sifting of America is successful, the nation cannot be disciplined. Instead, God will have to destroy us as we travel the path into the *Destruct Trail of Humanity.* (See chapter 15*).* All this means, is that the American people have entered into a gigantic struggle for the soul of our nation, and at stake is the very survival of human civilization. Yet, the nation does not have the knowledge or the faith; thusly, God has asked for these special intercessory teams to be set up. Even one team can save us! There is no turning back. And time is short. The Lord has given us a definitive date in which to establish the first intercessory team. Only severe defeat awaits us if we turn our back on this great need for intercession and fail to meet this deadline. Are there the necessary born again, Spirit filled, level three saints *(sanctified saints)*, each with their human spirit free and healthy, willing to be lifted to God the Father in true worship? These saints surely exist, and we pray that they can find one another. Indeed, there are no words that can adequately measure the magnitude of the moment in which we now live. The knowledge of the proper understanding and employment of true worship as found in the **Holy Junction** must spread across the land. And in this process, we must form these **Holy Junction** teams as the decisive weapon of the Lord, employed daily to rebuke and reverse the solicitation of the enemy for the spiritual and physical hegemony of America. This is a crucial and immediate need, necessary to save

America and with it, Christianity! Once Satan's initial sifting attack is turned back, these prayer teams can be utilized for the lifting of the 38 curses upon America. (See *Prototypical Kingdom.*) Then so armed with these victories over Satan's claim for the nation, and by using true worship to generate a sea of faith, we will be able to weather the Lord's discipline. From there we shall be able to lovingly accept the Spirit's outpouring Touch of Love. Hence, America will be enabled to move forward to the Third Great Awakening, enabling the first prototype of the kingdom of God brought to earth. This will be the next and highest level of human civilization: the culture of agape love. This is the true destiny of America as given by the Holy Spirit. However, let each saint or congregation validate this message before accepting it.

TIME LINE

A simple timeline will assist in understanding the events facing us:

Satan's request to sift America and several other nations:

- If the sifting is defeated, the Discipline of America arrives
- Release of the Hidden Manna
- Seven-fold outpouring of the Holy Spirit's Touch of Love
- Massive turning to Jesus
- Shift into the Subset Age of the Holy Spirit
- The implement of the first demonstration of the Kingdom of God adapted to earth as the Prototypical Kingdom of God.
- But if the sifting is not defeated, then we travel the Destruct Trail of Humanity.

OVERCHURCH

The corrective action of the church, i.e., its return to the true fighting army of God shall be via the emergence of the **Overchurch**. This new arrangement shall be ruled and governed exclusively by the Spirit of God. Human leadership shall be confined to anointed and appointed, **Teachers, Pointers, Collectors, Enablers and Adapters. Teachers** shall instruct on Jesus' vector to the kingdom of God adapted to the physical realm. **Pointers** shall reveal the Spirit's direction along that trail to the Kingdom. **Collectors** shall assemble the saints for the drive down the vector and the Holy Spirit shall provide the force that propels that drive using special human level-four, Spirit-filled **Enablers** to accomplish the task. **Adapters** will perform the necessary inner healing required for the human entity in order to reach this new closeness to God.

These anointed tasks transcend the five-fold ministry even as God has abandoned the old religious and failed methodologies for a new vigorous approach to achieving the mission goals of Jesus in the **Overchurch**, including invigorating new ministries. He would speak to us in a new lexicon, desired to stimulate anew our thinking. The saint must be careful to distinguish this new lexicon from that used by the New Age movement, remembering that Satan has operated to confuse the saints through the centuries by the use of prior parodies.

The lack of preaching will be the most obvious change in the **Overchurch**, reflecting the scarcity of preaching in the early church.[102] We are to switch from exhortation to action.

While members of the **Overchurch** are not expected to denounce their indigenous denomination, they are expected to leave the baggage of those denominations behind as they join their brothers and sisters of similar beliefs in the incarnation of the Son of God as Yeshua Ha-Mashiach. This baggage includes dogmas, canon beliefs, pagan influences and religiosity. Let us join with Jesus the carpenter, accepting only His redeeming sacrifice on the Cross, His resurrection and His dispatch of the Spirit of God to affect His vector to the Kingdom of God adapted to earth. Saints, so called forth, shall be committed to one cause: The drive to the kingdom of God.

Entrance to the **Overchurch** is exclusively through the Holy Spirit, mandated because only the Spirit of God can erase the impersonator and de-emphasize denominational dogmas, generating sensitivity to the Spirit's work.

The **Overchurch** shall operate as the most effective spiritual army the world has ever seen, even exceeding its original rise as the Grand Redemptive Engine of God in the first century. The army of God shall strongly utilize God's special end-time fighting weapons, the Spirit-check, and His hidden manna. When these gifts are combined with the binding of the enemy of God in all areas of human endeavor, they shall defeat the enemy spiritually, both internally and territorially, bringing about the millennium reign of Christ Jesus.[103]

---

102. Please do not associate the author as a founder or leader of the **Overchurch**. This development is of God, must be generated by Him and will be run by Him. Any human effort to form, organize and direct the **Overchurch** is destined to fail.

103. All saints that hold to the pre-tribulation rapture and Tribulation brainwashing of the religious populists about the coming of the millennium age possess an inadequate doctrine that shall preclude their usefulness to Jesus in the coming time of discipline. They will be marginalized in the drive to the first implementation of the kingdom of God adapted to earth. So says the Spirit of God! The Jewish Tribulation of Daniel 9:27 has

DISCOVERING THE CULTURAL ROLE OF THE IMPERSONATOR

The following life factors control the condition of any human:

- Cultural Beliefs
- Educational Conditioning
- Family Conditioning
- Religious beliefs
- Compulsive Sin
- Self
- Rationalism
- Emotionalism
- Psychic Influences
- Covert Urges of the Hidden Mind
- Temptations
- Inherited Sins
- Health
- Demonic Presence
- Inner Physical Environment
- Outer Physical Environment.

The personality of the human is determined by the interplay of these components. As any statistician can relate, the combinations within each component and between each component can be colossal, warranting our individual uniqueness. Into this scenario, we can add either the Holy Spirit or its impersonator. Now, each indwelling spirit, either the Holy Spirit or Satan's impersonator, has the capacity to overwhelm the other components of life, changing the personality of the human. If it is the impersonator that comes to dominate, the human victim can look and act as if her or she were upright and righteous but the truth will be dramatically different. If it is the Holy Spirit that indwells, the human can emerge as an instrument of the Lord, achieving a positive, God pleasing ledger in life. Indeed, as the Spirit of God grows within, that point can be reached where self no longer finds a voice. This is when the Christ Spirit is said to dominate; Christian Mysticism has been found, and that individual becomes the spiritual and cultural battle warrior of God. It is from the

---

already occurred in 66 to 73 AD. Study the comparison of events of the 70 holocaust with Mathew 24 shown in Appendix C.

critical mass of these warriors that the initial appearance of the kingdom of God will be constructed.

It always happens that when the impersonator comes to dominate the components within the individual, that the urge for denominational superiority comes to the forefront, preventing and averting the drive, in Christian unity, to the kingdom of God. Hence, we see a great secret of the enemy of God. His impersonator's primary task is to prevent the saint from seeking agape love unity with other, often dissimilar saints. Or in other words, the primary task of the impersonator is cultural not individual destruction. Satan is content to allow the host of the impersonator to rot in the Equity Adjustment Queue for millennia.

Why?

Because, when the kingdom of God's unique pumping capacities for the harvesting of souls is recognized,[104] the dimensions and objectives of the war between Satan and Jesus Christ will be identified and drawn. Then, humankind will be able to recognize the war strategy of the enemy of God, and become an active, perceptive player in this conflict for the first time in the history of the church.

The essence of the kingdom's great harvesting capacities is that the kingdom of God adapted to earth will process close to 100 percent of all its soul/spirits directly into the throne room of God, reloading each new generation with a new set of good seed. If we accept Origen's concept that God created a finite number of soul/spirit before the earth existed (see Ephesians 1:4) in what Jesus called *this generation* (see Mark 8:12), then the good seed of the world can be pumped out and harvested, from that large, but finite number in a relatively small number of generational iterations. This process would continue, through the switch from the Prototypical Kingdom to the Demonstration Kingdom through the time of Sorrows, until rapture. The Great Tribulation, not to be confused with the Jewish Tribulation, would then extinguish the separated bad seed from *this generation* of soul/spirits. Jesus would return with the New Jerusalem, the grown up adult of the raptured Demonstration Kingdom.

Currently, because of cheap salvation, only a trickle of soul/spirits reaches the throne room of God from each of our Christian generations. True, each saint that accepts Jesus as her or his personal Savior is saved to heaven, but only after spending a period of tenure in the Equity Adjustment Queue, a punishment queue. Hence, from this analysis, we can see the utter need to understand the

---

104. See the 'Great Vacuum Pump' in chapter 18 of Shults, *Prototypical Kingdom* for details, available from 1stbooks.com.

202

fullness of Jesus' eschatology, as well as the damage caused to that eschatology by the **second fall.**[105]

---

105. The first response to this chapter and the author was an angry: 'Fool, stone him.' It would appear that the impersonator is stirred viciously by its unveiling. This would seem to warrant the Lord's 1974 warning that critics would laugh and ridicule, then attack academically and use Bible-based debunking. This would be followed by pious pronouncements from persons of religious authority, followed by name-calling, hate mail and eventually, violence.

Chapter 21

End-Time Tools for Spiritual Warfare

As end-times approach and the forces of evil increase, God has revealed, through His Spirit, His desire that Jesus' beloved ones are not helpless in the coming spiritual and physical onslaught. Accordingly, the Spirit of God has revealed a set of weapons that the saint's can utilize to defend the Body of Christ. The problem is that God is calling for the execution of these weapons from a highly developed spiritual state, one that few saints today understand or dwell within. Basically, the Lord is asking His beloved ones to move closer to Him through His Spirit, there to become spiritual. (See 1 Corinthians 3:1 for an initial understanding of the difference between a carnal versus a spiritual saint. In the simplest definition, the carnal saint has the secular world as his or her top priority in life, even if it is proclaimed otherwise; wherein the spiritual saint has Jesus and the kingdom of God alone as the top priority of life, willing to sacrifice all, including life itself for God.) The method that God has introduced to the author for the conversion from carnal to spiritual status is the **Holy Junction**.

The **Holy Junction** is that special state of the Christian where the freed and independent human spirit is joined with the Spirit of its look alike Creator, the Holy Spirit, to be taken by the Spirit into the presence of the Father and the Son. There the human spirit is joined in an intimacy of love with God. **From this position the human spirit can conduct unsurpassed spiritual warfare upon Satan as well as other tasks of God.** But the human spirit must constantly recognize the privilege of this gift, remaining contrite and humble, even in the greatest display of God's power within that human. Human arrogance within this special junction with God could be fatal. Thus, the human mind must be tamed and collaborated before the human spirit can be successful in this extraordinary venture. Entrance to the **Holy Junction** is best achieved immediately after Holy Communion or intensive Biblical contemplation. It frequently occurs with the author even as the Blood of Jesus is being taken in Holy Communion. Each occurrence is confirmed by the anointing by the Spirit of God. It is the most powerful state of human quiet that can be found. The author has the privilege of participation in this spiritual journey with a team of intercessors. Frequent mental visions reveals that our human spirits can reach the doorway of the throne room of the Father and His Son. To date, we are unable to enter that brilliant light, but God wants that entrance. He has proclaimed such in words of knowledge, stating that we can make that step when our spiritual development reaches true sanctification, defined as destruction of carnal self and emancipation from the inner human. Today, the Lord tells us that there are only 6,000 such soul/spirits in the world, but with God's intervention to bring about the arrival of the subset age, it will be millions. The flow of kingdom spiritual power will be colossal. (To test this Holy Spirit led Holy Junction capacity, the author selected a sports team after the 9/11 attack on our nation and cleared out the spiritual trash that was descending on that team, the Chicago Bears. Several serious spiritual battles occurred, winning them only at the last few moments of the game. Dramatic wins then followed. Never conducting spiritual warfare for victory, just a level playing field, some started to call this team 'God's team.' Little did they know!)

ATTACKING SATAN'S SIFTING OF AMERICA

The Father, asked by the Son, has granted an end-time weapon to His beloved ones. This modern day gift is the deployment of the hidden manna of God. It appears that the Father's expectations are that this weapon is to be used in spiritual warfare to defeat the inroads of the enemy of God and the legacy blunders of the churches over the last eight hundred years. This is especially true since the thirteenth century failure of the Spiritual Franciscans, which effectively opened the floodgates to the sifting of America in modern times. These tools are urgently required to rebuke and reverse the sifting of America.

Here are the End-Time weapons that can be utilized in spiritual warfare. These deployments are:

The **Spirit-check shower**, this gift must be introduced by the saint to help that saint overcome the oppression of the impersonator and the daily oppression found in the secular world. In this application, the Spirit of God will flood over the requesting saint, driving out the impersonating enemy.

The **Holy Junction Attack**, the oppressing spirits of the enemy can be directly attacked from the **Holy Junction**. Here the unsurpassed power of the Father and His Son can be directed aggressively against these forces. The author's experience is that fallen angels that have operated for generations are traumatized upon being struck down by the Father, many of them having never been defeated in 2000 years of evil work. These workers will not return for a generation [35 years]. But in a surprise move, the Father revealed that from the **Holy Junction** the saints can completely eliminate the return of these evil spirits by the simple command: *Dance in front of the victim.* Apparently, in the spiritual realm this is a humiliation that transcends all humiliations for evil entities. So saints, find the **Holy Junction** and make those demonic entities dance. God bless!

Hidden Manna, from the Spirit of God it is revealed that the **hidden manna** is the *Love Touch of the Spirit of God*, functioning as ultimate grace for the unsaved and maximized indwelling of the Holy Spirit for the saved. End-time saints operative from the **Holy Junction** can utilize either capacity: vectored grace or the vectoring of the indwelling Spirit. In all instances, the permission of the Father and His Son is required.

Vectored Grace, **the first part of the hidden manna** can be set upon any human or social grouping for a short period of time. All receiving this grace will be pushed toward Jesus Christ. Again, human freewill will prevail and if the human does not desire this gift, it will be gone. If grace is accepted, that saint will be freed from the impersonator. Thus, if **Vectored Grace** is properly understood and utilized by the Body of Christ, huge numbers of the saints can be brought into the true presence of Christ through the Holy Spirit via this old, but previously concealed gift. This is because **Vectored Grace** is the directed impact of the Holy Spirit used as an offensive weapon for the Lord Jesus. In its true definition, grace is the Holy Spirit moving outside the human to bring that person into a relationship with Jesus Christ. Now, as an end-time weapon for the saints, God is allowing grace to be directed or targeted upon any given person when it is invoked from the close proximity to the Father and the Son as found in the **Holy Junction**. This form of controlled grace can be used in any fashion that normal, uncontrolled grace can be utilized. Saints able to operate from the **Holy Junction** can bless people, even strangers and especially the lost, via this special end-time gift of God. When the unsaved accept the touch of love, he or she becomes saved, filled with the Holy Spirit to level two, and freed from the yoke of Satan's request for their soul. What a mighty gift! Of course, the free will of the targeted person is still intact, remaining the final determinant. But importantly, **Vectored Grace** can be used to eliminate oppressive spirits in the unsaved, making that decision for Christ fairer. In addition, **Vectored Grace** can eliminate the impersonating spirits of the enemy of God that have deceived such a large group of saints for so long.

Vectored Deepening of the Indwelling Spirit, **the second part of the hidden manna** can be set upon any human or social grouping that already contains the indwelling Spirit of God, to dramatically increase that indwelling. This portion of the hidden manna has the capacities to clean out the hidden recesses of the mind, bringing self into control and eliminating all those secret sins so prevalent in the Body of Christ today, including the elimination of self-inflicted curses. This weapon of the Lord, the second portion of the hidden manna, will be a necessary tool in the cleansing of humanity, opening the way for

the construction of the kingdom of God. And to think this country, America, as well as the other selected countries, will have this gift given to it seven times within forty years. But even further, the Spirit has revealed that the Father is about to permit the projected utilization of the Love Touch, employed from within the intercessory teams at the **Holy Junction** level, before the first nationwide massive outpouring of the Holy Spirit's Touch of Love.
The initial release of this capacity is upon us.

ADVANTAGES DERIVED FROM THE UTILIZATION OF HIDDEN MANNA:

1. **Rebuking and reversing the sifting of the souls** by the enemy of God can be achieved best by deploying the **hidden manna** from the **Holy Junction.** Yet there are saints so brainwashed by their denominations that they cannot immediately step into the process of the **Holy Junction** even if called by God. Therefore, God will accept what those saints can offer until they can grow into a more powerful walk with Christ.

2. **Rebuking and reversing the sifting of social organizations** by the enemy of God can be, and must be, achieved. As given by the Holy Spirit, the most effective tool is the physical gathering of spiritual saints that synchronously enter the **Holy Junction** with an agreed target of intercession. The duration of the true worship is not a factor, just reaching it, even for a few minutes, is effective enough to deploy the hidden manna. The gathering of saints in any supporting intercessory efforts can be very effective, but to gather the saints in **Holy Junction** portents spiritual power not reached by the church for almost 2000 years. Our immediate intervention task is to save America in the intervening years before God's intervention arrives. Frequently, separated spiritual saints can reach synchronized **Holy Junction** via Internet, telephone or other technological communication connections.

3. **Each Holy Junction intercessory team, formed by the Spirit of God, represent the initial and foundation members of the Overchurch.** Each such team will have exponentially greater capacities to perform spiritual warfare, even to the point of cleansing the land of the presence of the enemy of God and his workers. The Father waits for us to come to Him to defeat the centuries-long invasion and perversion of America, especially the current sifting of America, thus opening up the last chance path for God's restoration plan via His Spirit's intervention. Understand what is being said here. We must hold the line against the attacks of the enemy, utilizing the end times tools of God, until the planned

intervention of the Holy Spirit can set Jesus' anointed ones back upon His vectored trail to paradise.

4. **Supporting Intercessory teams can be formed to assist the Holy Junction teams.** These teams will be formed around the progression towards the intercessory integration of the soul and spirit. *These steps represent the hierarchy of intercession with increasing dependency upon the human spirit as any given saint moves up the intercessory ladder.* Each step up this hierarchy releases more kingdom spiritual power as intercessory prayer power per saint. See Mark 5:30 to gain an insight on kingdom spiritual power. Here is that hierarchy:

HIERARCHY OF INTERCESSORY PRAYER GROUPS:

1. **Normal intercessory prayers** – These are agape prayers for others, and in this case for our nation.

2. **Singing in the Spirit** – This must be done through a prayer language, normally accomplished with Spirit-filled saints that have the gift of tongues. It is frequently seen among the Charismatic Christians. The Spirit desires to see this largely unused spiritual capacity directed at the sifting of America. Imagine the power of thousands of saint singing in the Spirit for God!

3. **Travailing in the Spirit** – Some saints are gifted with the capacity to weep for the Lord. Rather, the Lord uses the human entity to weep. Unbeknown to most, this capacity possesses great potential for intercession. The Spirit says that the saint can gain a 1000 to 1 increase in intercessory prayer power from this spiritual capacity.

4. **Scriptural Contemplation** – If the saint can bring the Holy Spirit into Biblical study and if the saint can let the Spirit have the lead, then contemplation can occur. Here the Holy Spirit, the human mind and, most importantly, the human spirit blend in an amalgamation of the Word. By the proper selection of Scripture this can be intercessory in intent. The Spirit says that the saint can gain an enormous increase in intercessory prayer power if he or she can really hit this contemplation.

5. **Holy Communion** – In the Last Supper our Lord gave us a blood covenant that He asked His followers to perform in His

remembrance. This function was initially carried out in the homes of the early followers as well as their assemblies. But as the institutional church developed, it retained the exclusive right to perform this blood covenant to themselves, serving the body and blood of the Lord as it desired. They even served the Body of Christ in the mouth of the peasants to avoid the dirty hands of the common people, refusing to disperse the blood of Christ to them. But now, the Holy Spirit wants to expand that Eucharistic capacity back to the people, to be performed at each family supper. Holy Communion can be dedicated to a cause, meaning it can be intercessory. Let us not fight over Transubstantiation (Catholic, featuring the actual transformation of the bread and wine into the body and blood of Jesus), Consubstantiation (Lutheran, representing the spiritual transformation of the bread and wine into the body and blood of Jesus) or Impanation (Christ is symbolically present without changing the physical characteristics of the bread and wine), rather let us simply join together in this great act of love. If the saint is successful - and you will know it - then, according to the Holy Spirit, the prayer power will temporarily jump to high levels of kingdom spiritual power. But a word of caution is needed. Let no one enter into Holy Communion with the Lord without first cleansing themselves of sin. To do otherwise is to place oneself in unnecessary spiritual jeopardy!

6. **Holy Junction** – This is the process where the soul yield the primacy of the human entity to the human spirit, which then joins with its look alike, the Holy Spirit, and is taken to the throne room door of the Father and the Son, there to feel the intimacy of God. This is a power position for the saints from which spiritual warfare can be maximized, especially through the employment of the **hidden manna** tools. The Holy Spirit says that the saint can reach a 50,000 to 1 increase in prayer power and a group together can reach exponential increases in prayer power that can exceed the combined prayer power of the entire nation in conventional intercessory prayer. While all of the intercessory teams represent our best hope to reverse the sifting of America, it is obvious that a large group of saints participating in the **Holy Junction** can be very victorious. The Spirit has told us that this effectiveness is peaked when the teams reach 7, 14, 21 or 28 members with the larger sized teams gaining extraordinary spiritual influence with God.

7. **Shekinah presence of God** – this is the coming of the glorious light of the Holy Spirit, which encases the saint(s). The Father and the Son exist within this light. This is a very rare occurrence, but it does happen. There is no measurement concerning this kingdom spiritual power; it is infinite.

Each team would specialize in one or more of the above spiritual battle formats. Individuals would join these teams as led by the Spirit of God, matching their gifts to the team. It is entirely feasible that each team would progress up the hierarchy of intercession as they grow spiritually, learning to deploy one or more of the intercessory formats in the same meeting.

God is not unjust: He will not forget your work and the love you have shown Him as you have helped His people (Hebrews 6:10).

THESE SHOULD BE THE GOALS OF THE INTERCESSORY PRAYER GROUPS:

- Reverse Satan's sifting of America.
- Prevent this conflict from escalating to a world war situation.
- Return America to its Christian status, openly acknowledged by the leaders of the land.
- Modification of the American Constitution to recognize Jesus as our King, eliminating forever the evil of the separation of Jesus from our land and governance.[106]
- Apologize to the Holy Spirit for the neglect and abuse He has experienced from the Body of Christ.
- Grieve with God over the sinfulness of America, seeking its reversal even if through God's chastisement.
- Conduct spiritual warfare to eliminate the curses over America to prevent the capture of our nation by the enemy of God before the intervention of God.[107]
- Pleading for the intervention of God to save humankind from itself, enabling:
- The spread of true worship through the human spirit even as outlined in John 4:24.

---

106. The separation of church and state is a concept that arose to prevent the dominance of one denomination over other denominations. It was never meant to separate the state from Christ Jesus, which is how the Christ-haters have twisted it.
107. The thirty-eight curses tyrannizing our nation are listed in *Prototypical Kingdom*.

- The return of the Body of Christ to the kingdom power level of the early church.
- The development of the **Overchurch**.
- The release of God's hidden manna (See Revelation 2:17).
- The shift into the subset age of the Holy Spirit.

(Note! Some of these gifts of God are old and others are new to the Body of Christ, being introduced by this text. Discern the validity of the gifts personally with the Holy Spirit before deploying them. Never attempt to deploy these gifts without the permission of God. If you cannot obtain that permission you will not be enabled to these gifts. And remember, no human can generated the Shekinah Glory of God, it is a pure and rare gift.)

SPECIAL END-TIME WEAPONS ABOUT TO BE ACTIVATED:

The Lord, in His compassion for His people, has revealed the existence of several new weapons of spiritual warfare. These weapons will be activated within the implementation drive to the Kingdom of God. These are the following:

Discernment - This gift of the Holy Spirit given in 1 Corinthians 12:10 will be expanded to the **Law of Identification**. This law states that God will identify the human and spiritual enemy confronting his people. Here, the saint in the **Holy Junction** will be enabled to know the following information about the enemy of God:

1. One, if the opponent is a soul/spirit allied with Satan incarnated out of Hell, referred to by the author as one of Satan's core souls. It is the constant reoccurrence of these core souls that has deteriorated the spiritual potential of America over the generations. In our ignorance of the spiritual realm, Christians have been unaware that this invasion could be stopped via the **Holy Junction**. Indeed, the author's intercessory team has asked for and received a moratorium of sixty years against core souls incarnating into America. However, these evil entities can still flood our land via immigration, signaling the urgency of a moratorium against immigration.
2. Two, identification of evil concepts and philosophies as they appear.
3. Three, identification of political moves as motivated by the enemy of God.
4. Four, identification of incorrect economic move instigated by the enemy of God.

5. Five, identification of insidious invasions of our land by core souls.
6. The numbers of the opposing forces, enabling the proper attacking force required to dislodge them.

Law of removal is the ability of the intercessory and spiritual warfare teams to remove any given human individual or group from warfare over the implementation of the kingdom of God. This capacity must be coupled with the Law of Identification and can only be enacted with the Holy Spirit's acquiescence.

Removal can take many different forms such as a job promotion or layoff, early retirement, health problems or death. The method and the timing is solely God's. But this is a serious tool of the Lord, to be deployed only under special prayers of compassion coupled with a request for salvation for the targeted soul/spirit. The scriptural basis for this law can be found in Act 5. Also examine this scripture:

Then Elijah commanded them, 'Seize the prophets of Baal....' Elijah had them ... slaughtered there (1 Kings 18:40).

The terrifying nature of this weapon emphasizes both the magnitude of the coming conflict and the utter necessity that God's fighting army prevails in this struggle. No longer will the people of God be extinguished by murder and execution such as happened when the Islamic invasions occurred. God will not tolerate a repeat of that abomination to occur to His army striving to bring about the coming of His Kingdom in its first adaptation to earth.

Law of Confirmation states that the Holy Spirit will confirm the following actions of Jesus beloved ones in their:

1. **Decisions**
2. **Worship**
3. **Assemblies**
4. **Revivals**
5. **Intercessions**
6. **Holy Junction**
7. **Use of the Hidden Manna**
8. **Interpretation of the Biblical Word enabling unity**
9. **Messages from God**
10. **Gifts of God**
11. **Faith**
12. **Healings**

13. Sacrifices

14. Martyrdoms.

Law of Angelic Protection states that no human or spiritual entity can harm a beloved of the Lord when engaged in kingdom implementation work, if that saint has asked for the Lord's angelic assistance and protection. Exceptions to this law will occur only when the Lord is calling the given saint home at the appointed time for that event.

Chapter 22

The Theology of the Holy Spirit

What is missing from the Christ Walk? The true representation of the Trinity, which can only be obtained by a theology of the Holy Spirit! Only this knowledge, absent all these centuries, can put together the different pieces of the Christian faith, presenting to the world a **united** Body of Christ determined to rediscover and accomplish the mission of Christ Jesus.

So what is the theology of the Holy Spirit? It is that kingdom force within Jesus' vector driving to the kingdom of God that also provides the direction of that vector. In other words, the theology of the Holy Spirit is the driving knowledge so necessary to reestablish our connection with Jesus' mission vector and to drive the Body of Christ up that vector toward the first adaptation of the kingdom of God to earth.

For the author, the knowledge of the theology of the Holy Spirit came in pieces over a period of twenty years until that fateful day on the 3rd of July 2001 in which the Spirit put all the pieces together. Perhaps it started on May 12, 1981 when the Lord Jesus gave this significant message:

They know not the Holy Spirit; they love not the Holy Spirit; hence, they are led not by the Holy Spirit.

Who? I asked. The reply was:

Leaders of church and state since the end of the first-century church! They love dogmas and laws, not me.

The astonishment was profound!

Any objective analysis of this message leads to the horrible conclusion that Christianity is out of control, led by the intellect of men instead of the Spirit of God. Years later, this message was validated when the author was able to grasp the significance of the rise of the church canon after the Pepusa incident of 172 AD, a process in which the Holy Spirit was squeezed out of His Jesus-appointed leadership role in the church.

Then these components fell into place, even while the author still lived in ignorant obliviousness. Each component is given with its reception date:

- The unique and singular appearance over the author of a thick white cloud that contained the personalities of the Father and the Son who dispatched the author on a mission of correction – experienced in 1938
- Powerful Baptism in the Holy Spirit – experienced in 1973
- Call to rebuild God's church on a new and solid foundation – heard in 1973
- Different levels of the indwelling Spirit – first heard in 1973
- Call to Spiritual Warfare – first heard in 1973
- Call to write for the Lord – heard in 1973 and rejected with the statement, 'you will have to force me before I would believe it'
- Subset age of the Holy Spirit – first heard in 1976
- Holy Spirit's Touch of Love (the hidden manna) – first experienced in 1977, 18 touches over six years, each overwhelmingly powerful
- Job-tests – first experienced in 1978
- First experience in Synchronized Spiritual Warfare 1979
- Inclusion in army-wide spiritual warfare, necessary to avoid a serious set of earthquakes as well as a pending nuclear conflict – 1979 [This attack on America was later confirmed as contemplated by the Soviets in the time frame of 1983 to 1986. The kingdom spiritual energy expended that night took three years to recover, dramatically introducing the concept of individual kingdom spiritual energy.]
- Message of the Holy Spirit's rejection – heard in 1981
- Message on the value of each soul – heard in 1981
- Second call to write – accepted, after author's material possessions and employment was taken by God, 1986
- Sanctified Justification – first dimly heard in 1986
- Overcoming struggle as given in Revelation, confirmed in its preeminent significance in 1986
- Spiritual insertion into the dark spiritual world for 45 seconds in 1986[108]
- Call to cultural confrontation – first heard in 1986
- Over 500 Spiritual Laws or their Corollaries, forming the fighting edge of the Christian cultural confrontational and

---

108. A physical breaking in great pain immediately followed this illustration of spiritual realm helplessness. In one amazing hour, the Lord demonstrated the author's complete dependency upon God in both realms of existence.

spiritual army for the coming of the kingdom of God – heard in two six months intervals with a five year separation, 1986 and 1991[109]

- Special, real-time commune with God via the Spirit of God – established in 1989 after an eight year introduction that started in 1981[110]
- Given the basis for the model of human civilization one cold day on the Nags Head beach in January 1990[111]
- Overcoming by emancipation – first heard in 1992
- Better grasp on Kingdom Spiritual Energy – 1993
- Dialectical Agapism – first heard in 1993
- Grieving of the Spirit – strongly felt in 1994
- Christian History broken into Minor Dispensations – first heard in 1994
- Impersonator – first dimly understood in 1995
- Validated Societal Commune – first heard in 1995
- Three stage implementation eschatology – first heard in 1995
- God's massive discipline – first heard in 1996
- Enormous outpouring of the Holy Spirit – first firmly heard in 1996
- Holy Junction – first heard in 1986 but firmly established as a dynamic, life and church changing function of the Holy Spirit while in extremely heavy 10-month-long spiritual warfare in 1997[112]

---

109. These laws are published in Shults, Eugene C. *Prototypical Kingdom: The Promise of Dialectical Agapism* available at 1stbooks.com. The five-year interval occurred because the author asked not to be awakened at night any longer, which was the method that the Lord used to convey these laws. The laws stopped coming immediately. Pondering the situation and feeling a mistake had been made, the author asked for the resumption of the laws. They did, five years later. Be careful how you pray!
110. This took so long because the author did not have an orientation that such a process could exist. It was against my brainwashing education.
111. This information can be found in *Prototypical Kingdom*.
112. The Lord wanted to teach me about Holy Junction to tell others, but once again, my brainwashed orientation stood in the way. Consequently, the author - already experienced in spiritual warfare - struggled and suffered terribly against the hordes of hell, in which struggle none of the conventional Christian defenses were effective. However, the victory found in the Holy Junction was swift and sweet, indeed, requiring one second to defeat all those hordes.

- That end-times events are held incorrectly by the fundamentalists – first firmly heard in 1998[113]
- That the only hope for humankind is the restored church led by the Spirit of God – first confirmed in 1999
- **Overchurch** – first heard in 1999
- Warning that the Bible does not contain all of God's knowledge, but that the Spirit of God who searches the mind of the Father and His Son does – first heard in 2000
- Unity of kingdom, redemptive and Jesus-lives-within theology via the indwelling of the Holy Spirit – first firmly heard in 2001
- That it is too late for human correction of the church – first heard in 2001
- That Jesus gave us a vector to the Kingdom of God brought to earth in which the Bible contains both the jump off position of that vector - but not the intellectual, societal, or spiritual position coordinates of that Kingdom - and the means of traveling down that vector, faith – first understood in 2001
- That humankind has lost the jump off position of Jesus' vector and cannot recover it via human reform or intellectual study of the Bible – first grasped in its total astonishment and horror in 2001
- God's intervention to reset the church on the correct path of Jesus' vector – first heard in 2001
- Harmonious organizations, the characteristic of Spirit-guided human organizations must be the characteristic of human travel down Jesus' vector – first heard in 2001
- That the world can survive only if it embraces the subset age of the Holy Spirit – definitively heard in January 2001 in the Lord's millennium message
- That the **Overchurch** established within the subset age of the Holy Spirit, via the Third Great Awakening, represents the required harmonious organization, which God has selected to bring humanity back to Jesus' faith vector. From there it is chosen to successfully travel that vector to the first implementation of that kingdom as the Prototypical Kingdom – first heard in 2001.

---

113. Perhaps, the biggest surprise was that the Tribulation spoken of by Daniel 9:27 occurred in the seven year Judean war of independence for 66 to 73 AD, a fact recognized only by a small minority of Christians.

PULLING IT TOGETHER

Now the author is presented with the task of pulling all of these events together into a coherent theology, obviously a task well beyond the capacities of a physics-trained individual. Yet, it is mandated that we try. So, in the humblest fashion, void of any pretensions, here is the best that the author can do. It is our prayer that a theologian of the future can bring these pieces together in a more meaningful and powerful fashion. Meanwhile, here are the inputs of the Holy Spirit.

CONSTRUCTION OF THE HOLY SPIRIT THEOLOGY

The Holy Spirit theology is based on these basic premises:

GOD'S MANDATES TO HIS SPIRIT:

Premise One: The Holy Spirit is that portion of the Trinity, existing before the creation of time, that currently inhabits the physical plane with the mandate to pursue the Father's Adamic restoration plan for humanity based on Jesus Christ's blood sacrifice and resurrection.

Premise Two: Part of the Holy Spirit's mandate is to uplift the Father and the Son.

Premise Three: Another part of the Holy Spirit's mandate is to spread agape love among the human inhabitants of the world, making the earth the unselfish, giving love planet, generating an agape civilization dedicated to the Son of God.

Premise Four: Another part of the Holy Spirit's mandate is His responsibilities to coordinate the work of the angels with His work for the benefit of the mission of the Son to redeem humanity.

Premise Five: The last part of the Holy Spirit's mandate is to integrate the two realms, the physical and the spiritual into the reality of the living. This is to be accomplished through the arrival of the kingdom of God adapted to earth.

CHARACTERISTICS OF THE HOLY SPIRIT:

Premise Six: The Holy Spirit is omnipresent.

Premise Seven: The Holy Spirit can be omnipotent under certain conditions of human cooperation under the blood of the Son, a qualification ordained by the Father.

Premise Eight: The Spirit of God functions as grace, which is assistance outside the human, pushing that human toward God.

Premise Nine: The Holy Spirit inhabits willing humans, turning those humans into the temple of God on earth. From His indwelling presence, the Spirit can manifest the foremost input of God's righteousness and maximize faith for that human.

Premise Ten: The Spirit of God loves and needs love, operating best within any human temple when loved.

Premise Eleven: The Spirit of God carries freedom and needs freedom to function to His fullness.

Premise Twelve: The optimum function of the Holy Spirit on earth is not as grace but as the highest indwelling presence surrounded by a bath of human love. Here faith abounds. Here, the Father's righteousness is optimized. Here, the saint reaches the highest justification as a battle warrior for God. Kingdom spiritual power is maintained, even as the miracles of God in healing and the exercise of the gifts of the Spirit are optimized.

Premise Thirteen: The Spirit of God is grieved by human sin, especially impurity, dishonesty, idol worship, deceit, cruelty, debauchery, cursing, murder, exploitation and gossip, all which cause His retreat.

Premise Fourteen: The Holy Spirit is moved by compassion and generates compassion.

Premise Fifteen: The Holy Spirit embraces human forgiveness, moving Him to compassion.

Premise Sixteen: The Spirit of God is truth, embodies truth and inspires truth.

Premise Seventeen: The Spirit of God soothes, advises, anoints and comforts God's beloved ones.

Premise Eighteen: The Holy Spirit does not honor obscenities directed at God, grieving when they are uttered.

Premise Nineteen: The Holy Spirit does not favor being called a *ghost*.

Premise Twenty: The Holy Spirit, representing God on earth, only communicates with humans via the human spirit, never through the human psychic capacities, which because of the Adamic fall are utilized exclusively by the enemy of God.

Premise Twenty-one: The Spirit of God is the vehicle for the communications between the human spirit and God, sometimes recognized as the small still voice.

Premise Twenty-two: The Holy Spirit incites the human conscience and moves human intuition.

Premise Twenty-three: The Holy Spirit cannot tolerate assertive and arrogant humans, frequently withdrawing from these humans.

Premise Twenty-four: The Holy Spirit cannot resist the humble human.

Premise Twenty-five: The Spirit of God frequently times the movements of God's beloved ones so that the work of God can be promoted.

Premise Twenty-six: The Holy Spirit encourages human health and human cleanness.

Premise Twenty-seven: The Holy Spirit is the source of joy and peace.

SANCTIFICATION:

Premise Twenty-eight: Working with the indwelling human's request, the Holy Spirit reaches into the inner mind of the beloved to bring that hidden portion of the human mind into the walk with Christ. This is the true process of sanctification.

GRIEVING THE HOLY SPIRIT

Premise Twenty-nine: The Holy Spirit grieves when humanity ignores Him and His unmerited assistance.

Premise Thirty: The Father will not tolerate or forgive blasphemy against the Holy Spirit.

Premise Thirty-one: The Holy Spirit grieves at the rejection of the Son, knowing that rejection now, means wrath expected tomorrow.

Premise Thirty-two: The Holy Spirit grieves at the misguided search for the natural Jesus, especially when the enemy of God turns this scholarly attempt into the destruction of the Christian faith.

Premise Thirty-three: The Holy Spirit still grieves over His third-century rejection.

Premise Thirty-four: To optimize the work of the Holy Spirit, an individual followed by a church wide apology for His centuries-long abuse and neglect must be given. Only the most sincere remorse, cloaked in deep and heartfelt prayer, can alleviate His grieving.

SPIRITUAL WARFARE

Premise Thirty-five: The Holy Spirit monitors all of God's spiritual and physical laws and possesses the capacity to override any law at any given time.

Premise Thirty-six: The Holy Spirit constantly seeks after souls for the Father and the Son, striking down the forces of the enemy of God to reach the lost soul/spirits.

Premise Thirty-seven: The Holy Spirit directs the work details of God's angels in the physical plane.

Premise Thirty-eight: The Holy Spirit directs the spiritual war with the enemy of God and his workers, utilizing both human and angelic forces in synchronized warfare.

Premise Thirty-nine: The Holy Spirit trains humans for synchronized spiritual warfare in localized scrimmages, whence, the beloved one cleanses his or her own house or place of business.

Premise Forty: Synchronized spiritual warfare is the total army of God, composed of humans and God's angels, functioning together as an integrated whole, in the spiritual realm, under the leadership of the Holy Spirit and the headship of Jesus Christ.

Premise Forty-one: When synchronized spiritual warfare is mastered by the church, the enemy of God and his workers, can be driven from targeted areas of the earth.

VIEWING THE HOLY SPIRIT

Premise Forty-two: The Holy Spirit normally cannot be seen, only felt by humans. That means that the secular world cannot see or know Him.

Premise Forty-three: The Holy Spirit can be seen in the Shekinah light, which is the exclusive visual manifestation of the Holy Spirit in the physical plane.

IMPERSONATORS OF THE HOLY SPIRIT:

Premise Forty-four: The Spirit of God detests and loathes deceiving impersonations of His presence by the evil workers of the enemy of God, which has gained such a powerful end-time presence among the saints.

Premise Forty-five: To combat this nemesis and the other activities of the enemy of God, the Spirit of God has provided a spiritual cleansing shower to all who seek spiritual cleanliness, urging all saints to shower daily. (The author has called this the Spirit-Check shower).

INDWELLING INTERACTIONS:

Premise Forty-six: The initial arrival of the Holy Spirit within the human occurs at the born-again experience, but neglect of this, His initially light presence, can lead to His departure, leaving the saint as a nominal infant Christian.

Premise Forty-seven: The Holy Spirit arrives in deep indwelling through Jesus' Baptism normally accomplished by the laying on of hands by a beloved one having a deeply indwelling presence.

Premise Forty-eight: The Holy Spirit can deeply indwell a human without the laying on of hands, but desires the human assist in this transfer, defining in this process His real church.

222

Premise Forty-nine: While the Holy Spirit goes where He will outside the human temple, His presence inside is constant and vigilant.

Premise Fifty: The Holy Spirit indwells each human up to four major levels, each level is further subdivided into multiple levels. The first level is reached by the born-again experience. The second level is reached by the Baptism of the Holy Spirit. The synchronized walk with Christ Jesus reaches levels three and four.

Premise Fifty-one: In the optimum status of a level four indwelling, the highest possible indwelling, the gifts and fruits of the Holy Spirit function free of human facades and deceptions.

JOB-TESTS:

Premise Fifty-two: As the saint climbs up the ladder of the Holy Spirit's indwelling presence, that saint will experience Job-tests in which the Spirit will seemingly withdraw all support.

Premise Fifty-three: In each Job-test, God is testing the value structure of the saint without the support of the Holy Spirit. God wants to ensure that His Son is the saint's highest value, a necessity in order to pass the test.

Premise Fifty-four: The saint can determine a Job-test from temptation by asking for the Holy Spirit's assistance. If it is not forthcoming quickly, know it is a Job-test.

Premise Fifty-five: Saints must successfully pass their Job-tests, each uniquely tailored to the saint, before that saint is permitted to major new levels.

CHURCH RELATIONS:

Premise Fifty-six: The Holy Spirit's real church is a spiritual church.

Premise Fifty-seven: The presence of Jesus' real church brings favor upon that nation which peacefully harbors that church.

Premise Fifty-eight: The Spirit of God's real church exists today across all denominational lines, existing where it can.

Premise Fifty-nine: The Holy Spirit shall procure Jesus' invigorated and renewed church exclusively by His introduction of the **Overchurch**.

Premise Sixty: The **Overchurch** shall be introduced to the secular and religious world via a colossal spiritual awakening.

Premise Sixty-one: The **Overchurch** will exercise Holy Communion as an integral function of its mission assignments.

Premise Sixty-two: Since the Spirit of God is the vehicle for the transformation of the bread and grace elements into the body and blood of the Lord Jesus, **Overchurch** Holy Communion services will become world famous for their fervor and blessings.

Premise Sixty-three: Only the Spirit of God can admit saints to the **Overchurch**.

CURSE BREAKING:

Premise Sixty-four: The Holy Spirit hates curses, compulsions and addictions that capture and control the soul/spirit of humans.

Premise Sixty-five: Only God can break curses, and the Spirit of God usually will break all curses not self-inflicted, when asked.

Premise Sixty-six: The Holy Spirit will break a self-inflicted curse when asked by the inflicted human, but this must be done from within the **Holy Junction** and as directed by the Father or the Son.

BOUNTIFUL BLESSINGS:

Premise Sixty-seven: While the Holy Spirit is the source of cultural prosperity, fulfilling and overseeing God's law of bountiful blessings, He can also provide for individuals if asked by the Father or the Son.

Premises Sixty-eight: When God's law of bountiful blessing is activated by the beloved ones within a societal entity, the Holy Spirit showers God's bounty upon all the members of that societal entity, saints as well as sinners, because the reward belongs to that civilization.

Premise Sixty-nine: Before the Holy Spirit is allowed to shower bountiful blessings upon any given cultural entity, that civilization must suffer and sacrifice for Jesus Christ.

Premise Seventy: A threshold of suffering and agape love is required before the Father will release His bountiful blessings through His Spirit.

Premise Seventy-one: A threshold of sinning against both the Son and the Holy Spirit is required before God will release His wrath upon any given cultural entity.

BIBLICAL ACUMEN:

Premise Seventy-two: The Holy Spirit grants to God's beloved ones, requesting His assistance, the correct interpretation of the Bible.

Premise Seventy-three: The Holy Spirit can enlighten the minds of the beloved to vast knowledge, if requested.

SPECIAL GIFTS:

Premise Seventy-four: The Holy Spirit grants His fruits to the beloved ones when they reach the overcoming indwelling level, which fruits are love, joy, peace, patience, kindness, goodness, faithfulness, gentleness, and self-control (Galatians 5:22-23).

Premise Seventy-five: The Holy Spirit grants His gifts to the beloved as He would. These gifts are wisdom, message of knowledge, faith, healing, miraculous powers, prophecy, discernment of spirits, different tongues, and the interpretation of tongues (1 Corinthians 12:8-10).

Premise Seventy-six: The Holy Spirit generates fervor for the Son of God, Jesus Christ, and for His mission.

PERSONAL INTERACTIONS:

Premise Seventy-seven: The Holy Spirit takes pleasure out of the accomplishments of humans when He is allowed to be a participant, regardless of human evaluation of the significance of those human achievements.

Premise Seventy-eight: The Holy Spirit greatly enjoys human thankfulness.

HOLY JUNCTION:

Premise Seventy-nine: When a human has reached true rebirth in Christ Jesus with the human spirit freed from the domination of the human mind, then the Holy Spirit will blend with that human spirit like a glove to a hand, taking that human spirit into the presence of the Father. This is called the **Holy Junction**, an optimum connection with God.

Premise Eighty: From the **Holy Junction**, all the enemies of God are helpless. The blessed saint does not pray in this junction; instead, he or she participates in true worship in which the human spirit communicates directly with the Father. The mind is allowed to participate in support, but its participation is not essential.

Premise Eighty-one: The elevation of the human spirit in the **Holy Junction** enables the human spirit to be engaged with the Father even while normal, sin-free, actions of the human occur.

Premise Eighty-two: The transfer of Spiritual Kingdom power (energy) is without limits while the saint remains in the **Holy Junction**.

Premise Eighty-three: When lifted to the **Holy Junction** by the Holy Spirit, our Father readily grants intercessory requests for others.

Premise Eighty-four: While in the **Holy Junction** the saint experiences a 50,000 to one increase in faith and energy power.

Premise Eighty-five: When lifted to the Father by the Holy Spirit in the **Holy Junction**, the saint is enabled to an equivalence of a level-four presence for the duration of the junction.

Premise Eighty-six: Frequent visits to the Father in the lifting of the human spirit in the **Holy Junction** will lift the permanent presence of the indwelling Holy Spirit.

Premise Eighty-seven: The Holy Spirit under certain conditions of Holy Communion or Biblical contemplation will lift saints to the **Holy Junction** that have not had an indwelling presence, leaving them with that presence.

Premise Eighty-eight: The Holy Spirit utilizes level-four saints for synchronized spiritual warfare, especially when that saint is in the **Holy Junction** with the Father. In effect, the overwhelming power of the Father can be directed into synchronized spiritual warfare with dramatic results. This is a form of spiritual warfare not yet understood or mastered by the human species but one, which is destined to help save the human species.

Premise Eighty-nine: If prayer solicitations can be agreed upon before the Holy Spirit carries the human spirit into the **Holy Junction**, the Father immediately grants them upon the arrival of the saint's spirit into His presence.

Premise Ninety: Because the responsibility is upon the Spirit of God, the granting of **Holy Junction** requests is not automatic.

SPECIAL END-TIME GIFTS

Premise Ninety-one: As a special end-time discernment gift to the beloved ones of Christ, the Holy Spirit has promised to identify the presence of inner impersonators to those saints desiring an introspective knowing.

Premise Ninety-two: As a special end-time gift to the beloved ones of Christ, the Holy Spirit has promised to provide the Hidden Manna as an anointed, aggressive spiritual cleansing weapon for the saints that frequent the **Holy Junction**.

Premise Ninety-three: The Hidden Manna functions in two modes: The second mode is as the projected Touch of Love of the Holy Spirit, which can be used from the **Holy Junction** as a cleansing blessing upon any given spirit-filled saint. Great cleansing benefits, including the removal of impersonators, will occur to any individual accepting this special cleansing blessing.

Premise Ninety-four: The first mode of the Hidden Manna functions from within the **Holy Junction** as vectored grace to the unsaved or carnal saints that are in spiritual need. Summarizing, the Hidden Manna provides grace for those not experienced in the indwelling presence and a greater indwelling to those saints that have a touch of this indwelling.

LIMITED LIFE CYCLES:

Premise Ninety-five: The Spirit of God desires to increase the knowledge of the Christian world to include the concepts of **Limited Life Cycles;** wherein, each soul repeats in a heathen cycle of life until that unique chance for a Christian life cycle occurs.

Premise Ninety-six: The Christian life cycle is the judgment cycle.

Premise Ninety-seven: To reach salvation, the soul/spirit must proclaim Jesus as that soul/spirit's personal Savior or face judgment, possibly to the Pit.

Premise Ninety-eight: Maximum judgment is the end of that soul's cycling, the second death, which carries an appointment to the Pit.

Premise Ninety-nine: God grieves over each assignment to the Pit.

Premise One Hundred: The Spirit states that God, under special exception, will grant a second opportunity to live this Christian judgment cycle. These second chance opportunities usually occur because of gross injustice in the initial Christian life, e.g., aborted fetus, retardation or murder.

Premise One Hundred and One: The Holy Spirit relates that sixteen retention centers exist in the spiritual realm of which one, the Equity Adjustment Queue, is the passage queue to the kingdom of God.

Premise One Hundred and Two: Because of the Father's great love, up to twelve retention centers exist enabling the qualifying soul/spirit another chance at life.

Premise One Hundred and Three: The Spirit states that six retention centers have the ability to process soul/spirits back into the Christian life cycles. These are the Innocent Queue (composed of the very young, the retarded and the aborted), the Murdered Queue with its special Warrior Queue (those killed in war unable to work out their salvation before their man-inflicted death), the Tyranny Conviction Queue, Backslide Queue and the Special-Exception Suicide Queue.

Premise One Hundred and Four: The burden for the release of these trapped soul/spirits has been placed by God on the living saints, working with the Spirit of God.

Premise One Hundred and Five: God has mandated that the living help the deceased stuck in those retention queues that can be recycled, by utilizing **Holy Junction** requests, with the expectation that the Spirit of God will direct and assist that effort.

Premise One Hundred and Six: To assist in this assignment the Spirit of God has a special notification methodology which will alert each living soul inclined and able to help the suffering soul/spirit, especially if a previous relationship of blood, marriage, friendship or association existed.

Premise One Hundred and Seven: Once the living saint has accepted the guidance of the Holy Spirit, that saint can be a vehicle to bring other living saints to the assistance of those souls/spirits stuck in one of several retention queues from which escape is possible.

Premise One Hundred and Eight: Three retention queues are of special interest to the Holy Spirit. These are the innocent queue of Christian aborted babies, the murdered queue of the innocent and the queue of those murdered by tyranny convictions, i.e., left outside the reach of the Holy Spirit by the deceptive (often indirect and educational) brainwashing by the enemy of God. (The Holy Spirit says that the last two queues have been untouched or unaided by the living since Jesus cleaned them out before His Resurrection in 30 AD, leaving extensive frustration among those poor victims.)

Premise One Hundred and Nine: The Spirit of God especially desires the assistance of the **Holy Junction**-capacitated saints in releasing the second chance aborted babies from their Innocent Queue. (This queue contains only soul/spirits aborted while entering the Christian life cycle.) Each such released soul/spirit dims the forthcoming discipline by reducing the expected death punishment by two living humans.

Premise One Hundred and Ten: The Spirit of God directs all soul/spirits - prayed out of the innocent queues by the living - into an incarnated Christian life. (While this process only has had a few soul/spirits released by the author and his prayer partners; knowledge of the theology of the Holy Spirit will generate a flood.)

Premise One Hundred and Eleven: A murdered-in-battle queue, the Warrior Queue, exists that contains most of the warriors of the past. It is a huge queue. The Spirit of God grieves over these victimized soul/spirits, asking for the living to consider their prayer assistance for these suffering souls, especially for each of those soul/spirits that qualify for another Christian incarnation.

Premise One Hundred and Twelve: The living saints have the option to request only those soul/spirits that will conform to the kingdom of God implementation work to be released from their retention.

Premise One Hundred and Thirteen: The Holy Spirit can and will quicken the mind of the living for prayer assistance for those soul/spirits stuck in a retention queue.

Premise One Hundred and Fourteen: The Spirit of God solicits prayers for unknown causes either on earth and in retention queues from all saints sensitized to Him.

MARTYRDOMSHIP

Premise One Hundred and Fifteen: Any soul/spirit willing to die for Jesus is lifted to heaven immediately.

Premise One Hundred and Sixteen: At the moment of martyrdom, the Holy Spirit provides extraordinary inner strength.

Premise One Hundred and Seventeen: The host of heaven grieves, along with the Holy Spirit, at each near-Martyr.

SOCIETAL INTERACTIONS: SUBSET AGE OF THE HOLY SPIRIT:

Premise One Hundred and Eighteen: The Spirit of God intends to lead the church once more, leading it back to the forgotten **redemptive capacities** of the rescue of Jesus Christ. From there He intends to reverse the Adamic fall individually and culturally. This will occur when the Spirit of God is able to touch enough souls to bring a critical mass of believers into the highest indwelling presence of the Holy Spirit. By resuming the leadership of the church, the **second fall** will be defeated.

Premise One Hundred and Nineteen: When the church embraces the forgotten redemptive capacities, the Holy Spirit will lead the church to victory over the Adamic Curse.

Premise One Hundred and Twenty: The Holy Spirit grieves over the differing doctrines of the Last Supper, desiring a common and daily communion among the faithful, with the body and blood of the Son becoming the Doorway to the **Holy Junction** with the Father.

Premise One Hundred and Twenty-one: The Spirit of God requires that the influences of the parodies of the pagans, especially of the Greek mystery religions, be disavowed and disowned as the condition for His resumption of the leadership of the church.

Premise One Hundred and Twenty-two: The Spirit of God requires that all pagan influences incurred over the centuries be purged from the church before He will be willing to resume leadership of the church.

Premise One Hundred and Twenty-three: The **Overchurch** shall function only under the leadership and direction of the Holy Spirit, dedicated to the mission of Jesus Christ. Human leadership shall operate only as **Teachers**, **Pointers**, **Collectors**, **Enablers** and **Adapters**, sanctioned by the anointing of the Holy Spirit to pursue Jesus vector to the kingdom of God.

Premise One Hundred and Twenty-four: The Spirit of God will anoint His **Teachers**, leading them in their teachings, especially in the correct interpretations of Holy Scripture.

Premise One Hundred and Twenty-five: The Holy Spirit will provide the task vector assignment to His **Pointers** who will then illuminate a given portion of Jesus' vector path.

Premise One Hundred and Twenty-six: The Holy Spirit will use His **Collector** to physically call the faithful ones assigned to this particular task as led by the Holy Spirit.

Premise One Hundred and Twenty-seven: When the team is assembled by the **Collector** and given its direction by the **Pointer**, the Holy Spirit will then provide the **Enablers**.

Premise One Hundred and Twenty-eight: **Enablers** will be level-four enables spiritual saints dedicated only to the mission vector work of Jesus, so filled with the Spirit of Christ that He truly lives within. These saints, both male and female, will be focused free from the distractions of life, able to provide spiritual strength for the tasks.

Premise One Hundred and Twenty-nine: **Adapters** are level-four spiritual saints appointed by the Spirit of God to heal the saints of inner conflicts, compulsions, addictions, curses and all other obstacles to the closeness to God that the arrival of agape civilization affords.

Premise One Hundred and Thirty: **Adapters** will make those social adaptations that humans will require in their adjustment to the kingdom of God brought to earth. Such adaptations will include no prisons or judges or police or leaders or evil activities.

Premise One Hundred and Thirty-one: The Holy Spirit will provide the force behind the vector task in the form of fervor and faith unexcelled.

Premise One Hundred and Thirty-two: The Father has used His Spirit to search the churches of the Body of Christ for purity of worship and has found them wanting. Fidelity and fervor to the Son is greatly dimmed. So, as mandated by the Father, the church must undergo a harsh cleansing discipline before the Holy Spirit can renew the church.

Premise One Hundred and Thirty-three: The Father has mandated that the church age ends as the subset age of the Holy Spirit. Here, human capacities are greatly expanded, enabling the successful completion of God's restoration plan from the grip of the Adamic fall.

Premise One Hundred and Thirty-four: The rule of law, which is superior to the rule of man, will be replace and enhanced by the rule of the commune in the subset age of the Holy Spirit.

HARMONIOUS ORGANIZATIONS:

Premise One Hundred and Thirty-five: When the Holy Spirit inhabits human social organizations He turns them into harmonious organizations capable of pursuing the mission of the Son of God, Christ Jesus.

Premise One Hundred and Thirty-six: After the Prototypical Kingdom arrives, the Holy Spirit will no longer withdraw from a harmonious organization, but instead, He will remove the offending human elements.

Premise One Hundred and Thirty-seven: Harmonious organizations, at their peak as the **Overchurch**, can successfully transform heathen societies into agape civilizations.

SUBSET AGE OF THE HOLY SPIRIT:

Premise One Hundred and Thirty-eight: Agape civilization, as the precursor to the coming of the kingdom of God, even in prototype, only can exist in the subset age of the Holy Spirit.

Premise One Hundred and Thirty-nine: In the subset age of the Holy Spirit, the thinking coordinates of humanity will be advanced to include the Spirit of God as a coordinate.

Premise One Hundred and Forty: In the subset age of the Holy Spirit, the human spirit will be elevated to the true status of a sensor in God's heavenly kingdom.

Premise One Hundred and Forty-one: As the subset age of the Holy Spirit approaches, the Holy Spirit will enable saints in the **Holy Junction** to restrict the incarnation flow of Satan's evil-dedicated soul/spirits into specifically targeted areas of the world, i.e., those areas set aside for the Prototypical Kingdom.

Premise One Hundred and Forty-two: In the subset age of the Holy Spirit, a validation process will be developed to monitor and check all messages received from God's spiritual kingdom.

Premise One Hundred and Forty-three: In the subset age of the Holy Spirit, a societal validated commune will arise that will enable the Son of God to rule His kingdom on earth even before His physical return.

Premise One Hundred and Forty-four: Societal Validation will be a blend of information technology and the **Holy Junction** formed and monitored by the Holy Spirit.

Premise One Hundred and Forty-five: The harmonious organization of humanity, functioning under the validated societal commune, will be the highest possible civilization that humanity can achieve. It will become the Bride of Christ.

Premise One Hundred and Forty-six: It was to reach the validated societal commune in the subset age of the Holy Spirit that God dedicated the last minor dispensation to technological advance.

Premise One Hundred and Forty-seven: Human discipline will become Spirit directed and controlled after the agape civilization shifts into the first prototype of the kingdom of God on earth.

Premise One Hundred and Forty-eight: Human knowledge will explode after the validation of the spiritual commune into the heavenly realm of God is tested and proven.

Premise One Hundred and Forty-nine: In the subset age of the Holy Spirit an army of battle warriors will be enabled to spiritual warfare that will cleanse the territory of the Prototypical Kingdom of the enemy of God and his workers.

Premise One Hundred and Fifty: In the subset age of the Holy Spirit, the human participants will be enabled to inner healing so that overcoming will be via emancipation instead of suppression. This is the supreme expression of overcoming and that of which Revelation 3:21 speaks.

Premise One Hundred and Fifty-one: When humanity reaches that status where a majority of humans in any given culture are operating at or near level four indwelling, frequently in the **Holy Junction** – a societal critical mass is reached. This unique situation generates an agape love explosion, which shall erupt throughout that entire culture. Under the wondrous support of the Holy Spirit, this explosion is fully capable of generating an agape civilization within days.

Premise One Hundred and Fifty-two: To raise humanity to the critical mass, God will implement the Spirit's Touch of Love. This will function in two modes. The first mode is as grace, touching the unbelieving soul/spirit from outside. The second mode is from the indwelling of the Holy Spirit, escalating the existing saint to the higher level indwelling presence in mere moments. In both instances, the affected soul/spirit can reject the Spirit's Touch of Love (defined as God's hidden manna) or accept it, becoming an entirely different human in a matter of seconds.

The Spirit driven explosion has never happened; although, it is felt that it was meant to happen around 70 AD and in 1287 - 1294 AD. The freewill decisions of humanity changed both of these precious dates, losing much. The lack of understanding and appreciation of the theology and role of the Holy Spirit throughout the centuries has contributed mightily to the demise of the potential of Jesus' mission. This must change, and change it; God shall. Study the premises of the theology of the Holy Spirit, and confirming them, make them part of your walk with God.

GOD'S INTERVENTION

Unfortunately, God's intervention must first generate immense human suffering. Tragically, human misery is a necessary prerequisite to rehabilitate human responsiveness to God. This suffering will be designed to eliminate our total, exclusive and arrogant reliance on our intellect. It is not that God wants to drive out our thinking capacities, He just wants a balance between the human spirit and soul, which does now exist rarely in humanity. Once this is accomplished, His outpouring, maximized love touch will follow. This outpouring will hit our country and other selected lands seven times, transforming the majority of those touched. However, human freewill will still be decisive, and the widespread rejection of the touch is the event that could instigate the trail of destruction. If the love touch is accepted, the reverse occurs, and the people of this land and those other specially selected nations shift into the subset age of the Holy Spirit, an age that will see the spiritual enlightenment of human existence. Here, we will know the fullness of Jesus' rescue, reversing the Adamic fall, eliminating human exploitation, dimming earth and animal exploitations, and implementing agape coexistence.

The vehicle for the explosion of the agape love focused on fulfilling Jesus' revolt will be the special implementation generation, arriving in great numbers since August 1999. It is important to grasp the following sequence of events, for the Lord God desires that you know this:

- In January of 1999, the host of heaven received an invitation from God to join in a special incarnation on earth - as John the Baptist did - to implement a generational correction on earth.
- Vast numbers of soul/spirits located in the three levels below the throne room of God volunteered.
- These babies have been pouring into our country ever since, including babies of non-Christian parents.
- The implementation generation will be led by the soul/spirit of Apostle Paul who incarnated from the throne room of God on Memorial Day 2001, scheduled for normal birth as the generational leader on January 28, 2002, fully protected by God's angels.

- The discipline of America will take the lives of million from our land, including many of the parents of the special implementation children.
- The implementation generation will be spared.
- Huge numbers of orphanages will develop in the post discipline era before the arrival of the subset age of the Holy Spirit.
- The Holy Spirit shall touch these orphans, who will then interact with each other, generating fervor never seen before on earth.
- As these orphans grow into maturity, they will reach a decisive critical mass of adult believers, which will then explode in a huge spiritual awakening, generating, first, a huge awakening then revival revolution.
- It is then that the Lord will shift the minor dispensation to the subset age of the Holy Spirit, inaugurating the drive for the initial implementation of His Kingdom adapted to earth. The plan of God featuring the sacrifice of His Son shall be fulfilled.

Once the targeted kingdom implementation generation of humanity is safely shifted into the dispensation of the Holy Spirit, we shall be able to synchronize our efforts with the Holy Spirit by the elevation of our human spirit. There the saints can precisely define and retune our thinking coordinates, adjusting it as the vector of Christ is fulfilled. Yet, the choice of the path is still ours; will we take it and move towards paradise, or do we fail again?

If as a nation, we allow the implementation babies to grow and prosper without poisoning their young minds with the vermin of materialism and humanism, then the people of this land shall shout an emphatic: Yes, we follow Jesus Christ! Let us as one people embrace the fullness of Jesus' mission vector and defeat the Adamic Curse, bringing on agape civilization, all for the good of humanity and the glory of God. Paradise approaches!

Chapter 23

Special Millennium Message from the Father
(This is a four-part message received early morning January 1, 2001 while in the Holy Junction with the Father.)

FIRST PART OF THE MILLENNIUM MESSAGE:

Hear Me! Until my beloved ones grasp my goal as initially expressed in the movement of my Spiritual Franciscans, my faithful ones are lost to my Son's plans to implement my kingdom upon this earth. I would speak to them!

SPIRITUAL FRANCISCANS

The movement of the Spiritual Franciscans was in direct response to the visitation of Jesus Christ to Francis of Assisi in 1205 in which Jesus requested a reconstruction of His church and His civilization with these words to Francis of Assisi: *Repair my House.* This request was coupled with Joachim of Flora's input about the need to shift into the age of the Holy Spirit, forming the essence of the movement of the Spiritual Franciscans.

What was the church's disrepair that so dramatically upset our Savior that He made a special appearance to correct it? The heart of this collapse resides in two basic mistakes, both covered by the text of this book as major portions of the *second fall.* The first huge mistake was **legacy blunder two** that forfeited the leadership of the Holy Spirit. The second huge mistake was **legacy blunder six** that sacrificed Jesus' implementation drive to the kingdom of God. These acts, especially the forfeiture of the drive to the kingdom, invalidated the Gospel - making inadvertent hypocrites of all saints saying the Lord's Prayer.

With the forfeiture of Gospel truth and the abandonment of the leadership of the Spirit, widespread true worship of God as defined in John 4:24, calling for the worship of God in spirit and truth, ceased. This terrible demise was solidified with the arrival of the church canon, which restricted the sovereignty of the Holy Spirit. Hence, the saints became enslaved in a worship syntax that negated the freedom and companionship of the Holy Spirit so essential to the human spirit's participation in true worship, stifling the first component of true worship. Then with the Gospel truth of the New Testament compromised in the Pact of Cooperation, the second component of true worship, truth, no longer existed.

Thus, widespread true worship of God ceased in the fourth century, substantially lowering the kingdom spiritual power potential of the saints.

Both of these serious mistakes also impacted the call to the age of the Holy Spirit, first heard in the second century Montanus movement. Montanism was deemed a heresy by the church - which, in its extreme, it was! But it contained much truth outside its extremes, and the call to the age of the Holy Spirit was one of these truths. The freedom of women to engage God directly and the concept of an ongoing commune with God were the other great teachings of the Montanists.

Why are these facts important to modern humanity?

Their importance stems from this crucial wisdom received January 1, 2001 from the Father in a continuation of the first message:

SECOND PART OF THE MILLENNIUM MESSAGE:

My beloved ones must understand that only the shift into the age of my Spirit can enable the coming of my kingdom.

The Spiritual Franciscans, called the dissentients, understood this wisdom. They knew that the mistakes of the past must be undone. So united, this movement succeeded in establishing the start to the kingdom of God on earth. Commencing in 1259, the dissentients eventually experienced up to 30-years of bliss, peace and agape love within significant portions of central Europe. Quoting from Will Durant:[114]

"Perhaps in excited expectation of the coming Kingdom, a mania of religious penitence flared up around Perugia in 1259, and swept through northern Italy. Thousands of penitents of every age and class marched in disorderly procession, dressed only in loincloths, weeping, praying to God for mercy, and scourging themselves with leather thongs. Thieves and usurers fell in, and restored their illegal gains; murderers, catching the contagion of repentance, knelt before their victim's kin and begged to be slain; prisoners were released, exiles were recalled, enmities were healed. The movement spread through Germany into Bohemia; and for a time it seemed that a new and mystical faith, ignoring the church, would inundate Europe. But in a little while the nature of man reasserted itself; new enmities developed, sinning and murder were renewed; and the flagellant craze disappeared into the psychic recesses from which it had emerged."

Here, we see the secular - thus an unbelieving and uncomprehending - view of the movement of the Holy Spirit; today, our only witness to this momentous movement of God. Throw off the ignorant bias of the secular report, reject the flagellation and then realize that this is the early and primitive portrait of the

---

114. Durant, Will *The Age of Faith*. New York: Simon and Schuster, 1950, Page 809.

future. But at the same time, let us never forget the ultimate mistake of this movement. It was deceived into rejecting the New Testament and Jesus, and with this rejection it sinned mightily, losing the guidance and the power of the Holy Spirit. Let us warrant to God that this can never happen again. We must take the positive from the dissentients and leave the negative. Let it be clear. The coming age of the Holy Spirit is a subset age, subsumed by and supported by the glory of the Lord, Christ Jesus, the beloved Son of the Father, our Savior.

THE CONFLICT

The Spiritual dissentients engaged the church in a fierce debate over poverty and the accumulated wealth of the church. They challenged the right of the church hierarchy to live like kings, contrasting this life of luxury with Jesus' life style while on earth, stating that the Lord Jesus was a dissentient, a Franciscan dedicated to poverty, in all but the habit. The church replied that even in the process of consuming food you did not own, you possessed it, disavowing absolute poverty. They could not agree.

Eventually driven from the church, the dissentients took the people with them, emptying the churches. This is when the bliss of God fell upon the people. Crime disappeared; compassion soared. The people embraced one another in brotherhood free of cynicism. And agape love marched through the land, changing that generation. Despite excesses like self-flagellation, it was a wondrous time to live, not seen since then. This movement approached the birth of the kingdom of God, nearly answering Jesus' request for church and societal reconstruction.

Still, those of intellect, both secular and religious, saw it as an anarchistic movement of rabbles, an evil happening - a view still reflected in most historical accounts of that time. Clearly, God's vision did not flow through the intelligentsia then, even as it does not now![115]

The dissentient's impact left the hierarchy of the church frightened and incensed - certain that the very survival of the church was at stake. Suddenly, a false gospel appeared among the dissentients, read to them since most dissentients were not literate. This spurious gospel, created by a monk, led the dissentients into serious apostasy. The essence of this false gospel was that the Bible and indeed, even Jesus' salvation, did not apply to the age of the Holy Spirit because all things would be new in this age. This was a lamentable mistake, a lie out of the depths of hell. By listening to this lie, the dissentients

---

115. Even now, it is easy to discern the suppression of, and the hate for, this movement of the Spiritual Franciscans in the history books.

failed Christ, proving they were unworthy. How God must have grieved! They should have heeded this Scripture:

Anyone who runs ahead and does not continue in the teaching of Christ does not have God; whoever continues in the teaching has both the Father and the Son (2 John 9).

The question of the centuries is, did the church hierarchical ecclesiastics manufacture this false gospel to break up the movement? The church denies it, but it operated to the advantage of the hierarchy.[116]

Grieved that the people so easily accepted this false teaching, the Holy Spirit withdrew as the apostasy spread, destroying the establishment of the age of the Holy Spirit for that time, killing this shift to a new minor dispensation before it was fully and truly implemented.

To finish the destruction of the dissentient movement, the church utilized a new methodology for faith persuasion modification, called the Inquisition, which, unfortunately, proved very effective.

The Roman Catholic Church has repudiated this false gospel, disclaiming any official connection with it, even imprisoning the authoring monk, thus blurring the lines of responsibility in this serious matter, at least in the eyes of humanity. But God sees all.

Interestingly, in the midst of this terrible struggle, God was able to install a supporting pope in July 1294 that temporarily reversed the campaign against the dissentients. This was Celestine V.[117] He rode on an ass to his coronation and slept on rough planks while pope. Yet in his innocence, the ecclesiastic couriers, champions of deception, took advantage of the man. He lasted five months before abdicating. Some question if he left voluntarily; others feel that he left because he perceived his own administrative weakness. Regardless, history records that he fled from his successor for two months before being captured and forcibly imprisoned in the tower of the castle of Fumone, where he died within months.

---

116. Hughes, Philip *A History of the Church* volume III, New York, Sheed & Ward 1927, page 187 relates that St. Bridget of Sweden felt that the Pope and Cardinals that persecuted the remnants of the dissentients were going to hell as greater traitors to Christ than Judas, 'more cruel than Pilate.'

117. Ibid. Page 53. Interestingly, before his coronation as Celestine V, Peter Murrone had written a letter to the Cardinals of Rome warning of God's wrath upon the church. Unable to escape the grasp of the king of Naples to effect these diverting decisions himself, his prophetic warning became reality over the next 350 years. The tragedy was enacted. Clearly, the confused and abbreviated reign of Celestine V was the linchpin for the Roman Catholic Church, that which set its path to violent breakup under the wrath of God.

The church cannot cover its sins over this pope or his support of the dissentients by making him a Saint.

Eventually, the church eradicated the dying movement by imprisoning all the dissentient leaders in 1317, burning four leaders at the stake in 1318.[118] God's anger was seriously provoked! In mere months after this church action, the Black Plague arrived in Europe. In less than half a century, huge numbers of Europeans perished. A huge sin had been committed both by the church that persecuted the dissentients as well as by the dissentients that, in their utter ignorance, were deceived into rejecting Christ. The magnitude of these sins has not yet been comprehended!

LEGACY OF THIS CONFLICT

Now, consider the legacy of this great sin of the church, yet unrecognized or repented: The modern churches' - both Protestant and Catholic - arrival into the contemporary world is founded upon misinformation, horror and torture, the tools of the enemy of God. Indeed, this concept is breathtaking in magnitude and scope. Yet, it is clearly specified and identified by all those dead modern churches that afflict Christianity today.

But why are the Protestants guilty? Their movement did not occur until two hundred years after these serious deceptions and inquisitional sins. The Protestant guilt is by inheritance, impacting them as the unrepentant descendents of the guilty church. Here finally, we can see as the Father sees:

THIRD PART OF THE MILLENNIUM MESSAGE:

The magnitude of the Roman Church's sin against my movement - and thusly, the return to my Son's plan to bring my kingdom to earth - is so great that complete disassociation from that mother church and its sin does not reach atonement for that sin in my eyes!

This means that this horrible sin is our common Christian inheritance, yet to be repudiated by either faith paradigm. The Greek and Russian Orthodox religions seem to be innocent of this responsibility.

Moreover, we, the modern world, have forgotten God's blessed movement of the thirteenth century and its utter importance to the comprehension of our current status and our future involvement with God. Here, we do not see as God sees! While recorded history has been blurred, the realities of those events live on in the mind of God.

---

118. Ibid. page 130.

To grasp what is happening in the world, we must cease thinking in 75-year cycles and start thinking in millennium cycles, just two days to God. This shift in thinking coordinates is imminently important to us, for uncompromisingly, Christian success in the future hinges on a modern reestablishment of that dissentient movement so beloved by God. But the events that would result in this reestablishment cannot commence unless this initial church sin is repudiated. Indeed, the Father says this prodigious sin remains today, as a curse upon all of our spiritual heads, a roadblock to the healing of Christianity. It functions as the **tenth church legacy blunder of humankind.**

Here is the fourth and critical portion of the Father's teaching given this first day of the new millennium:

FOURTH PART OF THE MILLENNIUM MESSAGE:

Seek atonement for my church's great offense in repudiating my Son's call to return the church into the anointed leadership of my Spirit. With my church and Spirit united again, my kingdom approaches within a new age of agape love and human cleansing, the age of my Spirit. This is the only permitted way the kingdom can be birthed on earth.

Today, modern Christians do not understand this teaching, but it is a teaching from God that must be mastered and redressed in order to move ahead in God's plan for humanity! The consequences of ignoring this call from the Father are too severe to contemplate.

Clearly, the dissentient's defeat at the hands of the Roman Catholic Church deeply angered God. He disciplined both the church and the culture for the next three hundred and fifty years; an event often referred to by historians as the most appalling years of European history. Europeans experienced unnatural deaths of up to fifty percent of their population. It was a time of mass horror and fear. The bodies of the suddenly dead piled up so high that it was impossible to bury them all before their stench overwhelmed the living. This discipline, and God's anger was terminated in the late seventeenth century. Yet, what stupidity enables humanity to so easily forget God's wrath? Rationality! Do we think for a moment that God's wrath could not find another means if the black plague had been understood and defeated by the equivalence of modern medicine? We dare not be arrogant before God!

So is the Father appeased? No! He would have us rejoin Jesus' push to the kingdom, commencing with the repudiation of those thirteenth & fourteenth century crimes against the expressed will of His Son, Jesus Christ.

To optimize the next attempt, the intervention in the affairs of humanity by the Spirit of God with His touch of love, God has permitted the eighteen, nineteen and twentieth centuries to be kingdom foundation centuries. Technology has been given to humanity to better assist our weak faith for another, and perhaps last, attempt to drive down the vector of Jesus to paradise, that which was killed off in the thirteenth century. Again permitted to drive toward agape civilization, the culture of optimized personal freedom and the return to paradise, all of humanity should rejoice. For clearly, the drive to return to paradise is instinctive within humanity, as recently illustrated by the intelligentsias' attempt to reach paradise via Marxism and its current push for the Global Village. All such movements are doomed to failure, lacking the presence and blessings of God. Even the Moslem revolt in Iran, although largely unknown to the West, was a revolution designed to bring paradise to earth. Today, its failure to reach its mission goals is evident by the contemporary events in Iran where the push to join the rest of the world is overwhelming.

Clearly, **agape civilization, defined as that culture in which each human deeply loves other humans free of the need for reciprocity or reward for that love,** is the highest possible culture obtainable by humanity. It is the true goal of humanity, representing a civilization free of the Adamic curse of exploitation. It is the first step in the establishment of the prototype of the kingdom of God adapted to earth. However, reaching this accomplishment can occur exclusively through Christ Jesus, and the Father has mandated that this shall happen only within the subset age of the Holy Spirit. *The huge emphasis on the continuance of the Gospel of Jesus Christ, His Divinity, and His salvation sacrifice on the Cross, followed by His Resurrection into the subset age of the Holy Spirit is the vast difference between that which will be in the future and that which failed in the thirteenth century.*

These truths must be grasped before we can reach agape civilization. For only in the subset age of the Holy Spirit can we experience Christ-led victories over sin. It is here, in this new but last minor dispensation of the Church Age, permitted by the Holy Spirit's intervention, that we can defeat, finally, the Adamic-generated curse of human exploitation, at last coming together as brothers and sisters in God's embrace as Jesus' **Overchurch.**

To grasp the significance of this word from God is to grasp the import of the Protestant Reformation. That reform movement, actually composed of three distinct movements, had the potential to undo the sin of the Roman Catholic Church, reversing not only the mistakes that generated the *second fall*, but the church's sin against Jesus' request to repair His church, the equivalence of a *third fall*. Instead, the Reformation ignored the lessons of the dissentients, disregarded Jesus' message, appearing indifferent, disbelieving, or perhaps ignorant of His 1205 appearance, an appearance that the Holy Spirit equates in importance to Jesus first century appearance to Saul on the road to Damascus.

Protestant leaders actually perpetuated the *second fall* by seeking their defense against the Catholic armies in the secular armies of the world. What might have been if the two leaders, Luther and Zwingli, had taken the road of the suffering Christ? But they did not! In fact, it is alleged that while both supported the Holy Spirit, neither man knew the deeper indwelling of the Spirit, generally holding spiritual Christians in contempt. Certainly, it is felt they had no grasp of the age of the Holy Spirit or of Jesus' appearance to Francis in 1205.

Yet, the Protestant Reformation had many successes. Indeed, it can be viewed as God's corrective step of prior weaknesses found within the movement of the thirteenth century dissentients. The Reformation introduced personal freedom to the world, producing widespread literacy by spreading the Bible among the people. (Clearly, with widespread Biblical literacy the mistakes of the dissentients could not be replicated.) The Reformation gave room for the Spirit to move within individuals, defeating, in large measure, the restrictions of the Roman Canon. It produced fervor and sincerity where previously, precious little existed. It triggered God's law of bountiful blessings, and it opened the door for great advances in science. In all this success, the Reformation looked like, and was, a great triumph.

However, the Protestant Reformation could have been much more. If it had listened to men like Conrad Grebel or Thomas Muntzer, it could have returned to the mission of the dissentients under the colossal blessings of God. Instead, it forfeited its great potential, generating **legacy blunders eleven and twelve** instead. In these blunders along with **legacy blunders thirteen and fourteen**, the Reformation became, instead, a harvester of Christian division, its fervor waning over the centuries.

This, then, is our situation. Both of the religious faith paradigms, Protestant and Catholic, are less than is needed. Today, after the Second Vatican Council, one is not better than the other! Suspicion and mistrust rules the Christian denominations. The Thirty-Year-War, the legacy of the Lord's wrath, is still clandestinely fought with brilliant human minds obstinately ruling both faith paradigms, ensuring future faith failures and cultural destruction. Both faith paradigms must overcome their feelings of elitism and exclusion. Both need to repent. Both can contribute to the drive to the kingdom by embracing the theology of the Holy Spirit with its emphasis upon the subset age of the Holy Spirit. In this fashion, these faith systems can become more than they currently are by moving into the spiritual status Jesus prefers. Yet, it is obvious that this will not happen if the churches remain under the intellectual control of humans, perpetuating division and disunity. Ecumenicalism, unity from the top, will not prove adequate.

To solve this problem, God intends to introduce the **Overchurch**, a church led only by the Spirit of God, not the intellect of humanity. The **Overchurch**, to be formed by the outpouring Spirit of God, will unify Christianity from the bottom up. It will also implement the shift into the subset age of the Holy Spirit, and impel a transformation of the culture of North America - and a few other nations - into the first prototype of the kingdom of God on earth.[119]

Now, that time approaches in which the Father and the Son shall order the outpouring of the Holy Spirit, God's intervention in the affair of humanity to save us. Only this intervention can reverse our sorry state of affairs in church and culture. To be ready, we must, each, fully understand the events of the Spiritual Franciscan movement, its successes and its apostasies, seeking atonement, personally and denominationally for the sins of our spiritual predecessors. Then, we must move closer to Jesus. Each saint and each denomination must plan for a spiritual jump to a new level with God, in effect shifting from a carnal saint and church to a spiritual one. This spiritual jump-start will be the massive outpouring of the Holy Spirit analogously equated to jump-starting a car. Let each saint prepare for this spiritual jump-start, realizing that exciting, even if turbulent events are now closing upon us in this new and exhilarating century. The path to this preparation and closeness to Jesus is the Christ-Walk, traversing that bridge between the carnal and the spiritual saint. Here, as a spiritual saint, the beloved of God can walk close to Jesus via the increasing indwelling presence of the Spirit of God.

Subsequently, we can see an important escape threshold from our current spiritual passivity: the knowledge and awareness that the Holy Spirit indwells to different levels.

Stop! Think about this! Here is knowledge that compels action. Actually, it is a dividing line between passivity and fervor - that pinnacle of spiritual knowledge sought after for centuries - always under our knowledge noses. Once this knowledge is absorbed, once we understand the theology of the Holy Spirit, it mandates each saint to seek after a higher indwelling level of the Holy Spirit,

---

119. Actually, the list of nations initially involved along with America is relatively small, but the number of nations that ultimately join is impressive, encompassing every continent but one. As given by the Holy Spirit, eight nations will split - each with portions joining the kingdom. This will sharply define the divide between the kingdom and the dark world even in the blood of the martyrs. Subject to human freewill decisions, the nations that will split are Mexico, Scotland, Russia, Norway, Sweden, China, Uruguay and the Philippines. Other nations that are involved without division are Korea, Poland, Finland, the Baltic nations, Argentina, Chile, Canada, England, Ireland, Australia, and New Zealand. Eventually, Israel will join after she finds her Messiah. There are several other nations that could join if the level of **Holy Junction** prayer within those nations reaches a required threshold. The number of developed nations that are excluded is shocking. The author has a map of the kingdom that will require the Lord's permission before it can be released.

even as instructed in Matthew 6:33. So proceed accordingly! Come to the appreciation of the Spirit and His potential work in you. Commence your closer walk now, today, always praising Jesus for the door He opened, so that jointly, as one people led by the Spirit, we enter that Door!

ADDENDUM TO THE MILLENNIUM MESSAGE:

Here is the order of critical events relative to the age of the Holy Spirit:
1. Jesus announces His departure and that He will send the Spirit with these words: And I will ask the Father, and He will give you another Counselor to be with you forever - the Spirit of truth. The world cannot accept Him, because it neither sees Him nor knows Him. But you know Him, for He lives with you and will be in you (John 14:16-17).
2. The Holy Spirit starts the church on Pentecost Sunday, powerfully indwelling the initial 120 Christ followers, then most of the subsequent converts. The primitive church is a spiritual church led by the Holy Spirit, operating in a de facto age of the Holy Spirit. It authors the New Testament.
3. The church splinters as many divergent groups emerge - mostly led by men of intellect who do not know the power of the indwelling Spirit. The original church, the Nazarenes, loses its struggle in the Judean culture and eventually dies out in the apostasy of Adoptionism. This is the **first legacy blunder**.
4. Before the death of the original Nazarene church, Jesus appears to Saul switching the anointed church to the Gentiles.
5. Still a struggling underground but spiritual church, the Gentile church, calling themselves Christians, effectively changes the world, defeating paganism.
6. Christians remain as an underground church with persecutions constantly coming and going. In between persecutions, Christians face their worst enemy, prosperity. The church slips from spiritual to carnal as articulated earlier by Paul in 1 Corinthian 3:1.
7. In 172, Montanus sought a return to the primitive church in which all saints heard the Spirit of God. He believed that God was calling the church into an age of the Holy Spirit. But in his efforts to hear the Spirit, Montanus confused the human psychic center with the human spirit. Deceived by Satan, Montanus leads his movement into apostasy, proclaiming the return of Jesus at Pepusa in 172 AD.
8. Although prominent thinkers of the church, men like Tertullian accepted the concepts of the Montanist, the church reacted strongly against the false prophesy, declaring Montanism a heresy.

9. The bishops developed a church canon to prevent the occurrence of another Pepusa. Unfortunately, the church, in its rejection of Montanism, lost both the leadership of the Holy Spirit and the knowledge and significance of the age of the Holy Spirit. This became the **second church legacy blunder**.

10. The fourth century brought the Pragmatic Cancer with its stepchild, the informal, but highly effective Pact of Cooperation between the church and the pagan society. This action, the **sixth legacy blunder** forfeited the drive for the kingdom of God - compromising the Gospels. In this compromise, the church surrendered its victory over paganism, betraying the cause of Christ. With Gospel truth comprised and the abandonment of the drive for the kingdom and the Spirit denied, the **third through the sixth of the church legacy blunders** were completed. Widespread true worship as defined by John 4:24 no longer existed. Those that fled this decision became the first monks of the church, inhabiting the caves of Egypt.

11. This **sixth legacy blunder** was a huge mistake generated by the fourth century church fathers seeking an end to Roman persecutions. With this shortsighted action, they invoked the anger of God, destroyed the keys to the Kingdom, and with it the anointed authority of the church. In effect, the organized church became a heresy void of the leadership of God. This word of truth comes from God, but validation of its truth can be seen in the subsequent history of the church, especially in the papacy, which frequently became a scandal and an embarrassment to Christ.

12. Much of this embarrassment arose from the excessive concentration of political and religious power in the hands of the few, the papacy, almost guaranteeing its abuse. This centralization occurred with the development of the False Decretals in Le Mans France in 850, the **ninth legacy blunder**. The first wrath of God resulted in the widespread demise of learning and knowledge, including the original church canon. So, three centuries later, the church authorities simply sat down and recreated it, attributing authorship to saints long dead.

13. However, the Spirit strongly warns that we must not let this indictment of the church hierarchy reflect on the good work for Christ Jesus performed over the centuries and still being performed at the pastoral level of this institutional church. With the Council of Trent and the Second Vatican Council this church has traveled a long distance in reconciliation with God and fellow man. What other church has publicly and officially apologized for its past mistakes? Let us remember the parable of the plank in our eye, Luke 6:41, and always accept those who see Jesus' divinity as the Son of God as brothers and sisters in the Lord.

14. With the **sixth legacy blunder**, God's discipline fell upon the church and surrounding culture, measured from the sacking of Rome in 410 to the appearance of Jesus to Francis of Assisi in 1205. It was a dark time for the Europeans.

15. At the end of the twelfth century, Joachim of Flora, a bishop of the church, had a vision in which he saw the history of faith divided into three ages. The first is the age of the Father, the second is the age of the Son, and the third is the age of the Holy Spirit. He identified the age of the Holy Spirit as the vehicle for the implementation of agape love and the future hope of humanity (which he felt would be implemented by monks). He reported his vision to Pope Innocent III, in 1200. That pope promptly rejected and suppressed it.

16. Five years later, in 1205, Jesus appeared to Francis with His request: *Repair my House*. Was this a request or a command? It was a command! Yet, His command that Christianity be repaired has been largely ignored for 795 years despite the fact that the Holy Spirit rates its importance to humanity equal with Jesus' appearance to Saul in the first century.

17. The rebellious movement of the Spiritual Franciscans, called the dissentients by the church, was inaugurated to answer Jesus' request, asserting that the age of the Holy Spirit would start in 1260.

18. The dissentients were amazingly successful, indicating the initial presence of the Holy Spirit in their movement. Their success drew the faithful out of the formal churches, emptying those churches.

19. The institutional church struggled against the success of the dissentients, facing the possibilities of collapse. They were saved when apostasy was induced into the movement from a fraudulent gospel. The movement of the dissentients dies at the hands of the church, becoming the **church's tenth major legacy blunder**.

20. The second minor dispensation of wrath started, measured from 1317 to the London fire in 1666.

21. In 1517, the Protestant Reformation broke out. It produced the Radical and Spiritual Reformation as schism reform movements. The Spiritual Reformation movement reached for a Spirit-filled church, but failed under the intolerance of the mainline Protestant leaders. This was the **fifteenth legacy blunder**.

22. In the sixteenth century, remnants of the Spiritual Reformation generated the Pilgrims who eventually settled America in the seventeenth century under covenant with God, a movement of great promise. Unfortunately, the Calvinists who followed did not fully understand this covenant. In their rush to prove they were predestined by God, validated only by

wealth, they polluted this covenant and its mission in their resultant avarice. This is the **sixteenth legacy blunder**.

23. Led by one of the founding fathers of this nation, a great denial of the divinity of Jesus Christ moved over America, only placed in check by the Second Great Awakening. This surge of disbelief, which still lingers in our country much as Arianism lingered in Rome, is the **seventeenth legacy blunder**.

24. After God's corrective action to save America with His Great Awakenings, the church has remained passive as the secular humanists have captured the American culture, shoving the Christians aside as second-class citizens. This is the **eighteenth legacy blunder**.

25. The humanists now running the Western world are rapidly generating God's wrath upon the entire world though the **nineteenth legacy blunder**, the attempt to spread God's bountiful blessings evenly across the entire world, even as they seek political world advantage.

In 1973, the author, blissfully unaware of Francis and his word from Jesus, heard God ask for a new church, one built upon a stone foundation with four great halls: 1) **True Worship**, later realized as reached through the Holy Junction love, 2) **Healing** and the exercise of the gifts and fruits of the Spirit, and 3) **Spiritual and Cultural Warfare**. The last hall would be named later. After many years the author became certain that this last hall of God's church is, 4) **Inner Cleansing**. Human cleansing is utterly necessary to form the kingdom of God, moving humanity from suppression of inherited or sin-acquired compulsions, addictions, and evil orientations to emancipation from these evil afflictions. The **Holy Junction** with God – the blending of the human spirit with the Holy Spirit after which the Holy Spirit takes the human spirit to the Father and the Son – is provided as the vehicle for success in all of the halls, operating as a fast track to kingdom spiritual power. Teaching the Word of God will also be prominent in this church. Twenty-five years after receiving the word on His unmovable church of stone, God revealed that His requested new church was the **Overchurch**, led exclusively by His Spirit.

In 1976, the author, still totally ignorant and indifferent to the movement of the dissentients, heard about the Lord's intention to bring about a Subset Age of the Holy Spirit. In the early hours of 2001 the Father delivered His new millennium message in which He defined the utter necessity to shift into the age of the Holy Spirit in order to reverse the Adamic as well as the **second fall.** By stirring His Spirit to intervene with a massive outpouring of the touch of love, the Father opens the door to the implementation of His Kingdom on earth in this new millennium, defeating the legacy blunders of humankind. However, His intervention will not be painless.

God is revealing that the reversal of the Adamic fall has been His ultimate but misunderstood, or sabotaged plan, since His Son, Jesus, initially walked this earth. The decision is now firmly made. God will move unwilling humanity into the greater state, the subset age of the Holy Spirit, leading to the first implementation of the Kingdom of God on earth. This is to be done by enabling the fullness of Jesus' redemptive capacities, thus eradicating the Adamic curses and cleansing His people, all accomplished by His Spirit's intervention. Our role is to become symphonized with His intervention, to accept it, and to optimize it. From this new subset age our progeny will look back and wonder at our lost wanderings, pondering how close we came to losing it all!

Appendix A

Human Exploitation

Human civilizations have had many political and organizational expressions: Monarchy, dictatorship, theocracy, oligarchy, totalitarianism and republicanism to name the most common ones. They all seem radically different. Yet they differ in degree not kind. Each of these civilizations is a primordial product of the Adamic curse. They are so judged, despite the highest expression of art, music, prose and poetry reached by any given civilization, because the determining trait for each of these cultural expressions always has been the exploitation of weaker humans. And with the arrival of sophisticated technology, the misuse of the earth for the benefit of the relative few must be included in that indictment, making the sin of exploitation generational.

THE IMPACT OF EXPLOITATION

An insidious drive, exploitation nurtures cynicism, breeding contempt of other human beings. Derision and contempt produces suspicion of the actions of others. The whole process destroys human trust and damages personal integrity. Democracy is a serious attempt to defeat this cycle of derision by redressing human mistreatment from a different perspective. The objective of democracy is to limit or to control the exploitation of the majority, by the powerful few, through the structured political activism of that majority. This, hopefully, elevates the status of a large number of persons in that culture, dampening the forces of cynicism and contempt. However, after an initial and successful start the goals of the world's foremost demonstration in democracy, the American experiment, are arguably, even if subjectively, judged as forfeited through special interest corruption. Thus this experiment, the only truly large-scale culturally exploratory experiment of modern times, has failed because of the political manipulation of the majority by the special interests of the few. Most significantly, the format of the failed American democracy has been spread throughout the world, offered as the road to bountiful prosperity. But do we know what we propagate?

Frequently, democratic and pseudo democratic cultures employ competitiveness to control and manipulate exploitation. These cultures push good sportsmanship, attempting to instill the concept of the reign of the superior human with good cheer. Thoroughly, this experiment has failed. All participants understand the ruthlessness of competitiveness. Each loser hates the personal defeat and expresses good wishes to the winner only as an expression of expected social facades. Thus, life in a democratic culture is nothing but the exploitation jungle once removed by a smile and twice removed by good manners.

Frustrated in its attempts to subdue human maltreatment, our modern version of democracy has degenerated into an attempt to conceal exploitation. In this effort, our American (and European) culture has equated concealment as the containment of human manipulation. In this ignoble action, our society has succeeded in concealing the realities of life, blanketing even the brutal finality of life that we must take life to live life. As an example, the average shopper picks up freshly killed carefully wrapped and refrigerated life forms without a fleeting thought about that life form's love of life.

Rarely does the thought of the rejection of exploitation, human, animal or earth, with its total encirclement upon each of us, embrace us, driving us forward toward something better. Indeed, our modern, polite civilization camouflages the unsavory aspects of existence, attempting to undo by facades, if we can, the results of the first fall of humankind. It is a ruse! We, its victims, navigate the ride as inauthentically as possible.

As we conceal reality behind our cultivated facades, pragmatically behind our economic and production cycles and societally behind our social programs, we generate a culture of deception. Thus ironically, the benefiting force in this trickery is human exploitation. Is this an accident or a horrible and clever fraud? And what price do we pay for this dead-end of cultural deception? This! Lost contact with the mission critical tasks of Jesus Christ, humankind's only hope for true freedom.

HUMAN EXPLOITATION: FOUNDATIONAL PREMISE FOR HUMAN CIVILIZATIONS

This conclusion remains. Human exploitation is the common denominator for all human civilizations and one of the chief tenets of the Adamic curse upon humankind. Clearly, within this overriding characteristic of all human cultures, it is certifiable human mistreatment, born as the by-product of the Adamic curse. That continues today motivated by economic and personal power drives. Hence, it is perfectly logical to argue that only by the elimination of human and earth exploitation can we reach that higher-level civilization, the quantum leap culture. Yet, blinded to this basic fact, the intellectuals of the West strive for economic advantage in globalization and a pragmatic and societal paradise in the global village. Tragically, this push, once again void of God, is the wrong direction, guaranteeing catastrophic failure! Mixed with the advent of weapons of mass destruction, our current decision point on the course of humanity is crucial to the continuation of human existence. We do not have the time to make another mistake; yet, that is happening.

It is essential that the present course of humanity be reversed to save the human species. Here is the primary premise for this salvation and the road to an advanced human civilization:

Exploitation must be eliminated as the defining feature of human civilization to reach the next level of human society. This level of civilization, the culture of agape love, can only arrive via the eradication of the Adamic curse. And this unique event occurs exclusively through the blood sacrifice of Jesus Christ and the full deployment of the redemptive capacities that Jesus gave to humanity. The problem is that all intellectual solutions are offered exclusively from the wrong frame of reference, which is the present day compromise to the Adamic curse. Today, all intellectuals are born and raised in this compromised systems, which they cannot perceive; hence, most of their ideas are useless.

It is important to understand that the single and sole hope for the exploited peoples of the world resides in the redemptive blood of Jesus Christ as it covers our culture and our persons.

When the saint affirms his or her personal salvation through Christ, the saint experiences inner freedom from the Adamic curse. But the culture in which that saint lives does not experience freedom from the Adamic curse. In fact, it continues in its human exploitation, unaware of the need to change. It is here that the church has been passive and timid.

Only by applying the redemptive blood of Jesus Christ to the culture, as well as the individual, can societal redemption from the Adamic curse occur. Culturally free, citizens can reach exploitation independence, experiencing a huge, dramatic and joyous shift in the adventures of life. This freedom shall be known as agape civilization, which as it evolves will focus the arrival of the kingdom of God.

SLAVERY AND ITS LEGACY

Human exploitation is a sin of the worse type because it makes a mockery of the judgment of God. And the worst manifestation of human abuse is slavery. At the time of Christ's incarnation, fully half the people of the Roman world were slaves. The good news that God loved them was 'good' indeed.

Slavery depends upon force and the human propensity to grovel in fear. American Korean War experiences validated the concept that every human can be made to grovel unless the Spirit of God intercedes. We are sheep, frightened sheep, which all of our societal and individualized bravado cannot hide. So when the mantle of Jesus' mission vector was shifted to the Gentiles, it found that after centuries of forced slavery the Gentile world had too many, too willing to grovel, too soon.

Then, there is the exploitation of the mind. Here, the exploiter effectively brainwashes the human target into actions of submission. When mental brainwashing reaches cultural levels and effectively prohibits the exploited from finding the salvation of Christ, that culture dooms itself to misery and eventual destruction. The modern media carries an extraordinarily important moral responsibility in this matter, a responsibility not yet recognized.

Clearly, the enemy of God is a major participant in the practice of human abuse. Hence, to break this abuse, the forces of Satan must be broken. This happens absolutely with the return of Jesus. But meanwhile, while we wait, the power capacities to realize a facsimile of these results, spectacularly and nationally, innately resides within the Christian churches. The saints must recognize that this innate power comes from the deeper presence of the indwelling Holy Spirit. Then, to suppress Satan, the saints must start individual and societal wide spiritual warfare.

AMERICAN DREAM: EXPANDING THE EXPLOITATION BASE

The American cultural experiment broke with the old country's [English] evolutionary approach to representative culture, instead reaching immediately for freedom and democracy. New, vigorous, and constricted only by a minimized handicap from its English cultural tradition, the American culture was free to inaugurate a cultural experiment even though it initially confined this experiment to wealthy white farmers. Its greatest feature was its encouragement of upward mobility from the ranks of the exploited to the lower ranks of the exploiters. And indeed, individual success stories of upward mobility dot American history. In aggregate, these actions have generated the notion of the American dream, best paraphrased as the escape from exploitation. This dream has attracted two types of persons. First there are those interested in escaping from exploitation. Second, there are those interested in becoming exploiters. The problem with the dream is that upward mobility has limits. By definition, in all cultures delineated by exploitation, which is in all primordial or semi-primordial cultures, not all participants can be exploiters; there must be some to exploit. This is true even in a massive network in which each person is both an exploiter and exploitee. Thusly, most American emigrants seeking to escape from terror manipulation became victims of polite exploitations. Obviously, these results are not compatible with God's vision for this land.

Consider this statement: Proportionally, no modern Western nation has a larger concentration of wealth held by the privileged few than America. And today, the American dream is a sham, a spurious surrogate of the real mission, although even in this Degradation, our nation is the optimized free culture in the world. God covenanted the true mission with the Pilgrim fathers: Develop the prototypical kingdom of God in the new world as a city on the hill, a light therein to illuminate the world by the radiance of Christ, opening the world to the harvest of the good-seed. In summary, the spurious American dream is the gut drive of greed, fostered and abetted by Satan, which has temporarily sidetracked the true mission of the land established by the Pilgrim Fathers.

AMERICA'S COVENANTED ABUNDANCE

Even as secular humanists were commandeering political and educational power within our culture, the faithful followers of Jesus Christ, mostly rural folks, remained loyal to Christ. This loyalty invoked the spiritual law of Bountiful Blessings, building a large heavenly treasure for our country.[120] Now and for several generations, America has lived on the payoff of that treasure, in which God has showered great economic abundance on the land, causing America to blossom. To its great credit, America has attempted to share this wealth, but to its great detriment, it has never understood the source of its abundance. Thus, we have yet to learn this lesson: Although the actions and decisions of humans (like congress or the Federal Reserve) can enhance or hinder economic abundance, humankind cannot directly fabricate it.

Unfortunately, the accidental recipients of this abundance, the secular humanists and their allies, the nominal Christian, non-devout Jewish or atheistic human and earth exploiters, now possess near total control of our civilization. Ignorant of the real reason for our nation's prosperity they believe their secular efforts promote economic growth. Various schools of economic theory concerning human monetary promotion and the maintenance of prosperity lace the universities of the land. And although their theories frequently challenge one another, they have chiefly developed one cultural economic theorem, which contributes the country's financial successes to economic exploitation controlled by democratic ethics. In effect, they promoted a system that grants the people the right to select their exploitation regulators, but not their exploitation, or the right to deny it. In this, the American experiment has equated democracy with exploitation. Is this a step-up in the evolution of human civilization? Yes, but it is still a civilization of human misuse, still the victim of the Adamic fall!

---

120. See Shults, Eugene C. *Mission-Critical* Wausau Fl, Pro-King Books, page 59.

Nonetheless, the American experiment is the apex of human freedom within our current minor dispensation of God, established to promote technology and personal freedom from groveling. As such, under the conditions of its establishment and the limitations of the current minor dispensation, our experiment is destined never to get better. So, all those who seek still greater freedom within our culture now face diminishing returns on their efforts. Void of the blessings of God, we now see the reverse effect of their effort, e.g., obvious criminals, eluding their punishment because they take advantage of this inane and unblessed effort to optimize that, which has already been optimized. To progress as a culture we must make the quantum jump to agape civilization. To affect this jump, we must turn to the New Covenant renewal, featured in the next minor dispensation - the subset age of the Holy Spirit. This age will be inaugurated through a vast spiritual awakening, led and brought about by the special intervention of God. In the language of the cultural scientists, we must go through a Cultural Transformation with the bifurcation point immediately ahead, in the form of a massive discipline, followed by a gigantic spiritual and cultural revival. Here, we must understand clearly that we face a revolution of thought, not an evolution of ideas. Our thinking coordinates must embrace a major adjustment in order to advance humanity toward the next higher level of human cooperative society. Unfortunately, humanity does not possess the inner capacities to reach this adjustment. Correspondingly, we are at the mercy of God for His assistance, which will be both painful and benevolent. Here, we shall see God, as He is, a God of balance, capable of both discipline and love.

ASSAULT OF THE CHRIST-HATERS

The people of America desperately need the New Covenant renewal. Today, a residue New Covenant faith remains in this country but under a vicious assault led by the educational and media cultural paradigms. Christ-hating atheists, humanists, and the people of a minority faith interested in the expiration of the Christian faith, despite vigorous Christian support for their homeland, staff these institutions. They fail to understand that the greatness of this land did not come from their ancestors nor their religious beliefs but from a relatively uncontaminated subset of Protestant Christianity.

Seriously ignorant of the real reasons for the residue of the nation's spiritual, moral and physical health, the secularists and their religious allies now act to remove the leftover hegemony of Christ from the land and to drive it from the hearts of the people. Increasingly, these special interests utilize the federal government and its court system as its enforcement tool in this drive. With victory, they will claim the land for their god, humanism, which is nothing but a front for Satan. Then they will turn and spit upon their religious allies who have so foolishly and enthusiastically supported them. When you see this happen, know that the hour is late, too late.

It is our call to resist the secular humanists and their religious allies to save our freedom democracy. *But for Christians this resistance must be hate-free and non-violent.* What victory for Christ can be consummated by force or in hate? Jesus would not tolerate it. Let us pray for our enemies even as we come against them with the spiritual force provided by God.

SECULAR HUMANISM

As stated before, the characteristic of secular humanism is exploitation. The deep irony of this religion is that it is named humanism, a faith that ostensibly rejects human mistreatment while vigorously pursuing it. Thus, even the definition of American secular humanism is hypocritical, an oxymoron. Here, we see the marriage of two heathenish ideologies maintaining the twin view that the operation of a culture should be void of personal religious beliefs while professing that the only real god that exists is humanity itself. This amalgamation has generated pseudo-secularism: A secular society that rejects religious faith, especially the Christian faith, even as it violates its basic premises by promoting its non-proclaimed faith: Humanism.

Gaining great strength since the late eighteenth and especially the middle nineteenth centuries, when humanism found that science - especially evolution - could be a useful ally, pseudo-secularism has waged unrequited war on Christianity.

THE CRY FOR JUSTICE

While the church sleeps and the saints remain passive, others, the exploited, the very poor, the ethnic and racial minorities, women, and the socially and economically deprived of this country and the Western nations have raised their voices. These people grow weary of the exploitation format, whether economic or hate oriented. For over a century they have demanded equality and the end of abuse, pushing for a solution without knowing that solution. Their push has generated a rising protest for equality and equivalence that has sensitized the intelligentsia and the political leaders of this land and, to a lesser extent, the world.

In response to this outcry, humankind, especially large numbers of the European intelligentsia of the twentieth century, selected Marxism as its path to exploitation freedom. But under Marxism, the problems of human abuse did not diminish but become more prominent, leading to its eventual collapse. Now, increasing dissatisfaction with human mistreatment continues, heating up in the female and black movements. This discontent, when combined with the appearance of the information age, is scattering the seeds of restlessness nationwide, fueling the possibilities of a huge collision over human mistreatment between the advantaged and the disadvantaged throughout the American cultural environment, spreading from there to the entire world. The third world peoples have heard and now join in a massive choir for the removal of their disadvantageous position. In this process they ask for the unmerited transfer of wealth to them. This, indeed, is another process of exploitation, for they ask for God's bountiful bounty without meriting it. Theirs would be exploitation by thievery.

NEW WORLD ORDER

The American and foreign humanists and industrialists are attempting to construct a New World Order; at present a vaguely defined international economic system based upon secular humanism and continued societal and individual exploitation. The New World Order will push the concept of economic democracy upon the world under the American format of fiscal freedom, constrained only by representative democracy and featuring individual human rights. The proclaimed reasons for this push are admirable. The problem resides in the hidden agenda of the promoters, exploiters all.

Ironically however, even as this push continues worldwide, secular humanism is collapsing at home in America. The root cause of this collapse is moral decay brought about by the rejection of Jesus Christ and His gospel of love and hope. The secularists, and their captive media, locked into a frame of reference that does not contain the spiritual realm, cannot possibly define the problems of America. Without the proper demarcation of the problems, including the appropriate frame of thinking references, they have zero chance to solve America's problems. They can only lead the country into greater immorality and a nightmare of crime with economic ruin as its inevitable conclusion. Program after program, law after law, regulation after regulation, as well as dollar after dollar cannot fix the basic problem. In this mounting American and, now, worldwide frustration, humanistic secularism will fail, doomed by definition as well as by action.

Consider this: The Lord would change the course of the world, bending it back to Jesus' mission vector. To do this He must destroy the world, as it presently exists. Two new orders, as polarized enemies, will be rebuilt in the place of the old order. These new orders shall be the kingdom of God adapted to earth and the New World Order as the great enemy of Christ. This new cultural arrangement will form a deeply polarized world of strong contrasts.

259

To grasp the magnitude of tomorrow listen to the word from Jesus heard by the author in an early morning Bible meditation on 2 November 1981: *Doomed!* Startled, I asked whom, me? *No, every major political, economic and military structure in the entire world is doomed!* Later, as a demonstration of the validity of His Word, God brought down the Soviet Union without violence. Beloved of God, prepare; be ready; move into a strong walk with Christ Jesus, for this was just a demonstration!

The question that lingered, and still lingers, does this destruction of the secular culture extend to the church as it is currently constructed? The commune validates that a jarring change in the church will unfold, shifting the church from carnal to spiritual. In this shift, God will instigate an enormous inner cleansing of both church and saint, enabling the faithful followers of Christ Jesus to enthusiastically embrace the arrival of the spiritual church in America. This will be the Spirit-led **Overchurch**, drawing its allegiance from every denomination without destroying those denominations. In effect, those denominations that transform into spiritual churches under the forthcoming discipline of the Lord will retain pastoral functions, while the **Overchurch** will conduct the spiritual and cultural confrontation against secular humanism destined to bring agape civilization to North America. To achieve this goal, God has dispatched a great flood of special soul/spirits, the implementation generation. They are arriving now. Truly, the world has forgotten the likes of these saints! Mark the calendar between 2020 and 2060, for it is then that this generation will come into maturity for the Lord Jesus. In this same period of time, 60 years, the arrival of Satan's core of soul/spirits from hell has been restricted over America. This combination of events will convulse the country and change the world. The civilization of man is about to take its next biggest step forward. We have traveled this long path:

- Anarchy and Savagery, the rule of the fittest
- Rule of the autocrat
- Rule of the law.

Now we approach the

- Rule of the commune, that system in which all citizens have a real-time interactive communication system with God, correcting, guiding and disciplining.

THE COMING SECULAR DEATH STRUGGLE

Here, in this special covenanted land of America, the time of secularism with its Adamic curse-based exploitation nears its conclusion. God has foreordained this action and the Spirit confirms it. Yet it will gain nothing to be naive about this situation. Secularism and its religious partner, humanism, will not fade away gracefully. Rather, these inbreeding ideologies will mount an enormous struggle to remain as the preeminent frame of reference for humankind's civilization. Its survival struggle will have the full weight of Satan and his evil kingdom behind it, generating a fury of disruptions and violence. Christians, prepare to die for Christ!

While no sane person wants to die, when your turn comes to die for Christ, consider it a great honor. We are all weak and frightened humans, mere sheep; yet, let there be no groveling! Let us hold our heads high, knowing that the Holy Spirit will be with us in great comfort.

The death struggle of secular humanism will be difficult for it currently possesses the capacity to capture the minds of men and women born into the Adamic curse by its brainwashing technologies, working diligently on eliminating the remaining influences of the second-fall-weakened Christian churches. It owns the culture; possesses the enforcement agencies; dominates the universities; rules the politics of the country; directs the media of the nation and has even penetrated some of the Christian denominations. It would seem invincible, the great problem of our time and our culture: Secular humanism, as the most sophisticated representation of demonic-based human exploitation ever created, will not just fade away. It must be killed, just as one would put down a rabid animal! Yet, the death of secular humanism is even more difficult when one realizes that it falls upon the saints and churches of this land to achieve this goal without instigating violence. Only a people truly walking with Christ can do this: a spiritual people. Hence, our first challenge is within, for we are not now a spiritual people. Only God's massive intervention can change this fearful situation.

So, the challenge of the church will be turbulent, generating clashes, both inner and external, that will set the pattern for the entire world even as it opens the door to the coming of the kingdom of God. After its Spirit-led conversion from carnal to spiritual, the church, as the **Overchurch**, will develop into the Antithesis to the Thesis, defined as modern secular humanism. It is then that the mode of these clashes shall come to be recognized as a dialectical process depicting the procedure for the widespread arrival of agape love as the synthesis.

Up till now, this task is beyond our current spiritual empowerment. This we must pray to change, looking forward to the shift from carnal to spiritual even as called forth by Paul in 1 Corinthians 3:1-2. To reach this goal, the churches of Jesus Christ, those that love Him without constraint, must renew themselves in the leadership of the Spirit of God as the **Overchurch**. Indeed, this shift will highlight the need to shed the dogmas of the denominations that divide the Body of Christ - a process that has been attempted several times in our past, but has never been successfully implemented.[121] So today, our nation, churches and people face great misery and personal suffering in God's conditioning punishment, as He prepares to cleanse His house. Truly, this misery could be avoided, in large part, if we could change our nation's course and find again the kingship of Jesus Christ for America. Be aware that this is not simply the biased statement of a Jesus-loving, Spirit-pulsing, Bible-reading fanatic - which of course it is - but it is also the solution to the problem of massive pain and premature chastisement deaths scheduled for this land, sadly, a time of tears and lost faith. As of this moment, two will be taken early in life for every baby this country has aborted.

Saints, we must think about what we do! Our comfort, prosperity, and religious passivity today will be paid for with our lives or the lives of our loved ones tomorrow. God has selected this nation, America, to work out the plan of God for all of humanity. The stakes are the highest, for beyond our personal and national problems, the very survival of the human species is to be determined by this nation in this century.[122] Take this warning most seriously. This is not an attempt at sensationalism, nor is it reductionism, but it is a most profound warning to the human species from the Spirit of God. Our current course is headed toward worldwide destruction of our race!

Do not think that the secularists can reform themselves out of this pending destiny. They have absolutely no chance to lead this country away from this path of destruction, unable to develop the country's potential spiritual greatness because they operate from false premises, functioning within a set of incorrect intellectual concepts, blind to the truth.

No human or group of humans can reach any given objective if the coordinates of that objective reside outside their thinking frame of reference.

As an example equate our vision analogously to our thinking coordinates. If humanity did not have cones in their eyes, imagine the difficulties we would have in grasping the concept of color! We probably would mock and scorn that one endeavoring to describe color to us. In this analogy, the frame of reference of color simply did not exist for us. Yet, color does exist. It is analogously the same, today. Our religious brainwashed frame of references blind us. At best we see only dimly. At worst, we believe those claiming to see are peculiar, carrying no information of significance. Also, it is possible that those claiming to see clearly

---

121. Bainton, Roland H. *The Reformation of the Sixteenth Century*. Boston: Beacon Press, 1952. See the discussion of religious freedom pages 215-227.
122. The Spirit is impatient at the low key of this serious warning.

are themselves deceived. So, we take the position: '*Do not disturb our comfortable and regulated lives.*' This attitude arises because challenging new information is not permitted in our present thinking coordinates. These denominational delineations have been presented as absolute truth, truly a great victory of the enemy of God over the Body of Christ. In most instances, we accept our brainwashing constriction with total confidence, rendering us truly captive to these demarcations.

How is it that everyone born into a faith system is most confident that his or her system is exclusively the correct and accurate system in the entire world? Why are Moslems fanatics about their faith even as are the Hindu? Why are the different Christian denominations so certain they have the absolute truth, and that poor man from the church across the street does not?

This confidence resides over the entire world with billions willing to die for their birth or educated beliefs. What is this but tyranny convictions? From this captivity, only a true spiritual and mental rebirth can liberate us. That is, only God can set us upon the correct thinking coordinates. And His coordinates are absolute; have done with relativism. But how can we be assured that we have reached this absolute frame of reference? There are so many claimants and so many directions! Only when agape love reigns as fundamental and integral to our culture, defining it, free from exploitation, can we rest in the assurance that we have reached God's absolutism, assured that we have become the Bride of Christ!

Appendix B

Mathematical Representation of Imputed Righteousness

(If mathematics, even at this, the lowest level, is frightening to you, skip this appendix.)

Fascinatingly, the question of grace, the indwelling of the Spirit and the imputed righteousness of God can be expressed mathematically. First, it is necessary to equate every kingdom energy level of the saint to a basic unit of kingdom spiritual energy, which we will call **fire**. From there we have these different levels of kingdom spiritual energy breakdowns:[123]

$Fi \implies$ fire, 1 fire unit
$DFi \implies$ decifire, 1/10 of fire unit
$cFi \implies$ centifire, 1/100 of fire unit
$DFi \implies$ millifire, 1/1000 of a fire unit
$\mu Fi \implies$ microfire, 1/1000000 of a fire unit
$\eta Fi \implies$ nanofire, 1/1000000000 of a fire unit.

Or expressed in nanofires:

$Fi \implies$ 1,000,000,000 nanofires
$DFi \implies$ 100,000,000 nanofires
$cFi \implies$ 10,000,000 nanofires
$MFi \implies$ 1,000,000 nanofires
$\mu Fi \implies$ 1,000 nanofires
$\eta Fi \implies$ 1 nanofire.

On the basis of the Holy Spirit's input, these transfer rates are assigned to the different Christian spiritual power practices measured in sub-units of Fire:

---

123. Taken from Shults, *Christ-Walk: Finding True Worship and the Kingdom of God* 1stbooks.com

KINGDOM SPIRITUAL POWER ACQUISITIONS

Power Source	Transfer Range
Decision for Christ	Millifire
Baptism by Water	Millifire
Rebirth of the Human spirit	Centifire
Baptism in the Spirit	Decifire
Reading the Word	Nanofire
Studying the Word	Microfire
Meditating on the Word	Millifire
Holy Communion	Microfire
Pleading the Blood of Jesus	Microfire
Adoption of the mind of Christ	Centifire
Praising God	Nanofire
Anointed Praise	Microfire
Singing to God	Nanofire
Anointed Singing	Microfire
Praying in the Spirit	Millifire
True worship of God	Decifire
Commune with God	Centifire
Community worship of God	Microfire
Baptism of Fire	Fire
Grace	Fire to Nanofire
Holy Junction	Millifire to fire

Since we have related the activities of the saint to energy attained and consumed, we can build a spiritual energy relationship that should faithfully represent these power accumulators at any given moment of the saint's life.

Now the calculation of Kingdom Spiritual power, as a subsumed derivative of the more comprehensive mathematical expression shown in *Christ-Walk,* would look like this.

$$\sum_{Sn=1}^{Sn=max} Fi = S[\sum_{Sn=1}^{Sn=max} G + \sum_{Sn=1}^{Sn=max} L + [\sum_{Sn=1}^{Sn=max}(g+e) - \sum_{Sn=1}^{Sn=max}(c+n+o+sin)]]$$

Or expressed for any given moment as:

$$Fi = S[G + L + [(g+e) - (c+n+o+sin)]]$$

Where sn stands for the indwelling step of the Holy Spirit and
max = the maximum step.

The other values are:

S is salvation in Jesus Christ, a binary number.
G is the Grace of God.
L is the Love-gift of God, due to arrive with the outpouring of the Holy Spirit.
g is the kingdom spiritual energy generated by human acceptance of the current level of the indwelling Spirit of God. When this acceptance value maximizes, the next indwelling step is reached.
e is the kingdom spiritual energy generated by kingdom spiritual energy acquisition acts (see the above table).
c is the consumption of nanofires in the kingdom activities such as pastorate work, witnessing, healing, preaching, teaching, prophesying, and casting out.
n is the leakage of nanofires by the hidden orientations and activities of the mind, including psychic activities and hidden or denied sin.
o is the diversion of nanofires by enemy activity, such as temptation, oppression, carnal desires, and addictions.
sin is the destruction of nanofires by overt sin, as determined by the kingdom decorum as found in Holy Scripture, starting first with the Ten Commandants.

Then we simplify further our expression for the moment,

$$Fi = S[G + L + [(g + e) - (c + n + o + sin)]]$$

to make those important relationships more understandable, equating the following:

Fi = KSP (Kingdom Spiritual Power)
Leaving out S thus limiting our relationship to saved souls and
Leaving out L since it is largely in our future.
Introducing C as curses and
Introducing Al as agape love for God and fellow humans and
Introducing Level as the indwelling level of the Holy Spirit, then
Adding what was missing, SF, as the factor of the second fall, even as we recognize that suffering and consumption of KSP by doing the Lord's work is missing, giving this relationship:

$$KSP = G + \{C[g\,(Al * Level)] + e\} * SF - (c + n + o + sin)$$

Where KSP = Kingdom Spiritual Power in units of fire
  C = Curses: inherited, sin induced or self-inflicted, a binary number
  g = Host acceptance of the Indwelling Spirit
  Al = Agape love of the host for the Spirit & man
  Level = Level of the indwelling Spirit, for example 2.5 would be the half-way point to level 3
  e = Acquisition of kingdom Spiritual Energy by the Saint's Acts
  c = consumption of KSP in kingdom activities
  sin = Sin life
  n = Secret sin
  o = Demonic Oppression.
  SF = Second Fall degradation factor (.1)
  G = Grace.

The righteousness of God is found through the integration of KSP (Kingdom Spiritual Power) over time, which is the mathematical representation for the imputation of God's righteousness via the indwelling Spirit. But most readers are not ready for this level of mathematics; hence for simplicity of understanding we will affix the imputation of God's righteousness to a threshold value of KSP. (Incidentally, this is the argument for grace, the imputation of righteousness free of time dependencies. This is the ultimately faulted dependency of Luther's theology, because, driven by capriciousness, grace, while it touches the imputation of God's righteousness, cannot sustain it. Nevertheless, for ease of understanding, it is our starting point.)

The problem is to find that threshold Kingdom Spiritual Power (KSP) that instigates this imputation, regardless of its source. To find this real life threshold, we combine the commune with God with the binary search technique. Shocked? Look beyond your brainwashing captivity to see the potential precursor of the future. Here, even at this elementary level, we can see the marriage of science and faith functioning for its great potential: the implementation of validated communes with God. Perfected, it will challenge the scientific method for preeminence as the chief instrument in recasting human civilizations, expanding the knowledge database and establishing absolute thinking coordinates, revolutionizing society for Christ.[124]

---

124. Watch for a greater description of this wondrous integration of science and faith for the advancement of society in Shults Eugene C *Odyssey to Agape Civilization* written and scheduled for publication soon.

We start this process by assuming the threshold KSP value imputing God's righteousness is 2.5 fires.

Now let us use a fictitious Brian Common to see how this relationship functions. Brian is 34, has a family of two kids and a loving, attractive wife. Brian serves as an usher in the large mainline Protestant church downtown, where his boss is an elder. Brian has accepted Jesus Christ as his personal savior, and he is born again by the standards of his church. He believes he is saved by Justification by Faith despite his sin faults. Brian is known throughout the community for his consistent tithing as well as his charitable work in a local soup kitchen. He is a respected and upright member of the medium-sized town in which he lives, a member of the local Masonic lodge.

Brian has flirted with the good-looking girl from the steno pool for over a year before it suddenly erupted into an affair. Brian also has a serious pornography and masturbating habit that he has concealed from his family and friends. His secret sin is driven by a self-inflicted curse[125] of which he is incapable of defeating. Here is his KSP (Kingdom Spiritual Power) calculation: Brian's walk with Christ has these values:

$$
\begin{aligned}
C &= \text{Curses} = 0 \text{ meaning a high level of curses} \\
g &= \text{Host acceptance of the Indwelling Spirit} = 0 \\
Al &= \text{Agape love of the host for the Spirit} = 0 \\
Level &= \text{Level of the indwelling Spirit} = 0 \\
sin &= \text{Sin life} = 2 \text{ (high)} \\
n &= \text{Secret sin} = 4 \text{ (very high)} \\
o &= \text{Demonic Oppression} = 3 \text{ (very significant)} \\
e &= 1 \text{ (Brian work in the soup kitchen)} \\
c &= 0.3 \text{ (consumption of KSP witnessing)} \\
SF &= \text{Second Fall degradation factor} = 0.1 \\
G &= \text{Grace} = 0.
\end{aligned}
$$

$$KSP = G + \{C[g\,(Al * Level)] + e\} * SF - (c + n + o + sin)$$
$$KSP = 0 + \{0[0\,(0 * 1) + 1\} * .1 - (.3 + 4 + 3 + 2)\}$$
$$KSP = .1 - 9.3$$
$$KSP = 0$$

At this moment in Brian's life, G (grace) is equal to 0, but at the time of his born again experience, G equaled 3 fires, which when equated to his sin life of -9.3 still would have given Brian a KSP of zero. The righteousness of God would

---

125. See Shults, Prototypical Kingdom page 286 -291 for a fuller examination of the viciousness of these forms of curses.

not have been imputed to Brian despite the high grace input. Instead of God's righteousness, Brian had the feeling and touch of God's power but not its fullness, which weakness would account for his present and future problems with sin. As the power of God's grace withdrew, Brian's fire for the Lord died out. He is bored in church but goes because it is a political and socially necessity in his life.

Then one week Brian is talked into going to a Spirit-filled church with the nephew of the boss. There, Brian is baptized in the Holy Spirit, completely changing his life. He repents of his affair, his pornography, the Lodge, and seeks freedom from his curses. Switching churches to the spirit-filled church Brian works into a 2.2 indwelling of the Spirit even as he delivers himself from the oppression of the enemy of God. This is Brian's KSP at the end of his first year as a true Spirit-filled saint:[126]

$$
\begin{aligned}
C &= \text{Curses} = 1 \text{ meaning he has defeated them} \\
g &= \text{Host acceptance of the Indwelling Spirit} = 1, \text{ a normal} \\
  &\quad \text{acceptance of the Holy Spirit} \\
Al &= \text{Agape love of the host for the Spirit} = 3, \text{ a high level love} \\
  &\quad \text{for the Spirit of God} \\
Level &= \text{Level of the indwelling Spirit} = 2.2 \\
e &= 1 \text{ (Brian work in the soup kitchen)} \\
c &= 0.4 \text{ (consumption of KSP by witnessing)} \\
sin &= \text{Sin life} = 0.5 \text{ (normal)} \\
n &= \text{Secret sin} = 0 \text{ (gone)} \\
o &= \text{Demonic Oppression} = 0 \\
SF &= \text{Second Fall degradation factor} = 0.2, \text{ an improvement} \\
G &= \text{Grace} = 0.
\end{aligned}
$$

KSP = G + {C[g (Al * Level)] + e} * SF – (c + n + o + sin)

KSP = 0 + {1[1 (3 * 2.2) + 1} *.2 – (.4 + 0 + 0 + .5)
KSP = {(6.6 + 1) * .2} - .9
KSP = 7.6 * .2 - .9
KSP = 1.52 – .9 fires.
KSP = 0.62 fires.

---

126. It must be recognized that impostors exist: those so anxious for the feel and love of the Spirit that they invite in false spirits.

Brian is alive and excited about Christ in His life, filled with the Spirit of God; he is a temple of God on earth. But what could Brian have been without the **second fall** curse?

Now ten years have passed. Brian has continued to master his curses, constantly guarding against oppression even frequently working to deliver others. He has moved up to a 2.8 level indwelling of the Holy Spirit. Apologizing personally to the Holy Spirit for the disabling legacy of the church, Brian's **second fall** handicap decreases, giving him 0.35. His sin level has dropped to 0.1. Here is Brian's KSP (Kingdom Spiritual Power):

KSP = G + { C[g (Al * Level)] + e} * SF – (c + n + o + sin)
KSP = 0 + {1[1(3 * 2.8) + 1} *.35 – (.4 + 0 + 0 + .1)
KSP = {9.4} *.35 - .5
KSP = 3.3 - .5
KSP = 2.8 fires.

Brian has passed the threshold for the imputation of God's righteousness, truly finding Overcoming Justification. He is now a battle warrior engaged in spiritual warfare, reaching a position in the Body of Christ where healing has become his ministry. In his efforts for the Lord, grace would once again flow into his life increasing his fighting capacities for Jesus even more. This is the shift in grace that occurs to senior saints; whence, grace now assists in spiritual combat.

Where would Brian be in KSP (Kingdom Spiritual Power) without the indwelling presence of the Holy Spirit and all that it portents? Look at the kingdom power that accumulated to Brian because he understood and personally repudiated the **second fall**. If Brian had not come to grips with the **second fall** his KSP would have been 0.44 units of fire, not decisive energy level for God's service. Clearly, the church needs to reconcile with God over the **second fall**!

Now this illustration has many conjectures and assumptions concerning the values used. Yet that day will arrive when humanity will be able to precisely measure these parameters, available as a new capacity of the kingdom of God adapted to earth. When that moment arrives, the new subset age for Christianity will dawn.

Appendix C

Evidence the Jewish Tribulation has Passed

Here is the evidence for the argument that the Jewish Tribulation has already occurred.[127]

Any objective observer not interested in building support for a preconceived bias can see that the 66-73 war with its 70 AD destruction of the temple is Tribulation, which means that it was always meant to be an exclusively Jewish punishment. Our attempt to make it into a future end-time set of events has led us into deep deception.

Josephus was a Jewish general that attempted to train and field a Judean army to face and defeat the Roman army. Instead, Josephus was severely defeated. Captured, he gained a measure of respect by flattery and prophecy. Looking for a task, he recorded the history of the Jews, especially of the 66 to 73 Judean War of Independence.

Using Josephus, the author has compared some of those events of the Judean war of Independence with Jesus' prediction found in Matthew 24. The author has have attempted to divide the events pertinent for that period from events that can reasonably be expected for our future, e.g., earthquakes and wars.

- **Deception (Matthew 24:4):** Deception was huge in both Jewish conflicts for independence, especially the deception that the Jewish messiah had arrived as Bar Kokhba. He proclaimed the anointing of God over the war of 132 AD, promising that God was with them, ensuring their victory over the Romans. Additionally, the Zealots used deception to lure the Idumeans into the pillaging of Jerusalem in 70 AD.
- **Wars and Rumors of Wars (Matthew 24:6):** Has this ever changed?
- **Nations will Rise Up Against Nations (Matthew 24:7):** The relative peace of the third decade was broken by wars in the Middle East, Germany, and elsewhere. This has continued as a general condition of humanity.
- **Famines (Matthew 24:7):** This is probably in our future as it has been in our past. However, the famine of the Jerusalem siege in 70

---

127. This same data appears in Shults, *Prototypical Kingdom.*

AD was so severe, that Josephus claimed that the elderly were in great peril of being eaten, and were eaten.[128]

- **Earthquakes (Matthew 24:7):** Unknown except for earthquakes recorded in Acts16: 26 and other ancient literature. It is certainly in our future.

- **Persecutions (Matthew 24:9):** Jewish followers of Christ were severely persecuted by both Romans and Jews, as were the Jews by the Romans. Even devote Jews, such as the Scribes and Pharisees, were persecuted by the Jewish Zealots in 70 AD, reaching the brink of extinction.

- **Turning Away From the Faith (Matthew 24:10):** In persecution, some of the Jewish followers of Christ, called the Nazarenes, did turn back and renounce Jesus. The remnant Jerusalem congregation melted into history. Unbelievably, God abandoned the original church of Jesus Christ when they abandoned Jesus' divine nature by accepting the fraudulent theology of Adoptionism. Significantly, this is the church that wrote the New Testament. Does that mean the validity of the New Testament is impaired? No, it means we must not be arrogant in our own denominational elitism, for in our stubbornness to accept God's truth, either as found in the revealed word or in the discoveries of science, in our arrogant clinging to our inherited denominational theology, in our proclamation that only our denomination carries the truth we could lose God's blessings tomorrow, and indeed, some will. Are we not all partially guilty as charged?

- **Betrayals (Matthew 24:10):** Many betrayals occurred in the 66-73 war. Most heinous is the Zealot betrayal of the vast multitudes of worshiping Jews gathered at Jerusalem for the feast of unleavened bread, estimated by Josephus as 2,700,200 Jews, practically the entire nation.[129] The Zealots revolted, trapping these worshipers by suddenly locking the gates of Jerusalem. A splinter group falsely

---

128. Whiston, William *Josephus, Complete Works.* Grand Rapids: Kregel Publications, 1976, Book 5, chapter 10, section 4, page 565 of this edition states, "they [Jewish Zealots] drank the blood of the populace ... and divided the dead bodies of the poor creatures between them."

129. Whiston, Book 6, chapter 9, section 3, page 588 of this edition. '*... upon the allowance of no more than ten that feast together, amounts to two millions seven hundred thousand and two hundred persons .... Accordingly, the multitude of those that therein perished exceeded all the destructions that either men or God ever brought upon the world ...*' up to that time.

infiltrated the temple causing much destruction and death.[130] Then the Zealots went on a killing frenzy. Now, even before the Romans appeared at the walls of Jerusalem, the Zealots managed to kill many prominent Judeans and practiced multiple abominations in their own Jewish Temple. When cornered in the Temple by the enraged population, the Zealots called in the Idumeans to assist them, using falsehoods to bring them to Jerusalem.[131] After the Romans started their siege of Jerusalem, those Jewish factions somehow divided up the defense of the city by awarding different parts of the wall to different groups. Yet, their assault on the civilians continued. Caught between these forces and living in sheer terror from the famine and the ongoing murderous debauchery and rape by the Zealots and Idumeans, the Jewish worshippers desperately sought flight. To escape they bribed the Roman solders each night of the siege, quietly slipping over the wall. Yet, their escape was just a cruel hoax. The Roman soldiers were laying a trap for them, capturing and disemboweling each escapee as the soldiers searched for swallowed precious jewels and gold coins. None, not even infants, were spared. All were disemboweled, as many as 2,000 a day for six months. Only the twentieth century Jewish holocaust can match this horror. Romans, composed of mostly German troops, were killing Jews. But perhaps because – besides the Romans - Jews were killing Jews, it had a measure of horror even greater the Nazi terror. It must have been horrible to die at the hands of other Jews gone mad in a blood delirium. Hauntingly, after the Romans arrived and laid siege to Jerusalem, it was the Germans in the Roman army that were responsible for much of the worshipper's betrayal into unchecked terror.

- **Flee. Do not even go back to the City to Get Your Cloak (Matthew 24:16):** The Zealots seized the gates of Jerusalem suddenly killing the sleeping guards, killing thousands that very

---

130. Whiston, Book 5, chapter 3, section 1, page 551 of this edition.
131. Whiston, Book 4, chapter 4, section 1, page 530 of this edition. 'However, it was resolved [by the Zealots] to call in the Idumeans; so they wrote a short letter to this effect: - That Ananus [Chief Priest] had imposed on the people and was betraying their metropolis to the Romans; that they themselves had revolted from the rest and were in custody in the temple, on account of the preservation of the liberty …'

same night.[132] The window of escape must have been very short, perhaps only minutes.

- **For the Sake of the Elect the Days of Suffering are cut Short (Matthew 24:22):** If the Roman siege had lasted several months longer, the entire population of Jerusalem could have perished. This potentiality loomed because the looting and raping Zealots and Idumeans had destroyed the food granaries of Jerusalem before the Roman army started the siege. Beyond the starvation that the population had to endure, the slaughter was excessive. Even before the Romans appeared, the Zealots exterminated the Sadducees and severely massacred the Pharisees.[133] Later, the Romans eliminated the Essenes.

- **False prophets (Matthew 24:23):** Bar Kokhba was accepted as the Jewish Messiah in 132 AD. Proclaiming God insured victory, he led Judea to its death as a nation. Several minor and false prophets, e.g., Theudas and The Egyptian, arose shortly after Jesus, killed by the Romans without trial.[134]

- **Increase in Wickedness (Matthew 24:12):** The wickedness of the Zealots and the Idumeans within the city of Jerusalem, inflicted upon the most devout of the Judean population, probably has not been surpassed since that time.

- **Love Grows Cold (Matthew 24:12):** Although it is immeasurable at this distance in time; yet it appears to be the situation of our time as well.

- **The Abomination will stand in the Holy Place (Matthew 24:15):** Zealots, Jews all, stood in the holy of Holies and raped, robbed and murdered therein.[135] Josephus records the tormented screams of the Jewish high priest, Ananus, bemoaning the abominations conducted by the Zealots. Ananus stood in the midst of them, and…said, 'Certainly it had been good for me to die before I had seen the house

---

132. Whiston, Book 6, chapter 9, section 3, page 587 of this edition. '…they were come up from all the country to the feast of unleavened bread, and were on a sudden shut up by an army …'

133. Garraty, John A. & Gay, Peter *The Columbia History of the World*, New York: Harper & Row, Publishers, 1972, page 220.

134. Sanders, E. P. *The Historical Figure of Jesus* New York: The Penguin Press, 1993, page 30.

135. Maier, Paul L *Josephus,* Grand Rapids: Kregel Publications, 1988, page 316. Josephus identified those who first desecrated the temple as the Jewish Zealots. This desecration included rape and murder in the holy of Holies.

of God full of so many abominations, or these sacred places...trodden on...with the feet of these blood-shedding villains [Zealots]; yet do I, who am clothed with the vestments of the high priesthood...still live...'[136]

- **Great Distress Unequalled since the Beginning of Time (Matthew 24:21):** The distress of the Jewish people, the most devout and good people of the land, still cries out from the pages of Josephus. One cannot read this terrible distress without innermost sorrow and sadness. Food deprivation so weakened the Judeans that frequently they fell dead into the graves of those they tried to bury. The siege of Jerusalem has been considered by some as an inferno of misery probably unparalleled in history.[137]

- **The presence of a False Christ Coming from the Desert and from the Inner Rooms (Matthew 24:26):** From the inner room, interpreted as from the Jewish nation of Judea, comes Bar Kokhba in 132 AD. From the inner room must be interpreted as from Judea. Judea accepted him as their messiah officially labeling him 'Son of a Star' on their coins. In 622 AD Mohammed came from the desert, significantly reducing the Christian population.

- **Gospel of the kingdom will be taught to the entire world (Matthew 24:14):** This was the primary task of the primitive and early church, which was initiated with much enthusiasm and success. It remains to be completed.

Hence, based on the above evidence, it is asserted that many of Jesus' prophecies were fulfilled by the year 135 AD. This warrants that we must be alert and not so confident that we understand the events of Parousia. In fact the Spirit indicates that all but the spiritually sanctified will be shocked and surprised at Jesus' forthcoming return. This means that our popularly held ideas of the end-time events are most certainly incorrect as to sequencing and timing. Indeed, the Spirit of God claims that we shall slip into the millennium reign of Christ in a far different manner than that currently held by the Christian fundamentalists. But, if the Body of Christ can defeat the sifting of Satan, (partially achieved by the small Holy Junction prayer team in February of 2002) endure the discipline of God, and accept the outpouring Love Touch of the Holy Spirit, we shall get there! Hallelujah!

---

136. Whiston, Book 4, chapter 3, section 10, page 528 of this edition.
137. Keller, Werner *The Bible as History*, New York: William Morrow and Company, 1981, page 364.

Index

About the Author

Eugene Shults was born in a rural area of Northwest Detroit just after the onset of the Great Depression. After college he served for five years in the Navy as an aviator followed by more than six years as a weekend warrior reservist. In the late 1950s he returned to school to earn an advanced degree in physics. Mr. Shults then joined IBM and began a career in computers and data processing. He taught information technology at the University of California Santa Barbara extension school, and later was president of his own computer company where he created many computer software innovations. In 1973 he received the baptism of the Holy Spirit which dramatically changed his life interests. In 1986, under the guidance of the Spirit of God, he gave up his life's vocation and began an intense study of church history, theology, and US History. This work is one of more than ten manuscripts he has produced with God's leadership. Father of eight children, Mr. Shults and his wife Carol, now live in Florida with two children still in the home.

Visit the author's website at kingdom-truth.com.